Fabulous Fallacies

"What is truth?" said jesting Pilate,
and would not stay for an answer.

—Francis Bacon

What I tell you three times is true.

—Lewis Carroll

Fabulous Fallacies

More Than 300 Popular Beliefs That Are Not True

BY TAD TULEJA

A Stonesong Press Book

Harmony Books / New York

Inquiries should be addressed to Harmony Books, a division of
Crown Publishers, Inc., One Park Avenue, New York, New York
10016. Harmony Books is a registered trademark of Crown Publishers, Inc.

A Stonesong Press Book

Published simultaneously in Canada by General Publishing Company
Limited

Library of Congress Cataloging in Publication Data
Tuleja, Thaddeus
   Fabulous fallacies.

   "A Stonesong Press book."
   Bibliography: p. 227
   1. Errors, Popular.   I. Title.
AZ999.T84 1982   001.9′6   81-13248
ISBN 0-517-543486 (Cloth)   AACR2
        0-517-547007 (Paper)

10 9 8 7 6 5

First Edition

CONTENTS

For my mother and father
who first stuck my nose in a book

INTRODUCTION

On Lincoln's Birthday a while back, some smart-aleck radio commentator smugly announced that Old Abe never wrote the Gettysburg Address on that envelope after all. The story was a piece of whimsy invented by a legend-monger who figured that the railsplitter-president's image could profit from one more example of his homespun genius. Actually, the radio announcer said, Lincoln had worked the speech over meticulously, letting the prepared text be only after he knew he could get every intonation right.

This news gave me a few miserable moments until I realized it might be a blessing in disguise. With several years of genteel education behind me, I was no slouch in the smugness department myself, and the more I thought about the envelope story turning out to be a hoax, the more attractive the debunking bandwagon looked to me. If I could dig up other cherished bits of wisdom that were in fact fabrications or distortions or mistakes, perhaps I could put them together in a collection.

I spent the next month in the library, searching for discrepancies between facts and what I had been taught in school. I paged through encyclopedias and the *Oxford English Dictionary.* I foraged through collections of fallacies, histories of error, and compendiums of superstitions, like a ferret making its way through a sclerotic pipe. After filling several packs of index cards with our species' more egregious misconceptions, I came to the conclusion that the radio announcer had been, if anything, not smug enough. As it turned out, the presidential myth he had exploded was just the appetizer of a feast.

Before beginning my research, I had tended, with sophomoric aplomb, to think of erroneous lore as being largely a thing of the past. The popular fallacies I expected to uncover were vestiges of an illiterate past, such as the medieval notions that the earth was flat or that lemmings were generated by clouds. We are more enlightened today and surely misconceptions such as the Lincoln myth would prove to be few and far between.

I could not have been more wrong. It quickly became obvious that we moderns were just as much enthralled by traditional ideas as our medieval ancestors had been. The ideas had changed, but not our willingness to swallow them without question. Our fifteenth-century European cousins looked west and said, "There be monsters"; we look into our fourth-grade textbooks and say, with as little justification, "Columbus discovered America." They believed lemmings dropped from the sky; we believe they run to the sea. Nobody checks the facts.

The resilience of traditional ideas is a governing force not only in history—which Voltaire called "the fable we agree on"—but in all realms of human endeavor. Whether you are talking about politics, mathematics, or religion, the given wisdom is ascendant. Fallacies are an integral part of a modern education.

After that first sobering month, I had two file boxes full of note cards. At that point the Great Debunker in the sky must have smiled on me, because one day, as I was reading about President Hiram U. Grant, my publishing friend, Paul Fargis, called. He was thinking of producing a book of popular fallacies. Would I be interested in writing it?

"Would I?" I responded. "I'm halfway there already. Did you know that Betsy Ross never sewed that flag?"

"Very happy to hear it," Paul replied. "And George Washington was not the first president of the United States."

"Wonderful!" I exclaimed. "Swiss cheese doesn't always have holes."

"And Lizzie Borden was acquitted."

We rattled on like this for twenty minutes or so and then got down to business. And this book is the result.

One of the most startling, and humbling, things about this project was the discovery that the information needed to correct most common misconceptions is extremely easy to locate. The facts, in many instances, are available in any good general encyclopedia. The trouble is that nobody bothers to check them. Lemming-like, we prefer to "think" in herds, rather than measure the given wisdom against the sources.

I hope this book will convince you to look again at things you have long believed and question both the content of our traditional information and the manner in which it is obtained. Wherever possible, I have tried to show not only that wrong beliefs exist, but also *how* and *why* they came about. Perhaps knowing an error's provenance will be, to those of you who want to go beyond *this* text, a stimulus to further thought.

One of the major drawbacks of universal education is that it tends to make all of us, not just the privileged, intellectually arrogant. If this compendium of modern mistakes evokes some humility in its readers, my time will have been well spent.

I want to thank the many friends who gave me moral support, encouragement, and entries while I was putting the book together. I am particularly indebted to Jeanne and Claude Nolen of Austin, Texas for sending me the excellent Cords/Gerster book, *Myth and the American Experience*. To Paul Fargis, who conceived the idea of the book and entrusted it to me, my warmest thanks and appreciation. To my wife, Andrée Nolen, my gratitude for reviewing the medical entries and for years of dancing eyes.

Most of this book was written in the Douglass College library in New Brunswick, New Jersey. To the librarians of that fine collection, and to those of the Princeton, Rutgers, St. Edward's, and Texas University collections, my thanks for indulging an eager, if unregistered, student. To the Douglass library workman who once said to me, "Boy, you must read a lot of books," a comradely smile and Amen.

T.F.T.

Austin
1981

Fabulous
Fallacies

FIRSTS:

ON THE STARTING LIE

WHO WAS THE FIRST PRESIDENT OF THE UNITED STATES?

He was not a Virginia planter, he never spent a night at Valley Forge, and although he was, technically speaking, our first truly national leader, he was far from first in the hearts of his countrymen. Indeed, aside from compilers of misinformation almanacs and sundry other pedants, few Americans have ever heard his name.

He was John Hanson of Maryland, whose ancestors had first seen these shores in 1642 as emissaries of Sweden's Queen Christina. Born in 1721, Hanson served in the Maryland assembly for over twenty years before being elected, in 1779, to the Continental Congress in Philadelphia. Once there he displayed the same dedication to colonial unity and defense which had characterized his tidewater career, and in the spring of 1781 he played a pivotal role in convincing Maryland, the only state still opposing the Articles of Confederation, to approve them. This ensured the adoption, in March, of what can reasonably be called the first American constitution.

Hanson's zeal was rewarded eight months later, when he became the first president of the Congress of the Confederation. His title, for the year in which he served, was "president of the United States in Congress assembled."

Between 1781 and 1789, when the current constitution was ratified and Washington was elected president, seven other men presided over the Congress. That really makes Old George not our first but our ninth president. *Dictionary of American Biography* (Scribner's, 1964).

WHO FIRST SAID THE WORLD WAS ROUND?

Remember all those stories you learned in school about Columbus having trouble finding a crew because sailors were afraid of falling off the edge of the earth? Remember how you were told that, alone among fifteenth-century Europeans, he had gotten it into his head that the world wasn't flat, but round? The story was, at least in my fourth-grade classroom, commonly brought up to demonstrate how "wild" ideas often turn out to be grounded in truth.

But Columbus was not alone. When he proposed his great "Enterprise of the Indies," very few people thought he was batty simply because he spoke of a round earth. Aristotle and the ancient geographer Strabo both claimed that you could sail from Europe to the Indies. In the Middle Ages, Pierre d'Ailly and Pope Pius II calculated the narrowness of the ocean, and Columbus's copies of their books are filled with his marginalia. The Florentine doctor Paolo dal Pozzo Toscanelli, two decades before the 1492 voyage, also postulated a small distance between Spain and the East; Columbus corresponded with him, and the Toscanelli assertion became his main ammunition when arguing that the journey was feasible. According to the admiral's biographer, in the late fifteenth century, "since there was no doubt of the world being a sphere, almost everyone admitted that Columbus's theory was valid; his originality lay in proposing to do something about it."

Why then did he have such trouble in securing the needed backing? Because although most agreed the world was round, few agreed with the Genoan about the narrowness of the ocean. The pessimists were right, too. Toscanelli, for example, put the east-west distance from the Canary Islands to Japan at 3,000 nautical miles; Columbus, fudging his calculations to make it appear even smaller, came up with 2,400; the actual distance, by air, is over 10,000 miles.

"Columbus' calculations were illogical," says Samuel Eliot Morison, "but his mind never followed rules of logic. He *knew* he could make it, and had to put the mileage low in order to attract support." To the everlasting glory of Spain, Ferdinand and Isabella had perhaps less rigorous mathematicians than those of the princes who rebuffed him. The strength of his convictions aside, it is still a lucky thing that in the midst of his 10,000-mile journey

America got in the way.   Samuel Eliot Morison, *Admiral of the Ocean Sea* (Little, Brown, 1943); and his *The European Discovery of America* (Oxford, 1974).

IN THE BIBLE, WHAT WAS THE FIRST MAN'S NAME?

Genesis speaks of Adam, yes, but few commentators on the Bible take that as the first man's given name. The word *adham* in Hebrew means "man," and most Biblical scholars agree that it is to be read as a generic, not a proper, name. There are few places in the Old Testament where the word can reasonably be interpreted as a personal name, and according to *The Interpreter's Dictionary of the Bible,* this was not accidental: "The choice of the generic term indicates the intention of the biblical writers to portray, not just the story of one man, but the universal story of mankind."

Eve, on the other hand, is a proper name, although its derivation is not clearly established. Some scholars say it comes from the Hebrew *hawwah,* meaning "to live," and is thus meant to suggest the woman as the origin of life. Others see it as similar to the Aramaic for "serpent," thus emphasizing Eve's connection with the snake.   *The Interpreter's Dictionary of the Bible* (Abingdon, 1962).

WHO FIRST SAID THAT THE EARTH REVOLVED AROUND THE SUN?

The Polish astronomer Nicolaus Copernicus (1473–1543) has long been regarded as one of the founders of modern science, and rightly so: his treatise *The Revolutions of the Heavenly Spheres* is one of that select group of books—like Marx's, Darwin's, and Newton's—that radically altered the way we humans view our world. Taken up by Kepler and later Galileo, his heliocentric theory not only demolished the Ptolemaic world view, but acted as the thin edge of the wedge that was to divest Europe of religious absolutism and bring its Christian population skittering uneasily toward modernity.

But even though it is hard to overestimate his importance, Copernicus was not the originator of the heliocentric view, only a particularly convincing expounder of its revolutionary tenets. The idea that the earth moves around the sun, and not vice versa, was not a popular one in the sixteenth century, but in the words of Thomas Kuhn, "it was scarcely unprecedented." The fifteenth-century cardinal Nicholas of Cusa was only one of several who had, shortly before Copernicus, suggested that the earth was not stable. A millennium and a half before him, heliocentricity was a Greek hypothesis, and it was only after Ptolemy of Alexandria, around 150 B.C., wrote his noted defense of geocentricity, the *Almagest,* that the "solar system" thinking began to decline.

A century before Ptolemy, a Greek named Aristarchus of Samos proposed both of the principal innovations of the Copernican model: one, that the earth revolves on its own axis; and two, that it moves about the sun. Copernicus was familiar with Aristarchus, and, in fact, mentioned his work in a preface to his own magnum opus. The Greek's influence on his own thinking was profound, although Aristarchus is not popularly remembered today. Historians of science, however, call him "the ancient Copernicus." Angus Armitage, *The World of Copernicus* (Signet, 1963); Sir Thomas Heath, *Aristarchus of Samos* (Oxford, 1959); Thomas Kuhn, *The Copernican Revolution* (Harvard, 1957).

WHO FIRST FLEW NONSTOP ACROSS THE ATLANTIC?

When Charles "Lone Eagle" Lindbergh touched down at Paris's Le Bourget airport on May 21, 1927, he became an immediate sensation; he soon received a $25,000 prize, a tumultuous stateside welcome, and the Congressional Medal of Honor. Overnight he was transformed from an obscure mail pilot to the very image of American individualism. Long after the tragedy of his son's kidnapping and murder, and after the subtler tragedy of his own crypto-fascist leanings had surfaced, he remained one of the nation's true heroes.

But the event which catapulted him to fame is frequently misapprehended. Lindbergh was not the first flyer to cross the Atlantic nonstop, but the first to do it *alone.* Eight years before his *Spirit of St. Louis* took off, Capt. John Alcock and Lt. Arthur Whitten-Brown had co-piloted a Vichers-Vimy twin-engine plane from Newfoundland to Ireland's Galway. It took them sixteen and a half hours, on June 14 to 15, 1919. The extraordinary thing about Lindbergh was that he managed to stay alert enough to fly almost twice as long as that, by himself. Leonard Mosley, *Lindbergh: A Biography* (Doubleday, 1976); Walter Ross, *The Last Hero* (Harper & Row, 1968).

WHO SEWED THE FIRST AMERICAN FLAG?

On March 14, 1870, the Pennsylvania Historical Society was treated to a charming tale of colonial industry by one William J. Canby, the grandson of Betsy Ross. According to Canby, just before the signing of the Declaration of Independence in the summer of 1776, his grandmother was visited by Robert Morris, George Ross, and George Washington himself in her seamstress's shop in Philadelphia, and asked if she would sew a flag to the gentlemen's design. The result of her labors, Betsy herself had told him, was adopted by the Congress as the country's first Stars and Stripes.

This delicious tale the Historical Society took in as if it had been waiting to hear it. Then preparing for the 1876 centennial, Philadelphia was delighted that one of its own daughters had made the first Old Glory, and the story soon became common knowledge. Within a short time it was appearing in textbooks everywhere, and by the time the centennial rolled around, it was already on its way to becoming a national legend.

But legend it was, and remains. There's not a thread of evidence that the story was more than a family anecdote—though no one could say for certain whether it was the grandson or Betsy herself who had made it up. Betsy did make flags for the Pennsylvania navy, in 1777, but that was hardly the stuff of which patriotic images were sewn. David Wallechinsky and Irving Wallace, *The People's Almanac #2* (Bantam, 1978).

WHERE WAS THE FIRST SHOT OF THE CIVIL WAR FIRED?

"Fort Sumter" is equivalent in our national mythology to "Lexington and Concord" or "Pearl Harbor," but it comes by its fame a little dishonestly. The Confederate shots which were fired on the South Carolina fort on April 12, 1861, are usually said to be the opening salvos of the Civil War, but they were actually the second round. Three months before the incident, on January 9, a Union ship steaming toward Fort Sumter with supplies was fired upon by a rebel battery on nearby Morris Island, and forced to abort its mission. The ship's name was the *Star of the West,* and although its crew sustained no casualties, two of the seventeen volleys fired did connect. One reason that the war did not then begin in earnest may have been that the South was still preparing an army, and preferred to bide its time.

Most historians, reasonably enough, date the beginning of the war from Fort Sumter, since three days after the April incident President Lincoln issued a "state of insurrection" proclamation. A respectable minority view, though, takes the *Star of the West* episode as the opener, and credits the Morris Island cadet George Haynesworth as having initiated the proceedings. Military historian Mark Boatner calls the January 9 incident "the first overt act of the war."   Mark Mayo Boatner III, *The Civil War Dictionary* (David McKay, 1959); Joseph N. Kane, *Famous First Facts* (H. W. Wilson, 1964).

WHERE WERE THE FIRST CONCENTRATION CAMPS?

The term "concentration camps" became widely known only after Hitler's SS used them to murder millions of Jews and other "ethnic undesirables" during the 1930s and 1940s. The existence of death camps, however, predates the monstrosities of the Third Reich by almost a dozen years. According to the writer Mihaljo Mihajlov, the first internment camp in history whose "sole purpose was the physical destruction of the prisoners" was Holmogor, established in the Soviet Gulag archipelago around 1921. In this and other camps Stalin's henchmen liquidated an estimated 10 to 19 million prisoners between 1921 and 1953.

The designation "concentration camp" arose in the 1890s to describe first the Spanish internment centers in Cuba, and then the British equivalent in South Africa during the Boer War; it was a product thus not of totalitarianism, but of democratic and royal imperialism. These camps, however, were restrictive rather than punitive—like those set up in California after Pearl Harbor, or in Belfast today. The Nazi propaganda minister Joseph Goebbels, a genius at misrepresentation, seized on the Boer War example during the 1930s to draw attention away from the carnage at Auschwitz and Dachau. On his orders Nazi propaganda postcards formerly labeled "genuine Russian concentration camp scenes" were relabeled as "genuine British scenes" set in troubled South Africa.

Goebbels's ingenuity in rearranging history was matched by his Stalinist counterparts, who as late as the mid 1950s were denying that the Gulag ever happened. Astonishingly, some contemporary "revisionist" historians are now claiming the same thing about the Holocaust. Never underestimate the power of wishful thinking.   Patrick Robertson, *The Book of Firsts* (Clarkson Potter, 1974).

WHO PERFORMED THE FIRST SUCCESSFUL SMALLPOX INOCULATION?

Because he popularized his experiments in the 1798 volume *Inquiry into the Causes and Effects of the Variolae Vaccinae,* the English physician Edward Jenner (1745–1823) is often credited with being the first person to successfully vaccinate anyone against smallpox. He did perform successful vaccinations, and even opened several London clinics for that purpose in 1803, but he was not the first in the field. That honor belongs to a Dr. Downe of Bridgeport, England; in 1771 he vaccinated a butcher, Robert Fooks, who thereafter was in frequent proximity to smallpox but never contracted the disease.

Downe, like Jenner, used cowpox pustules to induce immunity against the more severe disease. The more hazardous variolous inoculation—inoculation with smallpox pustules themselves—had been practiced with varying results long before either of the English doctors was born. It was known in Wales in the seventeenth century, and in various non-European countries—among them India, China, Turkey, Persia, and North Africa—for an unknown period before that.

Another English doctor, this one named Kennedy, first described the Turkish method in his *Essay on External Remedies* (1715). According to him, physicians in Constantinople scarred the wrists, legs, and forehead of the patient, placed "a fresh and kindly pock" in each incision, and bound it there for eight or ten

days. After this time, he was "credibly informed," the patient
developed a mild case of smallpox, recovered, and was thereafter
immune. The operation apparently had a mortality rate of only
one in a thousand. Two years after Kennedy's description appeared, Dr. Charles Maitland successfully inoculated the wife of
the British ambassador to the Turkish court, and four years after
that, he introduced the practice to England. Patrick Robertson,
The Book of Firsts (Clarkson Potter, 1974).

WHEN WAS THE FIRST OFFICIAL CELEBRATION OF THANKSGIVING?

Although it's true that the Pilgrims held *a* thanksgiving (the
feast actually lasted three days) in 1621, the celebration did not
become nationally recognized until 1789—and was not a regular
occurrence until almost a century after that. Throughout the seventeenth and eighteenth centuries, days of thanksgiving were observed only sporadically, at the conclusion, for example, of a
successful battle or after a particularly good harvest. The first
national thanksgiving proclamation was issued in 1789 by the
new president, George Washington, and he repeated the order in
1795. As a national holiday, however, it was a long time taking
hold, since some political leaders, including Thomas Jefferson,
didn't much like the idea. Many state governors shied away from
it even in the nineteenth century, thinking it a civil interference
with religion.

However, thanks to the efforts of an insistent magazine editor,
Thanksgiving finally became a national holiday during the Civil
War. The editor was Sarah Josepha Hale, and beginning in 1827
she campaigned in her Boston-based *Ladies' Magazine* to have a
regular day set aside for the observance of the "Pilgrim" celebration. When the magazine merged with the popular *Godey's
Lady's Book,* her crusade reached a vast readership, and on October 3, 1863, President Lincoln proclaimed the fourth Thursday in
November as henceforth "a day of thanksgiving and praise to our
beneficent Father who dwelleth in the heavens."

In 1939 and 1940, Franklin Roosevelt set aside the *third* Thursday as Thanksgiving, to give merchants more time after the holiday to prepare for the Christmas rush. Aside from that brief
concession to the commercial spirit, the day has been observed

since 1863 on November's fourth Thursday, in accordance with Sarah Hale's design.   Robert J. Myers, *Celebrations: The Complete Book of American Holidays* (Doubleday, 1972).

WHO ORIGINATED THE THEORY OF EVOLUTION?

Charles Darwin's great *Origin of Species* (1859) so astounded and transformed Victorian society that nearly a century and a quarter after its appearance, many continue to think of its author as "the father of evolutionary theory." But as Gertrude Himmelfarb shows in her study of Darwinism, and as the naturalist himself acknowledged, Darwin was indebted to numerous predecessors. The notion that species were not fixed but mutable was one that had been entertained seriously for centuries, and Darwin's forceful reiteration of it "was not so much a case of Athena emerging full blown from the brow of Zeus as of the Phoenix rising once again from its ashes."

Among those who had paved the way for Darwin were the Greek philosophers Anaximander and Empedocles, who outlined a theory of adaptation; the Enlightenment thinkers Newton, Leibniz, and de Maillet, all of whom hinted that the "great chain of being" had been forged by mutating links; and, most notably, several fellow naturalists and scientists. Georges Buffon and Carolus Linnaeus, for example, had debated the immutability of species in the eighteenth century. Darwin's own grandfather, Erasmus Darwin, fifteen years before Charles was born, had suggested in a book that was placed on the Catholic Index that the animal world might have "arisen from one filament" with the power of "continuing to improve by its own inherent activity, and of delivering down those improvements by generation to its posterity." The naturalist Lamarck, the paleontologists Cuvier and Geoffroy-Saint-Hilaire, and the geologist Charles Lyell were among those to whom evolutionary theory was a matter of constant concern long before Darwin sailed on the *Beagle*. Geoffroy, in fact, used the term "evolution" in 1831, in referring to fossil reptiles.

So common in educated circles were "Darwinian" ideas by the 1850s that a year before the *Origin* appeared, an obscure English naturalist named Alfred Russel Wallace sent Darwin a paper in which the basic evolutionary theory—including Darwin's major innovation, the process of natural selection—was outlined with unnerving exactness. To Darwin's credit he treated this rival formulation honorably, agreeing to allow Wallace's paper and one of his own early abstracts to be presented, in 1858, to the same meeting of the Linnaean Society. Thus he and Wallace can be seen as joint "originators" of the theory—although, as Wallace acknowledged, without Darwin's massive body of evidence, the theory would have been received as no more than "ingenious speculation." Gertrude Himmelfarb, *Darwin and the Darwinian Revolution* (Norton, 1968).

WHAT WAS THE FIRST "TALKIE" PICTURE?

As every film buff knows, the first nonsilent movie was Al Jolson's *The Jazz Singer* (1927). Only it wasn't. The Jolson picture was a first, all right, but it wasn't the first real "talkie." In fact, by 1927 sound film had been around for two decades. The French inventor Eugene Augustin Lauste had demonstrated a practical system as early as 1910, while American innovators were developing sound technology throughout the 1920s. Lee De Forest first displayed his Phonofilm—presenting audio-visual records of vaudeville acts—in 1923. Warner Brothers' similar Vitaphone shorts were in distribution by 1926. And in 1927 William Fox began to produce not only scored features (the first was *What Price Glory?*), but sound newsreels as well.

The first all-talking long film was actually *Lights of New York*, which showed in 1928 and was forgotten. *The Jazz Singer* was not: using only minimal dialogue, it created the modern sound audience almost singlehandedly. The film's distinction, therefore, was not its date of appearance but its demonstration that sound technology could be successfully employed in a full-length dramatic film. Arthur Knight, *The Liveliest Art* (Macmillan, 1957).

WHAT EXPLORER FIRST SAILED AROUND THE WORLD?

There is no question that it was the genius and perseverance of the Portuguese seaman Fernão de Magalhães, whom we call Magellan, that led to the first circumnavigation of the world.

Setting out in 1519 from Spain (his own king would not sponsor him), he brought a frequently mutinous entourage through the straits that bear his name, then on into the Pacific, becoming the first European to sail it. Under his often cruel but unswerving captaincy, his ships discovered Guam, and then the Philippines, where they landed for rest and supplies.

It was a fateful stopover, for the indigenous Filipinos bridled at Magellan's attempt to convert them, and in a confrontation on the beach killed the captain and several of his men. So the man who is spoken of as the first circumnavigator of the world actually sailed only partway around it; one of his mutinous officers, Juan Sebastian del Cano, actually led the expedition, in 1522, home to a Spanish harbor.

Magellan's reputation, though restored today, suffered badly by the accident of his death, as political rivals (among them del Cano) denounced him to Spain's King Charles and belittled his accomplishments: The Straits of Magellan they described as "no more than a useless bay." The king, irked that the three-year voyage had netted him no gold, accepted these prevarications, and it was not until much later that the significance of the navigator's vision became generally accepted. Aside from its many cartographic contributions, the journey he began but never finished proved beyond reasonable doubt that the globe *could* be circumnavigated. According to Ian Cameron, "There could, from now on, be no going back to such bizarre conceptions as the Christian Fathers' non-concentric globe or uninhabited Antipodes: the basic structure of our planet had been for all time unquestionably ascertained." Ian Cameron, *Magellan and the First Circumnavigation of the World* (Saturday Review Press, 1973).

ORIGINS:

THE ORIGIN OF SPECIOUS

WHERE DOES INDIA INK COME FROM?

Most people call it Indian ink. The preferred term is India ink, and the only really accurate term is the seldom-used China ink. For it was from China, and occasionally Japan, that the original "India ink" found its way to the West. A mixture of lampblack (soot) and gum, it was first recorded as "Indian ink," according to the *Oxford English Dictionary,* in 1665, by no less an authority than Samuel Pepys. Horace Walpole and William Makepeace Thackeray, in later centuries, continued the diarist's error, and today it has become fixed convention.

Compare the similar misnomer India rubber, which in the nineteenth century was used to make both overshoes and erasers. The elastic gum from which the substance was made comes not from an Indian plant, but from trees found in the East Indies, Africa, and Latin America. A confusion we can blame on Columbus. *Oxford English Dictionary* (Oxford, 1961).

THE RICKSHAW IS NOT CHINESE.

In spite of its appearance in numerous films about Old China, the rickshaw came originally from Japan—and was a Western not an Oriental idea. The human-drawn, two-wheeled carriage seems to have made its first appearance in Japan around 1870, and though no one seems certain who invented it, it's agreed that some Western missionary was responsible. The *Oxford English Dictionary* cites C. Roper, author of *Zigzag Travels* (1895), crediting the missionary W. Goble; Patrick Robertson gives the nod to an American Baptist preacher, Jonathan Scobie, who was supposed to have devised the contraption to have his invalid wife carted around the streets of Yokohama. In either case it was the Church's doing.

Based on the eighteenth-century French *brouette,* which was a sedan chair with wheels, the rickshaw remained popular in the East until the advent of the pedicab made all those strong arms obsolete. The original form of the name was *jinrikisha,* from the Japanese for man (*jin*), strength (*riki*), and vehicle (*sha*).   Patrick Robertson, *The Book of Firsts* (Clarkson Potter, 1974).

THE BAGPIPE IS NOT SCOTTISH.

Since Scottish pipers have popularized the bagpipe in modern times, it's often assumed that the instrument is native to the highlands. Actually, the first primitive version was constructed by a Middle Eastern (probably Hittite) music lover several hundred years before Christ. It was a crude affair, composed of reeds stuck into a goatskin bag, but proud Scots should be wary of mocking its lack of sophistication: In the first millennium B.C. their ancestors were still *wearing* skins.

From the Mediterranean the bagpipe gradually spread throughout Europe, reaching Italy in the thirteenth century, England in the fourteenth, and Scotland, alas, not until the early fifteenth. Clearly, Scottish pipers should be congratulated for having done so much with so little so soon.

The French call the instrument a *musette,* the Italians a *piffero,* the Norwegians a *Penbrock,* and the Germans (with unintended drollery) a *Dudelsack.* The best name of all, though, was devised by Victor Hugo. In his novel *Travailleurs de la Mer,* evidently attempting to impress his readers with his grasp of English, he called the thing a *bugpipe.*   Percy A. Scholes, *The Oxford Companion to Music* (Oxford, 1970).

WHERE DID THE GUILLOTINE ORIGINATE?

Although it is widely believed that the inventor of the guillotine—that most horrid symbol of the French Revolution—was Dr. Joseph Guillotin , he did not himself invent it, but only recommended to the French National Assembly that it be adopted as the country's official killing device, since it provided the condemned a swift and humane end. The Assembly approved, the device was tested on corpses, and on April 25, 1792, it claimed its first live victim, the highwayman Pelletier; within a year, it had become the overworked servant of the Terror.

The instrument's makers were a German mechanic called Schmidt and the French doctor Antonin Louise, in whose honor it was originally called the "Louison" or "Louisette." These two, however, had only adapted a design that had been used throughout Europe for centuries, generally to execute criminals of noble birth. As the "maiden" it was used in Scotland throughout the Middle Ages, and notably in 1581, when it decapitated the regent Morton. In Germany, where it was called variously the *Diele,* the *Hobel,* and the *Dolabra,* it was also a common medieval device. In Italy, where Dr. Guillotin probably learned of it, it went under the name of *Mannaia,* and was in vogue, according to the *Encyclopaedia Britannica,* in the thirteenth century. (The earliest recorded use of the maiden in Patrick Robertson's *Book of Firsts,* however, is in Ireland in 1307.)

Dr. Guillotin had a political as well as a humanitarian argument for the instrument's adoption. A good republican, he felt that employing a "noble" head chopper on all persons regardless of rank would be a sign of revolutionary equity. Within a short time after the Assembly agreed, he was to see the device democratized beyond his wildest hopes.   Tom Burnam, *The Dictionary of Misinformation* (Crowell, 1975); *Encyclopaedia Britannica* (1970).

WHAT PEOPLE DEVELOPED KARATE?

Thanks to Bruce Lee and David Carradine, most people think of all the Oriental martial arts as having originated in China. Others, with little better justification, say that kung-fu is the original Chinese form, and karate its Japanese equivalent, of fighting methods that started in prehistory. It's true that the Japanese were largely responsible, early in this century, for popularizing karate in the West, and the term itself, which means "empty hand," is also Japanese. But the form began in Okinawa, as a means of fighting *against* the Japanese.

This was in the fifteenth and sixteenth centuries, when the Ryukyu Islands, of which Okinawa is the largest, were suffering under Japanese domination. Fearful of popular rebellion, the overlords had prohibited the Okinawans from bearing arms, so they bared fists and feet instead, perfecting the weaponless art in small, secret bands. The moves they practiced evolved from Shaolin boxing techniques, which had recently been imported from China. These in turn had been, according to legend, brought to China in the sixth century by the Indian monk Bodhidharma.

Karate became a public art relatively recently. Shortly after World War I the Okinawan techniques, called Okinawa-te, were demonstrated in Tokyo by the master Gichin Funakoshi, who became head of the Japan Karate Association. From Japan they spread to other parts of Asia, and ultimately to the West.   John Goodbody, ed., *The Japanese Fighting Arts* (Barnes, 1969)

THE GUITAR CAME FROM A) EGYPT, B) TURKEY, OR C) SPAIN?

The classical guitar is almost as firmly associated with Spain as the bagpipe is with Scotland; the image of the hidalgo serenading his lady beneath a balcony, *guitarra* in hand, remains a central icon of Iberian culture. But the instrument was not invented there, only perfected. Its ancient precursors, the lyre (*cithara*) and the lute (*pandoura*), arose in Mesopotamia millennia before the birth of Christ.

As to the guitar's exact origin, that depends pretty much on definition. If by guitar you mean merely a fretted instrument with strings stretched over a sounding board, the earliest known example comes from what is modern-day Turkey: Bas-relief sculptures at Alaca Höyük clearly depict an hourglass-shaped lute with a fretted fingerboard, and some authorities claim this Hittite model as the earliest true guitar. German musicologist Ernst Biernath suggests it was the instrument that the Israelites hung up by the waters of Babylon.

But the Hittite model had a skin-covered body, and its neck joined that body in a rather primitive fashion; it was simply thrust through it, like a spear through a gourd. Because this is not typical of the modern guitar, other authorities claim Egypt as the source of the instrument, pointing out that in the Coptic era (ca. 800–300 B.C.), the African kingdom's inhabitants played a flat-bodied wooden lute whose construction more closely resembled that of the modern guitar.

Just when this proto-guitar was transformed into the instrument of Segovia is impossible to say, but it is likely that its basic features were introduced to Spain by the Arabs during their medieval hegemony of the Mediterranean. Structurally, the modern *guitarra* has its beginnings around the thirteenth century, when Moorish influence on the peninsula was profound. The Moors' exact role in its development is uncertain (some, claiming it developed from the Roman *fidicula,* even deny the Arab connection), but a cautious estimate is that Moorish influence at least "prepared the ground for the advent of the guitar." From the Fertile Crescent, by way of the Nile, to Seville. Frederic V. Grunfeld, *The Art and Times of the Guitar* (Macmillan, 1969).

THE TURKEY DOES NOT COME FROM TURKEY.

Our preeminent symbol of Thanksgiving is, fortuitously, truly an American bird. Species of wild turkeys roamed the entire North American continent long before Columbus landed, and the conquistadors discovered in Mexico that the Aztecs had domesticated the *Meleagris gallopavo* variety. The designation "turkey" came about because Europeans confused the American import with a bird that had been known in Europe since ancient times. This was the Guinea cock or Guinea fowl, which didn't come from Turkey either, but had been brought to Europe *through* Turkey by Portuguese travelers who had gotten it from Guinea in West Africa. When the two birds were finally distinguished, the American bird somehow got stuck with the African bird's false nickname.

That is the conventional explanation. A more charming, though possibly apocryphal, one ascribes the name to the Portuguese Jewish interpreter of Columbus's first journey, one José de Torres. Upon seeing his first specimen of the bird in the New World, he is supposed to have cried out "Tukki, tukki," which means "big bird" in Hebrew. A pretty story, if true. *Oxford English Dictionary* (Oxford, 1961).

WHERE DID THE PONY EXPRESS ORIGINATE?

With Buffalo Bill Cody and Wild Bill Hickok among its alumni, the American pony express is justly counted among the

Wild West's most memorable heroic enterprises. The young riders who covered the stretches of sagebrush between St. Joseph, Missouri, and California have gone down in legend as paragons of rugged individualism, and their feats comprise one of the most romantic chapters in the history of the westward movement.

Given the mythic aura that surrounds the pony express, it's easy to forget that the venture was short-lived and financially disastrous for the promoters. Those record-breaking runs lasted less than two years (1860–1861), at the end of which time the riders were put out of business by the completion of the first transcontinental telegraph.

Nor was the operation the madcap American idea it often seems. Pony express courier teams were, by 1860, ancient history, having made their first appearance in Outer Mongolia thousands of years before and having been successful since then in Cyrus the Great's Persia (around 540 B.C.) and Alexander's empire two centuries after that. The pony express reached its fullest development among the nomads of the Asiatic steppes, and it thrived in Outer Mongolia until the 1920s.   G. N. Georgano, ed., *Transportation Through the Ages* (McGraw-Hill, 1972); George P. Oslin, "Pony Express," in *Encyclopedia Americana* (1980).

WHERE DID THE ARYANS COME FROM?

The term Aryan, which was elevated by Hitler's henchmen into a synonym for racial purity, started out as a linguistic, not an ethnic, designation in the writings of the German philologist Max Müller. His *Science of Language* (1861) postulated the existence of an original "Aryan" tongue from which had derived the languages we call today Indo-European—including the Latin tongues, the Germanic, and Sanskrit. This mother tongue, he went on, may have been spoken by an Aryan "race" of fair-skinned Asians from whom the European peoples descended.

Both the linguistic and the racial theories were speculative, and it is to Müller's credit that he later repudiated the latter. In 1888 he said that "an ethnologist who speaks of Aryan race, Aryan blood, Aryan eyes and hair, is as great a sinner as a linguist who speaks of a dolichocephalic dictionary or a brachecephalic grammar." By the 1880s he had good cause to revise, for by that time there was already developing in Europe the "Nordic stock" the-

ory which, two generations later, would lead to the Nazi holocaust.

The chief proponent of the Nordic humbug was the French
count Joseph Arthur Gobineau (1816–1882). His controversial essay *The Inequality of Human Races* (1855) suggested that the
Nordic peoples—the blond, blue-eyed caricatures of Nazi legend—were the rightful heirs of "Aryanism," and that they were
being dangerously watered down by interbreeding (Gobineau
called it "semitization") with yellow and dark-skinned people.
Taken up by European racists, including Richard Wagner, the
essay became a principal text in the development of the "Nordic
blood" myth.

It is a measure of how tendentious that myth was that Hitler's
scholars, ill at ease with the notion that the modern Valkyrie had
descended from Asians, modified the Aryan theory so that the
prehistoric Nordic homeland was in the pure heart of Europe.
This was nonsense: The name Aryan itself comes from the
Sanskrit for "noble," and it was clear even in Müller's day that
the ancestral home of the Aryans was near the Caspian Sea. They
migrated west into Europe and east into India in the second millennium B.C. Jacques Barzun, *Race: A Study in Superstition*
(Harper & Row, 1965); Ashley Montagu and Edward Darling,
The Prevalence of Nonsense (Harper & Row, 1967); Margaret and
James Stutley, *A Dictionary of Hinduism* (Routledge & Kegan
Paul, 1977).

WHAT COUNTRY GAVE US THE STORY OF THE LITTLE BOY WITH HIS FINGER IN THE DIKE?

This favorite tale of old Holland, in which an urchin saves a
nation from the sea, came not from Holland but America. It
appeared for the first time in Mary Mapes Dodge's juvenile classic *Hans Brinker, or the Silver Skates,* published in 1865. Mrs.
Dodge, editor of the children's magazine *St. Nicholas,* put the
gem in the book's eighteenth chapter, where it is read aloud in a
schoolroom by suitably choked-up students. As Hans Brinker's
fame spread, the story was accepted as Dutch, and ultimately
brought to the Netherlands by tourists who wanted to know, from
every citizen of Haarlem, where the spot in the dike actually was
that the young hero's finger had plugged.

Understandably, this annoyed the Dutch, who resented having

constantly to explain that the story was an imported fiction. For many years they cried down the tale until, in 1950, they gave in to popular pressure (and the lure of tourists' dollars) and erected a statue to the lad near the Spaarndem lock. This made the Spaarndem merchants happy, and perhaps softened the aggravation of telling American tourists that if the boy had been as smart as he was noble, he might have stopped up the trickle with a stone. Bergen Evans, *The Spoor of Spooks and Other Nonsense* (Knopf, 1954).

WHERE DOES THE BOOMERANG COME FROM?

Contrary to popular opinion, not all boomerangs are designed to return to the thrower. Those that do, made flat on one side and curved on the other, were perfected by Australian aborigines, who have used them since prehistoric times in hunting, sport, and war. The name "boomerang" itself is a modern spelling of an aboriginal name.

But Australia is not the boomerang's only home. Curved hunting sticks which produce the characteristic whirring sound, and which can be just as deadly as the Australian variety, have been discovered in at least four other regions of the earth, where their history is equally ancient. These regions are Indonesia (particularly Borneo and the Celebes); eastern Africa (Egypt and Ethiopia); the Indian subcontinent; and the southwestern United States, where the Hopi, Acoma, and Zuni Indians use the weapons still to hunt small game. Their common term for the device is "rabbit stick." There is also a suggestion by Strabo, the ancient Greek geographer, that the Gauls may have used them to hunt birds. According to Philip Ward, the Australians also aim them *above* flights of ducks, who mistake the shadows for hawks and, trying to escape, dive into prearranged nets.   Joseph J. Cornish III, "The Mystery of the Boomerang," in *Natural History* (May 1956); Philip Ward, *A Dictionary of Common Fallacies* (Oleander Press, 1980).

THE TURKISH BATH IS NOT TURKISH.

To the European Crusaders, high with the odor of sanctity, the baths of the Ottoman Empire must have been an astonishing revelation. Imagine being accustomed to bathing a couple of times a year, and then with half your garments on, and finding a huge steam-cleaning establishment in which your every pore is left tingling with the novelty of health. It's no wonder they brought the innovation back with them when they returned to Europe.

But Europe was not ready just then for open pores, and it was several centuries before the Turkish bath took hold in the Western mind. From the end of the Middle Ages to the beginning of the nineteenth century, perfume was more popular than soap, while puritanism helped keep Europe from being too clean. Spain destroyed its Moorish baths around 1500, public baths in the sixteenth century were denounced by Protestants and Catholics alike as morally unsound, and by the eighteenth century, according to Reginald Reynolds, "European standards of cleanliness were at their nadir." It was only after the imperialism of the post-Renaissance world had reintroduced Europeans to the East that bathing came back into favor. The Turkish bath specifically was brought to London in 1862, by David Urquhart, who had spent much time in the East.

What is not generally recognized about this development is that in bringing the steam bath to the West, Europeans were really only taking *back* an institution that Europe had sent out to the East many centuries before. The great bathers of the ancient world were the Romans, and the Turkish steam bath was basically a variant of baths which they had brought to Asia Minor—as well as to London, Charlemagne's capital Aachen, and of course the Somerset borough of Bath—back in imperial times. The Turkish steam chambers were an outgrowth of the Roman *laconicum,* and "the elaboration of the sweat bath," says Reynolds, "was the outstanding feature of the Roman system."   Reginald Reynolds, "Baths and Bathing," in *Encyclopedia Americana* (1980); and his *Cleanliness and Godliness* (Doubleday, 1946).

CHESS IS NEITHER EUROPEAN NOR MEDIEVAL.

I used to have a chess set in which the rook, or castle, was represented by an elephant with a turret on its back. Ridiculous, I thought. All the other pieces were properly traditional, with the corner pieces alone eccentric. Everybody knows elephants had no place on a European medieval battlefield.

My pique dissolved years later, when I discovered that chess, far from being the feudalistic war game it seemed, was not European at all. The knights and bishops were a sham: Chess had been created in the East, centuries before the Normans heard of castles, by a people to whom elephants were no oddity.

Although claims have been made for the Persians, the Chinese, the Egyptians, and the Welsh as the inventors of the game, it seems most probable that it grew out of the game *chaturanga,* played first in sixth-century India. *Chaturanga,* which in Sanskrit means "four arms," is also the word for "army," and it referred in the game as in life to the chariots, cavalry, infantry, and elephants then used in large-pitched battles. These four "arms," modified by Europeans, came gradually to be known as the bishops, knights, pawns, and rooks of modern play. This transformation took place sometime between the tenth century, when Arab invaders brought the game to Europe, and the sixteenth, when it acquired its present form.

The Arabs also gave it a name, since in Arabic it was called *al-schah-mat,* meaning "the king is dead." You can see the similarity between this term and the current usage "checkmate." The Arab connection is even more obvious in other languages' names for the game. The Germans call it *Schachspiel,* the Italians *Scacchi,* and the Russians, most closely, *Shahkmat.* I. A. Horowitz and P. L. Rothenberg, *The Complete Book of Chess* (Collier Books, 1969).

THE CHRISTMAS TREE IS NOT CHRISTIAN.

The Christmas tree as we know it today originated in Germany, where a "Paradise tree," usually a fir, was hung with apples and used as a prop in a medieval mystery play about Adam and Eve. In the fifteenth century many homes contained similar Paradise trees, decorated not only with fruit but also with small eucharist wafers. From Germany the custom spread gradually through Europe and ultimately to the New World.

But trees had been important in religious celebration long before the Germans ever heard of Eden. As emblems of eternal life, evergreens were appreciated in various pagan countries, including Egypt and China, even in ancient times. In northern Europe, the pre-Christian religions considered trees to be sacred; in southern Europe devotees of the Attic religion hung images of the slain god Attis on pine trees, since it was into a pine that he had been turned by Cybele. Evergreens suggested magical survival, then, to people long before Christmas was invented. Robert Myers notes that divinity was often attributed, especially at the turning point of the year, to "the fir trees which weathered the bitterest storms without succumbing to the cold winter darkness." Robert J. Myers, *Celebrations: The Complete Book of American Holidays* (Doubleday, 1972); *Encyclopaedia Britannica* (1974).

THE ENCYCLOPAEDIA BRITANNICA *IS NOT BRITISH.*

That most distinguished example of British scholarship, the paragon of encyclopedists and the bane of lesser-known rivals, the *Encyclopaedia Britannica* is not now, nor has it ever really been, a British institution. Not even its inception was British, since its founders—the printer Colin Macfarquhar, the illustrator Andrew Bell, and the scholar William Smellie—were Scottish entrepreneurs; the title page of the first edition (1771) credited "a Society of Gentlemen in Scotland." Bell and Macfarquhar ran it until 1815; control then passed first to Archibald Constable, then to A. and C. Black, both of them Edinburgh firms. It wasn't until the eleventh edition (1910) that the British got involved, and then as partners with Americans, who since the 1920s have been central to its management. From 1928 to 1943 Britannica was owned, believe it or not, by Sears, Roebuck, and since then it has been owned by the University of Chicago. The vastly popular Britannica 3 (1974) was proposed by Mortimer Adler, who continues as its *eminence gris.* Like many of the over four thousand contributors, he is an American.   David Wallechinsky and Irving Wallace, *The People's Almanac #2* (Bantam, 1978).

WHAT IS THE ORIGIN OF THE SWASTIKA?

The first time I saw a swastika on a Tibetan wall hanging I thought it was a neo-fascist forgery. Like most people, I associated the broken cross with one thing and one thing only: that defilement of decency and reason that called itself National Socialism. But the swastika, I later discovered, was not invented by Hitler—only appropriated from among a host of ancient symbols.

Erroneously believing that it had been used by the pure-stock "Aryans," the Nazis made it stand, in the popular imagination, for all it had not stood for before.

Among many traditions, the swastika was a symbol of good fortune (the name itself, from the Sanskrit, translates as "It is well"). It has been found on ancient Greek and Mesopotamian coins, Celtic and Scandinavian artifacts, and objects of art and/or worship from India, China, Byzantium, Egypt, and pre-Columbian America. Early Christians, who used it during Roman persecution, called it the *crux dissimulata;* it is also known as the *crux gammata,* because its twisted arms resemble four Greek gammas. As late as 1930 the German scholar Rudolf Koch noted its connection with sun worship, saying it had derived from the "sun wheel." A scant five years later, the Nazis adopted it as their emblem, twisting it, as they twisted so many things, so its arms pointed right and not left.   Stanley and Ruth Freed, "The Origin of the Swastika," in *Natural History* (January 1980); Rudolf Koch, *The Book of Signs* (Dover reprint, 1955).

WHERE IS DRESDEN CHINA MADE?

In the nineteenth century numerous factories in and around the German city of Dresden produced porcelain ware of varying quality, and much of this is commonly, and correctly, designated "Dresden ware." What most people mean when they speak of Dresden ware, however, is porcelain produced not in Dresden, but in the nearby town of Meissen, home of the oldest porcelain factory in Europe and the origin of some of the finest, most delicately crafted china anywhere in the world.

Meissen porcelain was first produced in 1708 by craftsmen sponsored by Augustus the Strong, elector of Saxony, the region of which Dresden was the capital. The work of the Saxon factory established at Meissen two years later became known in France as *Saxe,* and among ceramicists *Saxe au point* and *Saxe à l'étoile* are known even today as particularly distinguished examples of the European potters' art: They are identified by crossed swords on the base of the piece, with a dot near the intersection in the first and a star near it in the second.

China actually made in Dresden includes pieces known as "Crown Dresden," which is frequently confused with Meissen ware. Made by Helena Wolfsohn in the 1870s, Crown Dresden originally copied the very rare "AR" mark of Augustus Rex Meissen ware but, after a Meissen suit, shifted to a crown with "Dresden" written beneath. None of this would be terribly important if it were not for the fact that antiques appreciate with age, so that eighteenth-century "Dresden" is considerably more valuable than Crown Dresden of a century later. George Savage and Harold Newman, *An Illustrated Dictionary of Ceramics* (Van Nostrand Reinhold, 1976).

WHERE DID THE LIMERICK COME FROM?

The comic, often bawdy light verse form known as the limerick has been called "the last surviving folk poetry in the machine age." Although the description would flatter the Irish (who pride themselves as much on being out of date as on having the gift of gab), there is no evidence that the form originated in the town whose name it shares—or anywhere else in the Emerald Isle. Old dictionaries, including the *Oxford English Dictionary,* suggest it may have been a French verse form brought *to* Limerick by Irish soldiers returning from foreign wars. A more common explanation is that it grew out of the traditional refrain "Will you come up to Limerick?" Both explanations are conjectural.

Among the earliest English limericks is the "Hickory Dickory Dock" rhyme which appeared in the early eighteenth century; the earliest collection of these fanciful rhymes appear in *The History of Sixteen Wonderful Old Women* (1821) and *Anecdotes and Adventures of Fifteen Gentlemen* (1822). The latter volume inspired Edward Lear to turn to the form, and it was from his first *Book of Nonsense* (1846) that its modern popularity derived. Lear never claimed to have invented the form, although it is frequently ascribed to him. The first recorded use of the term "limerick," in fact (according to the *Oxford English Dictionary*), was in 1898—ten years after Lear died. Karl Beckson and Arthur Ganz, *Literary Terms: A Dictionary* (Farrar, Straus, & Giroux, 1977); Alex Preminger, ed., *Princeton Encyclopedia of Poetry and Poetics* (Princeton, 1974); James Reeves, "Limerick," in *Encyclopedia Americana* (1980).

THE BULLFIGHT IS NOT SPANISH.

In the Picasso museum in Barcelona there is a series of drawings of bullfights in which the original, primitive magic of the
sport appears with eccentric clarity. The *toreros,* in their frilly
"suits of light," are like so many mincing elves, while the bulls
are phantasms of flesh, far more minotaur than cow. Looming
clumsily amid the dancing men, they are monuments to the solid,
the unyielding. Seeing those drawings makes you realize that the
bullfight is not so much a game as an ancient purgative ritual, in
which surrogate heroes prance for the assembled masses with an
energy that is both life and death.

Spain was the last European nation to abandon feudalism, to
deny the strong man ethos—and so it is predictable that the bullfight should have found a permanent home here. A people
among whom *la muerte* is seen as a kind of blessing naturally
took up the *corrida* as an appropriate national game. Better than
the Church and better than monarchy, it shows the peninsula's
luxuriant backwardness.

But the bullfight was not born in Spain. The bull was a symbol
of strength, endurance, and fertility throughout the prehistoric
world, and early versions of the bullfight were found among peoples as diverse as the Greeks, Romans, Egyptians, Cretans,
Koreans, and Chinese. The ancient Persians paid homage to the
animal, people of the eastern Mediterranean slaughtered it in a
vegetation ceremony, and modern African Zulus killed it and
drank its gall. All of these customs were a means of ensuring
prosperity by assuming the animal's power. Spain may have gotten the bullfight as part of an ancient vegetation ceremony, or it
may have been introduced by the Moors. Whichever route it
came by, it was not unique to Iberia.   Rudolf Brasch, *How Did
Sports Begin?* (David McKay, 1974).

WHERE DID GOLF ORIGINATE?

It was in Scotland, around 1552, that the world's most celebrated golf course, St. Andrews, was established, and it has been
the Scots, for most of the subsequent four centuries, that have
most conspicuously distinguished themselves as addicts of the
game. This has led many to suppose that golf was invented in the

highlands, and some, as Rudolf Brasch contends, have even seen in it evidence of that nation's "reserve, caution, and meticulous care. Only a Scot, it has been contended, could have created a contest that combined such features as hitting a small ball across rough country to a hole in the ground, without his opponent having the right to interfere in any way."

The cliché about Scottish reserve may or may not be accurate, but in any event the Scots did not invent the game; they only organized the mania. Versions of golf employing a stick and stone, instead of the modern club and ball, had probably been played before written history began, and in Imperial Rome the game *paganica,* "the country game," involved whacking a bent stick at a leather ball stuffed with feathers: It was very likely brought to northern Europe by Roman legions, who may have pushed it in the direction of Scotland.

Both the Dutch and the Flemish have been credited with the invention of golf, the former because of their game *kolf* or *kolven,* in which one tallies the number of strokes it takes to hit a standing post; the latter because of their game *chole,* a cross-country game in which the clubs resembled the modern version. In neither of these games, however, does the player sink balls into a hole. The best estimate of golf's origin, then, may be that it was the Scottish variant, developed into a national passion by the fifteenth century, of a game that had long been played on the Continent.

That passion, incidentally, was not immediately shared by all Scots. In 1457, the Scottish Parliament under James II became so alarmed that his subjects were neglecting their archery practice (a necessity for the national defense) that they outlawed the stick-and-ball game, demanding that it be "utterly cryit doun and nocht usit." The injunction had at best a short-lived effect. Rudolf Brasch, *How Did Sports Begin?* (David McKay, 1974).

THE ENGLISH HORN IS NOT ENGLISH.

Not only is the English horn not English, but it is not even a horn. Horns (such as trumpets and tubas) are what musical taxonomists call "lip-vibrated aerophones," while the English horn is a double-reed pipe, related to the oboe and bassoon. The precursors of the double-reed family originated in the ancient Near

East, from where they were brought to Europe by Crusaders in the early Middle Ages. In the poignant, if somewhat fulsome, phrasing of H. W. Schwartz, "they have preserved their oriental character and suggest an expatriated people who will not forget and who still yearn for the homeland."

How this descendant of the Levant came to be called an English horn is not entirely certain. The most informed conjecture is that when the peculiarly curved instrument began to appear in Italy and Vienna around the middle of the eighteenth century, the French called it *cor anglais* to distinguish it from their own *cor,* or horn—not because it was English, but because it was at that time "angled" so a player could reach the lower keys. Some authorities claim the "anglais" meant "English" right from the start, and that the "horn" was so called because it sounded like an English hornpipe. Others think the instrument was used as a substitute for an English hunting horn, and so received an imitative name.

For whatever reason, by the 1760s musicians throughout Europe had taken the misnomer to heart. The Italians called the woodwind *corno inglese;* the Germans wrote *englisches Waldhorn.* In the welter of analysis, perhaps we should recall Schwartz's humble quip: "All of this controversy is really unimportant, for regardless of what name it goes by, it will sound just as sad and melancholy." Pining, no doubt, for the East.   Sibyl Marcuse, *A Survey of Musical Instruments* (Harper & Row, 1975); H. W. Schwartz, *The Story of Musical Instruments* (Garden City Publishing Company, 1943).

WHERE IS THE UKULELE FROM?

Few instruments are so firmly associated with a specific locale as the ukulele is with Hawaii, but the idea that it originated in the islands is, to put it bluntly, a lei. It evolved from a small Portuguese guitar, was taken to Hawaii (then the Sandwich Islands) in the nineteenth century by Portuguese sailors, and found its way back to Europe and then the United States between the two world wars, when it enjoyed a brief vogue among flappers. Its Portuguese predecessor went by the name of *machete,* a curious term which designates not only the musical instrument but also a saber, a type of popular song, and (as in Spanish) a machete. And you thought English was confusing.   Anthony Baines, ed., *Musical Instruments Through the Ages* (Walker, 1976); Karl Geiringer, *Musical Instruments* (Allen & Unwin, 1943).

WHAT IS THE ORIGIN OF KILTS?

This most Celtic of Scottish accoutrements originated not in the misty highlands, but in the sultry eastern Mediterranean, at a time when the Scottish clans had not yet been imagined. Both in Egypt's Old Kingdom (third millennium B.C.) and in the mysterious Minoan culture, based on the island of Crete, men wore a skirtlike garment that Millia Davenport describes as a kilt; in the days of Persian glory (the sixth century B.C.), the Medes were similarly garbed.

Kiltlike skirts seem to have reached the highlands by way of Roman Britain. Among the innovations that Roman legions brought to the British Isles was the *laena,* a large cloak worn by the capital's common people. Secured at the waist by a belt, this cloak divided into a copious shawl for the head and a long skirt, or kilt, hanging down. Adapted by the indigenous people, the garment became the highland kilt and plaid.   Millia Davenport, *The Book of Costume* (Crown, 1948); Herbert Morris, *Costume and Fashion* (Dutton, 1924).

WHERE DO PANAMA HATS COME FROM?

Popular among nineteenth-century British imperialists and plantation owners in the American prebellum South (where they were known as "planters' hats"), Panama hats were popularized in North America in the 1890s by soldiers who had bought them on the isthmus. They did not, however, originate in Panama, but in the Ecuadorian town of Jipijapa, where the *Carludovica palmata* tree, from whose leaves the hats were plaited, grows in equatorial abundance. In turn-of-the-century Central America, they were even called "jipijapa hats," in honor of their place of manufacture. Turner Wilcox says they are made in Peru and Colombia as well as Ecuador, but not in Panama itself.   R. Turner Wilcox, *The Dictionary of Costume* (Scribner's, 1969).

WHERE DID DUNGAREES (BLUE JEANS) ORIGINATE?

No article of clothing seems as quintessentially American as dungarees. In the 1960s blue jeans became the uniform of a generation, and in the past few years, thanks to the pioneering efforts of various designers, the "look" has become de rigueur on two continents.

But dungarees do not come from these shores; nor are jeans, or even denim, peculiarly American. It's true that Levi Strauss made the first so-called blue jeans in San Francisco in 1850—and made a fortune selling them to frayed-pants miners. But the dungaree cloth which went into them had come originally from India, where as early as the seventeenth century it was being used to make clothing both for the natives and for British sailors. The word itself comes from *dungri,* the Hindi term for the suburb of Bombay where the blue cloth was manufactured.

"Denim," another seventeenth-century term, drives from *serge de Nismes,* a cloth produced in the southern French town of Nismes. "Jeans" is an American corruption of *jene* or *geane fustian*—sixteenth-century terms for a cloth produced in Genoa. The countrymen of Columbus could well have set the stage for old Levi.   *Oxford English Dictionary* (Oxford, 1961); George Stimpson, *A Book About a Thousand Things* (Harper, 1946).

RULERS:

UNEASY LIES THE HEAD

WHEN IS GEORGE WASHINGTON'S BIRTHDAY?

I always liked February as a child. On the twelfth you got off school to celebrate Lincoln's birthday and ten days later it was Washington's turn. Since both birthdays were national holidays, and since February was already short, it was a recreational prelude to the longer, more significant Easter break.

But celebrating Washington's birthday on February 22 was, and is, a concession to a fairly recent calendar reform. George was actually born on February 11, 1732, and it wasn't until his twentieth year that his birthday got shifted eleven days ahead. This came about because in 1752 the English nation and its colonies finally got around to dropping the Julian calendar and adopting the reformed calendar that had been proposed in 1582 by Pope Gregory XIII. George's birth date had to be "adjusted" to fit into the new system, and as a result he kept his age intact, but lost over a week of work time. So, of course, did everyone else: to schoolchildren it must have seemed a divine boon.

The birthday of the Revolutionary War hero was celebrated as early as 1782 in Virginia, but on the Old Style February 11. It only began being observed on February 22 in 1796, the year he left the presidency. Today it is celebrated, like nearly everything else, on the nearest Monday, to give all of us more time to kill ourselves on the roads. Robert J. Myers, *Celebrations: The Complete Book of American Holidays* (Doubleday, 1972).

WHAT WERE PRESIDENT GRANT'S GIVEN NAMES?

"U. S. Grant." It has such a stentorian, patriotic ring to it that it seems eminently well suited to the man who saved the Union and became our eighteenth president. But U.S. were not his original initials; nor were "Ulysses" and "Simpson" his given names. He was born Hiram Ulysses Grant, and it wasn't until he went to West Point as a cadet that he adopted the now familiar "U. S."

What happened was that the congressman who sponsored him for the academy, in reporting his name to the registrar, dropped the Hiram, retained the Ulysses (that one seemed martial enough), and added Simpson, which was the boy's mother's maiden name. Why he did this we don't know, but evidently young Hiram saw the advantage in the revision, because he retained it from then on. A good thing, perhaps, for the Union: Is it likely that Hiram would have commanded quite the loyalty that Ulysses did from his troops?

Grant was not the only president with a problematic S. Harry Truman, born a year before Grant died, is known as Harry S. Truman, but it is not generally known that the S doesn't stand for anything. At his birth his parents were undecided whether to give him the middle name Shippe (the middle name of his paternal grandfather) or Solomon (the first name of his maternal grandfather). They settled on the letter alone.   David Donald, "Ulysses Simpson Grant," and Richard S. Kirkendall, "Harry S. Truman," in *Encyclopedia Americana* (1980).

AFTER WHOM IS "CAESAREAN SECTION" NAMED?

A longstanding tradition holds that Julius Caesar was, like Macduff in Shakespeare's play, "from his mother's womb untimely ripp'd"—that is, delivered by caesarean section. Considering the sanitary practices of the ancient world, and the fact that Caesar's mother lived for many years after his birth, this is at best unlikely. Infection was so common in premodern C-section cases that virtually all of the women so delivered died shortly after giving birth. So the notion that "caesarean" derives from "Caesar"—or that the reverse is true—is etymologically tenuous.

More likely, the term derives from the *lex caesarea* of the seventh century B.C., which stipulated that a woman dying close to term should be delivered abdominally to save the child; performing such a posthumous operation quickly would of course involve cutting, and *lex caesarea* may be approximately translated as "the law of incision." There is no certainty, though, that Caesar got his name from this custom. Latinists disagree whether "Caesar"

(from which of course we get both "Kaiser" and "Czar") comes
from the verb *caedo* (to cut); the noun *caesaries* (a head of dark
hair); or the adjectives *caesius* or *caeruleus* (shades of blue, as in
eyes). Since we do not know what Caesar looked like as an infant,
the point remains unresolved. Charlton Lewis and Charles
Short, *A Latin Dictionary* (Oxford, 1969).

KING ARTHUR WAS NOT A KING.

   The ultimate British regent, the defender of the soil and the
faith, the incomparable, legendary ruler of the land that would
become England, Arthur, the king of the Britons, has been celebrated in song and story for so long that no one seems to know
any longer whether he was a real or fictional character. Books
have been written placing him, and misplacing him, at this or
that battle site, and the debate is sure to go on. I won't add to the
muddle here, except to comment on one fact.

   Historical figure or not, it is at least generally agreed that
"Arthur" was king of the Britons sometime during the sixth
Christian century. The title "king" is coupled with his name as
readily, and unarguably, as "generalissimo" was coupled with
Franco's. According to a major Arthurian source, however, he
may not have been a king at all.

   Leslie Alcock identifies, apart from oral histories, three principal medieval sources for the Arthurian legends: the history of the
monk Gildas, the Anglo-Saxon Chronicle, and the text commonly referred to as Nennius's history of the Britons, which he
calls the British Historical Miscellany. It is in this miscellany of
British Museum manuscripts that Arthur had an alternate title:
dux bellorum, or "leader of battles."

   The phrasing goes like this: *Tunc Arthur pugnabat cum regibus
Brittonum sed ipse dux erat bellorum.* Which means "At that time
Arthur was fighting with the kings of the Britons, but was himself
leader of battles." It has been much debated who these "kings of
the Britons" were, but in any case it is clear that Arthur was not
one of their number. He was rather a kind of warlord, working
for many British princes to stop the Anglo-Saxon invasions then
threatening the common realm. If he indeed existed, we might
see him then as a very good mercenary soldier—so good, in fact,
that the actual rulers of the land were able to rely upon him to

take care of the island's defense.   Leslie Alcock, *Arthur's Britain*
(Allen Lane, 1971).

WHO WAS THE YOUNGEST UNITED STATES
PRESIDENT?

Next to his patrician charm, his age was John F. Kennedy's
principal drawing card in the 1960 presidential race. After the
avuncular Eisenhower, JFK seemed the epitome of youthful
vigor; his detractors said that showed he was too green for the
job, but his supporters saw it as a sign of renewal. Kennedy was
not, however, the youngest man ever to occupy the presidential
office—though that is still widely believed. On Inaugural Day,
1961, he was 43 years old. When Theodore Roosevelt took the
oath in 1901 upon the assassination of William McKinley, he was
only 42. Kennedy was, though, the youngest person ever *elected*
to the office.   James T. Patterson, "John F. Kennedy," and
Robert F. Wesser, "Theodore Roosevelt," in *Academic American
Encyclopedia* (1980).

NERO NEVER FIDDLED WHILE ROME BURNED.

My seventh-grade history teacher, an animated classroom
clown, once hopped on top of his desk with a delirious smile to
mime Nero's famous fiddling act. It is a moment I have never
forgotten, but the episode it etched in my memory turns out to
have been pure fiction.

Of course it's easy to believe almost anything about someone
who killed both his wife and his mother. Setting fire to Rome and
dancing amid the flames would be nothing for the deranged boy
emperor, if he was really as bad as he was painted. He was bad
all right, and later Christians may have been justified in thinking
of him as Antichrist, but it's unlikely he set the blaze. According
to the *Annals* of the contemporary historian Tacitus, Nero, at the
time of the conflagration, was in his villa at Antium—thirty-five
miles from Rome. It's true that he took advantage of the fire to
rebuild the city in a splendid new Greek style, but the idea that
he set it himself is a later invention.

As for the fiddling story, it's obviously a fanciful tale. Nero did style himself a musician, but his instrument was probably the lyre. The violin was not developed in Italy until fifteen centuries after his death. *Encyclopaedia Britannica* (1974).

CLEOPATRA WAS NOT EGYPTIAN.

There were several queens of Egypt by this name. The one who ruled the Nile kingdom in the days of Antony and Caesar was Cleopatra VII Philopator, who was born in 69 B.C. and died by her own hand not quite forty years later. The legend that she killed herself with an asp (the Egyptian cobra) is unverifiable but not unlikely: The snake was the symbol of Egyptian royalty, and it would have been fitting for the queen to dispatch herself in this manner. With her died the Ptolemy dynasty, Egyptian independence, and the Roman republic. She might with more justice than Louis XV have said, "After me the deluge."

The Ptolemies, whose line she ended, were not Egyptian but Macedonian—they came from the same region that had given the world Alexander the Great—the mountainous area north of the Aegean Sea that is now shared by Yugoslavia, Bulgaria, and Greece. When Egypt became a Roman province after the queen's death, hegemony had merely shifted from one Mediterranean power to another. Cleopatra herself was part Macedonian, part Greek, and part Iranian.   Caroline N. Peck, "Cleopatra," in *Encyclopedia Americana* (1980).

WHAT WERE HITLER'S FAMILY NAME AND ORIGINAL PROFESSION?

In an attempt to trivialize the principal monster of our age, some have claimed that Adolf Hitler's family name was the ridiculous-sounding "Schicklgruber," and that the crowd-intoxicated Führer who bore it was originally a house painter or paperhanger. Neither assertion is based on fact.

Hitler's family name was, as he claimed, Hitler. This was a modern variation of the fifteenth-century Hiedler, which was possibly Czech in origin. His father, Alois Hitler, had been known as Alois Schicklgruber until he was forty, because he had been born out of wedlock in 1837, and had been given his

mother's maiden name. Although Alois's paternity is not absolutely certain, it's been pretty well established that his father (Adolf's grandfather) was Johann Georg Hiedler, who married Maria
Schicklgruber in 1842 and who gave Alois the name "Hitler" in
1877. That was twelve years before Adolf was born. According to
historian Alan Bullock, Adolf "was never known by any other
name until his opponents dug up this long-forgotten village scan-
dal and tried, without justification, to label him with his grandmother's name of Schicklgruber."

As for the house painter story, that too is evidently a myth. As
a young man in Vienna, Hitler had aspirations to be an architect,
and supported himself by painting picture postcards, which he
peddled with a friend in taverns. He also did posters, advertise-
ments, and drawings of no great distinction; these last could still
be found in Vienna in the 1930s, "when they had acquired the
value of collectors' pieces."   Alan Bullock, *Hitler: A Study in
Tyranny* (Bantam, 1961).

WHAT "WICKED KING" SIGNED MAGNA CARTA?

Medieval England's King John is one of those "bad sovereigns" whom we all grow up despising. Because of the Robin
Hood legends, he has had a terrible press for centuries, while his
brother Richard the Lion-Hearted, Robin's and Hollywood's favorite, has come down to us as a model ruler: equitable, wise,
and even-tempered. This is a gross distortion of the facts.

John was no paragon of virtue, it's true. He granted the charter
under duress and repudiated it the same summer. But the whole
episode had been Richard's fault. Had he managed his kingdom
with the slightest degree of care, Runnymede might never have
occurred. Instead he spent virtually his entire reign in the Cru-
sades, indulging a homicidal mania.

His exploits bled the nation dry, and in the process under-
mined the crown, leaving it open to baronial attack. John was too
vacillating a regent to pick up the pieces successfully, but he was
hardly the back-stabber of legend. In the estimation of the English scholar Frank Barlow, the nation declined in John's reign
largely because Richard was "a heroic fool."

As for the signing of the Great Charter, it's doubtful that John
could write, and in any case the document was not signed. It was

"sealed" by the cornered king on June 15, 1215. Frank Barlow, *The Feudal Kingdom of England* (Longmans, 1955); George Stimpson, *Information Roundup* (Harper, 1948).

ON WHAT DID LINCOLN WRITE THE GETTYSBURG ADDRESS?

Abraham Lincoln seems to have had inordinate difficulty in finding decent writing equipment. There's the stock image of the young rail-splitter on his belly before a fire, scrawling figures in coal on the back of a shovel. At the other end of his life, there's the image of the war-weary president hastily jotting down a masterpiece on the back of a used envelope, hours before arriving at Gettysburg.

I don't know about the shovel, but the idea that he wrote the Gettysburg Address on an envelope, or anything else, on the train is without question a myth. In fact the speech was finished, and written down, at least a day before the battlefield dedication ceremony. As long ago as 1906 Henry Sweetser Burrage noted that the address was probably finished on November 18, 1863—the evening before it was delivered. He noted, too, that according to Lincoln's private secretary, no writing at all was done on the train—it was simply too bumpy a ride to permit writing, with or without an envelope. Lincoln drafted the address, as might be expected of the president, on executive letterhead.

The homespun Lincoln dies hard because it's flattering to a democratic people to think of their favorite man of the people spinning out those deathless words practically off the cuff, as he would have an Illinois yarn. In Robert Lowell's opinion, though, Lincoln may have been "the last president of the United States who could genuinely use words." You're not born with a gift like that; you acquire it with practice, and Lincoln was far too conscious of the dignity of the Gettysburg occasion to have relegated his speech's transcription to an eleventh-hour jolting envelope. Henry Sweetser Burrage, *Gettysburg and Lincoln* (Putnam's, 1906); Allan Nevins, *Lincoln and the Gettysburg Address* (University of Illinois Press, 1964).

WHAT EGYPTIAN RULER ERECTED "CLEOPATRA'S NEEDLES"?

"Cleopatra's Needles" are a pair of 70-foot tall granite obelisks which stood originally before the temple of the sun at Heliopolis, near the present city of Cairo. One of the pair now stands in London, the other in New York City. They were constructed in the fifteenth century B.C. by the pharaoh Thutmose III, and up until the Middle Ages were known as "Pharaoh's great needles." Perhaps because Cleopatra was among the most famous of Egypt's rulers, the obelisks later became associated with her; this erroneous association was abetted by the fact that from 22 B.C. until the late nineteenth century, they were situated in her capital city of Alexandria. Thutmose had them constructed, though, fifteen hundred years before she was born. Caroline N. Peck, "Cleopatra's Needles," in *Encyclopedia Americana* (1980).

WHAT MONSTROUS ENGLISH KING KILLED THE "PRINCES IN THE TOWER"?

He is one of the arch villains of all English history, a man with such a deficient moral sense that in order to secure a crown, he murders not only his own brother the Duke of Clarence but also their dead brother Edward's heirs, the young boys Edward, Prince of Wales, and Richard, Duke of York. He can't even do it himself, either, so he engages a hireling, one John Tyrell, to smother the lads for him. No wonder his defeat and ignominious death at Bosworth Field seems a stroke of justice in an otherwise sordid tale.

Or so the schoolbooks, William Shakespeare, and the sainted Sir Thomas More, from whose *History of Richard III* the picture of the last Plantagenet as a hunchbacked, vicious monster was first drawn, would have us believe. Is it an accurate picture? Several historians, including Horace Walpole, have thought not.

According to the minority view, Richard III was the victim of a gigantic deception, engineered by his usurper Henry Tudor (Henry VII) after Bosworth to discredit the house of York and consolidate Tudor power. In her ingeniously reasoned investigation of the case, *The Daughter of Time*, Josephine Tey demonstrates that while Richard had absolutely nothing to gain from his

young nephews' deaths, Henry Tudor had everything—making
him a much more likely suspect than Richard. Furthermore, she
shows, there was no contemporary accusation of Richard for the
crime (not even by Henry, who certainly could have used this
trump card), nor any evidence that after the deed had supposedly
been done, Richard and the boys' mother were ever anything but
perfectly cordial to each other.

The conclusion Ms. Tey draws is that the boys were murdered
after Bosworth, by Tyrell, but on *Henry's* orders. The supposedly
deformed, rapacious tyrant was merely a Tudor invention, concocted by Henry's scholars as a smoke screen for his own iniquity.
Thomas More's account, the "horse's mouth" for subsequent historians, was "a damned piece of hearsay and a swindle"—the
good Sir Thomas himself was eight when Richard died.

A minority report, yes, but an astonishingly convincing one.
Not only does it lay the blame for the boys' death at the door of a
man who, having no legitimate claim to the throne himself,
needed them out of the way; it also effectively explains what even
Richard's many detractors have never been able to explain: how
a king of acknowledged ability, generosity, and popularity could
have turned into a madman overnight. The answer is simple: He
didn't.   Josephine Tey, *The Daughter of Time* (Pocket Books,
1977).

"SILENT CAL" COOLIDGE LOVED TO TALK.

The Vermont Yankee Calvin Coolidge is as closely identified
with taciturnity as Harry Truman is with a readiness to say exactly what was on his mind. "Silent Cal," many of his contemporaries called him, and the nickname has stuck. He is the ultimate
White House exemplar of that dogged, laconic grittiness which is
supposed to have forged a civilization out of the rock-hard hills
of New England.

I am indebted to Ashley Montagu and Edward Darling's *The
Prevalence of Nonsense* for pointing me to a book that dispels the
"Silent Cal" legend with admirable humor. Thirty years after the
thirtieth president's death in 1933, researchers Robert Ferrell and
Howard Quint unearthed in Coolidge's last home, Northhamp-
ton, Massachusetts, the transcripts of the off-the-record press conferences he had held while president; these proved to be an

unusually revealing source of information about a quite talkative, even garrulous, chief executive.

Coolidge, evidently, was perfectly willing to chat at length about both domestic and international topics—but only if he could first set up the format of discussion and control the drift of interrogation. To that end he established that marvelous modern combination of carnival barker and defensive lineman, the post of presidential press secretary; to that end, too, he held biweekly press conferences throughout his administration in which he displayed not only the famous laconic wit but also a broad and detailed acquaintance with "a wide variety of subjects" which he treated "with a degree of expertise that historians of a later generation not always have appreciated."

Not that he mouthed off indiscriminately. The carefully engineered conferences were a way of presenting his administration in a favorable, not necessarily a candid, light, and although he was uncharacteristically voluble to the press corps, he was not exactly wed to "full disclosure." Questions were fielded and screened; the president frowned upon "follow-up" questions; and many topics were avoided almost entirely, among them such hot issues as prohibition, the Sacco-Vanzetti case, the Scopes monkey trial, and the bullish New York Stock Exchange. As Ferrell and Quint remark, "When one compares what President Coolidge and the historian Frederick Lewis Allen had to say about the twenties, it seems at times that they were not talking about the same era."   Robert H. Ferrell and Howard H. Quint, *The Talkative President* (Garland Publishing, 1979).

WHAT WAS GEORGE VI'S FIRST NAME?

The tumultuous years of George VI's reign, during which his kingdom nearly became a fief of Nazi Germany, are remembered as the years of Churchill, not the king himself. This is fitting, since even without comparison to the dynamic Sir Winston, George was a quiet and largely colorless personality. He traveled widely with his consort, the current Queen Mother, and was a focus of patriotic hope during the war by visiting bombed areas of the country and inspecting defense plants.

His quiet, self-effacing nature was nowhere better demonstrated than in his willingness, upon ascending the throne in

1936, to put family considerations ahead of his own personal custom. His given names were, in order, Albert, Frederick, Arthur, and George; one would have expected him to become England's King Albert I. His great-grandmother Queen Victoria, however, upon the death of her beloved Albert in 1861, had made it known that she would be most grieved if the name "Albert" were ever to grace the throne of England. This royal equivalent of retiring a favorite ball player's number the new Albert honored with appropriate filial dignity, changing his name so that he ruled not as Albert I but as George VI. *The Columbia Encyclopedia* (1963); *The Academic American Encyclopedia* (1980).

WHO IS BURIED IN GRANT'S TOMB?

This was a favorite consolation question on the old Groucho Marx TV show *You Bet Your Life.* If a contestant had failed to answer anything correctly and was thus in danger of leaving the show without winnings, Groucho would drag this one out, the guest would sheepishly say, "Grant"—and go home fifty dollars richer.

But "Grant" is only half the answer. The tomb, which sits on Riverside Drive in New York City, was designed by John H. Duncan, paid for by public subscription, and dedicated in 1897 by President William McKinley. It contains the remains not only of the Civil War hero, but of his wife, Julia, as well. "Grant's Tomb" in *Encyclopedia Americana* (1980).

PEOPLE:

PERSONS AND PERSONAS

WHAT NATIONALITY WAS ST. PATRICK?

Patrick is the patron saint of Ireland not because he is Irish but because he converted the island to the Faith. The details of his life are unclear, but we do know he was born in Roman Britain early in the fifth century A.D., the son of an imperial official and the grandson of a Christian priest. So he was clearly British although the place of his birth is uncertain. He called it "Bannavem Taberniae," but scholars disagree about its location, some claiming Dunbarton on the Clyde, others Cumberland near Hadrian's Wall, still others the mouth of the Severn. A long way from Ireland, in any case.

Patrick's mission to Ireland later in the century was actually his second visit there; at the age of sixteen he had been kidnapped by Irish pirates and sold into slavery as a shepherd. Six years later he escaped, returned to Britain, and then to Gaul, where he undertook the religious studies that were to prepare him for his life's work: the conversion of his heathen captors. On his ordination he was given the sobriquet Patricius, meaning nobleman, "as a kind of cancellation of his slave background and deficient education"; he had been raised Magonus Sucatus.

Under his direction the Irish monastic system rivaled the ancient clan structure in importance, although Patrick, ever a stranger in a strange land, never quite forgot his original visit. "Even at the end of his life," according to E. J. Dillon, "he expected daily a violent death, to be robbed or reduced to slavery." Today's Irish embrace him with the fervor of children claiming a long-lost father, but the welcome was a long time coming.   E. J. Dillon, "St. Patrick," in *Encyclopedic Dictionary of Religion* (Corpus Publications, 1979).

WHAT KIND OF NAME IS "CONFUCIUS"?

The man who is generally considered China's greatest teacher
was born in 551 B.C. in Shantung province. Although he is known
in the West as Confucius, that name is a Latinization, and not a
very good one at that. His family name was K'ung, his personal
name Ch'iu, and in China he has always been known by the
simple honorific K'ung Tzu, which translates as Master K'ung.

The name "Confucius" was the invention of Portuguese Jesuit
scholars who, around the fifteenth century, tried to approximate
the sound of K'ung Tzu with the letters of the Latin alphabet.
According to Carl Crow that was not their only mistake. To him
Master K'ung was a "sincere, lovable entirely human scholar and
gentleman" who "lived a blameless life, suffered more disillu-
sionments and disappointments than usually fall to the lot of men
and died feeling that his life had been a failure," while Confucius
was a bloodless deification, "an intellectual Frankenstein monster" created by readers who had lost track of the man.   Carl
Crow, *Master Kung* (Harper, 1938); Fung Yu-lan, *A Short History of Chinese Philosophy* (Free Press, 1966).

WHEN DID ROBIN HOOD LIVE?

Robin Hood is generally identified today as a champion of the
tax-oppressed English people at the turn of the thirteenth century. His champion in turn is Richard I, and his enemy the king's
brother, John. Medieval sources, however, are far less clear than
Hollywood about when the outlaw may have lived—and indeed
whether or not he was a historical character at all. He is celebrated in numerous ballads, of which the most famous, the *Lytell
Geste of Robyn Hode,* appeared only in 1495; the earliest printed
reference to the popular hero is in William Langland's *Piers
Plowman,* written in the 1370s. Although numerous attempts
have been made to identify him with this or that historical outlaw
(of which there were many at the time), no conclusive evidence
has been given to help us decide whether he was an actual person
(or persons), the outgrowth of preliterary myth, or simply a poet's
fancy.

As for the date of his deeds, pinning that down is like trying to
say when democracy was born. English social outlawry, like de-

mocracy, evolved over several centuries, and it cannot be stated with certainty that Robin lived under, before, or after King John. All we know is that he was a focus for popular resentment at social inequities by the time of the Peasants' Revolt (1381). He has, of course, continued so to this day, and maybe that is the most significant thing about him: whenever or wherever he shot his last arrow, it has yet to land.   P. Valentine Harris, *The Truth About Robin Hood* (Linneys of Mansfield, 1973); Maurice Keen, *The Outlaws of Medieval Legend* (Routledge & Kegan Paul, 1979).

JOHN CABOT WAS NOT AN ENGLISH EXPLORER.

In the late fifteenth century, when Mediterranean sailors were at the forefront of maritime exploration, John Cabot stood alone as an exemplar of British enterprise: His pluck and courage in braving the North Atlantic winds brought England a foothold in the New World less than ten years after Columbus's first voyage. That he reached Newfoundland in 1497 by following Bristol-based venturers' courses west only confirms the notion, so dear to British schoolboy pride, that the Anglo-Saxons had as genuine a claim to be the discoverers of America as their more publicized Latin rivals.

Unfortunately for this interpretation, Cabot (like Columbus) was Italian. His given name was Giovanni Caboto, he was evidently born in Genoa, and from the middle 1470s he was a citizen of maritime Venice. There he married, had two sons, and busied himself as a merchant. Around 1490 he moved to Valencia in Spain, where he was known as Juan Caboto Montecalunya, and where he tried to convince officials that a westward journey to the Indies was possible. After Columbus beat him to this, he moved his family to Bristol, where he ultimately had better fortune.

The British, impressed by Columbus, were persuaded by the man now called "Cabot" that a northern Atlantic route, following the English fishing routes, would be cheaper and therefore more profitable than Columbus's southern path. In 1496, after he had already made one preliminary voyage, Cabot received a royal patent from England's Henry VII; on the authority of the king, he then set out to the west, hoping to find what he called the Isle of Brasil. Reaching Newfoundland instead, he brought back news of phenomenal fishing off the Banks. This made him briefly rich, until on his third voyage (1498) he was lost at sea. David Beers Quinn, *England and the Discovery of America, 1481–1620* (Knopf, 1974).

CAPTAIN BLIGH WAS NOT THE VILLAIN OF THE BOUNTY MUTINY.

Thanks largely to Charles Laughton's masterful portrayal of him in the 1935 film, William Bligh remains, almost two centuries after the notorious *Bounty* mutiny, an archetypal overbearing officer, as cracked and inflexible in his way as Humphrey Bogart's Queeg. According to Gavin Kennedy, this is a false picture enshrined in the Nordhoff/Hall book and originally concocted by the influential family of Fletcher Christian, the "heroic" head mutineer immortalized by dashing Clark Gable.

The mutiny, says Kennedy, resulted less from Bligh's dictatorial tactics—common enough on eighteenth-century British ships—than from overcrowding, a shortage of able hands, and (most of all) Christian's mental instability. Criticized by the captain for ill performance of his duties, mate Christian fomented the rebellion as revenge and was so unsure of its acceptance among the crew that he had "tied a heavy weight round his neck to bring a speedy end to his life if the mutiny failed and he had to jump over the side." Compare to this the dogged professional Bligh, who navigated an open boat over thousands of miles of ocean after being set adrift, and you can see why Kennedy thinks of the pro-Christian tale as special pleading.

The British admiralty had a similar view of the matter. Far from condemning the "tyrannical" captain, they stood by him through a second mutiny, and retired him as a vice-admiral. Gavin Kennedy, *Bligh* (London, 1978); Philip Ward, *A Dictionary of Common Fallacies* (Oleander Press, 1980).

WHO DISCOVERED HUDSON'S BAY?

Because the Dutch East India Company sponsored his momentous *Half Moon* voyage of 1609, it is often erroneously assumed that Henry Hudson was himself Dutch. Actually he was English, and he had already made two voyages for the English-run Muscovy Company before the 1609 venture: On both of them he had failed to find the northeast passage to the Indies for which he had been commissioned. On his fourth and final voyage, too, during which his crew mutinied and set him adrift, he was sponsored by his own nation.

Although he was a courageous and resourceful navigator, he discovered neither the river, the straits, nor the bay that bear his name. The Hudson River was first sighted by Giovanni da Verrazano, after whom the New York City bridge is named, in 1524, and the following year Estevan Gomez, a Portuguese sailing for Spain, also noted its existence; for a while, at least in Spain, it was known as the Rio de Gomez. Hudson's extensive exploration of the river, almost a century later, gave the eponymous honor to him.

Both Hudson Strait and Hudson Bay were also known long before Hudson. Hudson's own biographer, G. M. Asher, credits the Portuguese with finding both bodies of water in the mid-sixteenth century, and Lawrence Burpee speculates that John Cabot, the Genoan who sailed for the English, may have reached the strait as early as 1498. Hudson did not see the bay until 1610, on his ill-fated last voyage on the *Discovery.* Robert H. Boyle, *The Hudson River* (Norton, 1969); Lawrence J. Burpee, *The Search for the Western Sea* (Macmillan, 1935).

WHAT NATIONALITY WAS JEAN-PAUL MARAT?

Jean-Paul Marat, whose name became widely known in the 1960s because of Peter Weiss's play *Marat-Sade,* has long been considered a French national hero. Although his attacks on the aristocracy and his fear of counter-revolution were seen as extremist at the time, his martyrdom at the hands of the conservative Charlotte Corday secured him a place in history as one of the French Revolution's most popular figures. Jacques Louis David's famous painting *Death of Marat* (1793) was only the first of many tributes that have been paid to the fallen leader since his murder.

The irony in this is that he was Swiss, not French. Born in Boudry, Switzerland, on May 24, 1743, he spent an obscure youth on the Continent before going to London in the 1770s, where he became a successful physician. His early philosophical and political tracts were written in English, not French. It wasn't until 1777 that he returned to France, where he began to write in French and became the personal physician to, of all people, the guards of Louis XVI's younger brother—the young man who would become Charles X after the Bourbon restoration. His editorship of *L'Ami du Peuple,* beginning in 1789, was the step that was to bring him, within four years, a revolutionary's death. *Encyclopaedia Britannica* (1974).

WHOM DID POCAHONTAS MARRY?

Since Pocahontas is a genuine American heroine, a dream in the eye of the nation, it should not be surprising that her legend, over the centuries, has accumulated the patina of sentimental romance. So compelling is the image of the young Indian princess offering her life for her lover that we often forget that the man she ultimately married was not the one she had rescued. In fact, Pocahontas was married twice—and neither time to John Smith. We have only the captain's word for it, moreover, that she had rescued him at all—and there is no compelling evidence that they had ever been lovers.

A contemporary of Shakespeare and Elizabeth, Pocahontas was called Matoaka by her tribe; Pocahontas, meaning "playful one," was her father Powhatan's pet name for her. She was twelve, reputedly, when Smith was about to be sacrificed and she threw her body over his. A couple of years later she became the wife of Kocoum, whose fate, like his life, is obscure. Presumably, he died or the couple was divorced soon after the wedding, because in April 1614 Pocahontas, now baptized Rebecca, became the Christian wife of Smith's fellow colonist John Rolfe. Rolfe took her to England with him, where she was a brief celebrity and where, in 1617, she died at the age of twenty-two.

Rolfe returned to the New World, remarried, and was killed four years later by Pocahontas's kinsmen. The Rolfe-Pocahontas line, through a son, Thomas, who was raised in England, is rumored to have included the Marshalls, the Jeffersons, and the Lees—an ostensibly more illustrious company than the descendants of the famous Captain Smith. David Wallechinsky and Irving Wallace, *The People's Almanac* (Bantam, 1975).

WHAT DOES ATLAS HOLD ON HIS SHOULDERS?

It was the sky, not the world, that broad-shouldered Atlas was condemned to support. Numerous classical authors mention the hapless Titan, some making him a guardian of the pillars of heaven but most agreeing that his job was to hold up the sky. He was given this not exactly plum position either by Zeus, as a punishment for participating in Uranus's rebellion, or by Perseus, who turned him into stone by showing him the head of the Gorgon. He is called the father of the Hesperides, and is associated with North Africa's Atlas Mountains; the ancients saw those cloud-nudging peaks as images of his straining shoulders.

Atlas was brawny but slow. When Heracles was searching for the apples of the Hesperides, the Titan offered to get them for him (the Hesperides were his daughters) if the hero would hold up the sky until he returned. The deal was struck, but upon his return Atlas refused to resume his burden. "Just until I get a pad for my shoulders," said the cagy Heracles—and Atlas fell for the ruse. He's been holding up the sky ever since, although he is commonly depicted, in atlases and gazetteers, as shouldering the world instead.   *The Oxford Classical Dictionary* (Oxford, 1970).

BENJAMIN FRANKLIN DID NOT FOUND THE SATURDAY EVENING POST.

Contrary both to popular opinion and to the magazine's own claim, Franklin had nothing to do with the founding of the *Post.* As Tom Burnam points out, he did own and operate a small newspaper, the *Pennsylvania Gazette,* after 1729, turning it from a failing enterprise into such a successful one that it lasted until 1815, twenty-five years after Franklin's own death. But the connection between this paper and the *Post* was slight. The *Gazette* was not the forerunner of the *Post;* the two publications were merely printed in the same print shop at different times, and, in fact, the *Gazette* had already been out of business for six years when the first issue of the *Post* appeared in 1821. By that time Ben had been gone for thirty-one years.

The Franklin connection was apparently invented toward the end of the nineteenth century, possibly as a way of drumming up business in the midst of the yellow-press news wars. The cover first started carrying the phrase "Founded A.D. 1728 by Benjamin Franklin" in 1899, under the editorship of George Horace Lorimer. Such a claim would no doubt have scandalized the original publishers, but it has been accepted unquestioned ever since. Tom Burnam, *The Dictionary of Misinformation* (Crowell, 1975).

ON THE "18TH OF APRIL IN '75," WHO WARNED THE AMERICAN COLONISTS THAT THE BRITISH WERE COMING?

Thanks to Longfellow's famous ballad, the reputation of a doughty Boston silversmith has been firmly engraved in the minds of generations of schoolchildren. Ask anybody over twelve who warned the minutemen that the redcoats were on the way, and the answer will be swift: Paul Revere.

But Revere was only one of three riders that momentous night. The other two, William Dawes and Samuel Prescott, have been forgotten in the hooplah about Revere, and yet it was their efforts, at least as much as his, that made the April 19 stand at Concord Bridge possible.

On April 18, 1775, the provisional commander of the colonial insurrectionary forces was Joseph Warren, a doctor among whose most trusted confederates were Revere and Dawes, a cobbler. When Warren learned of British troop movements that were clearly a prelude to an attack on the rebels' arms stores, he ordered the two to mount up and warn the countryside west of Boston. Dawes started his ride that day, and Revere left later in the evening. Around midnight, with Lexington already alerted, they were joined by Prescott, another doctor, and the three set out for Concord.

On the way, however, they were accosted by British soldiers who, naturally curious about their midnight excursion, demanded to know their business. The trio scattered, with mixed results. Dawes and Prescott escaped, the former returning to Lexington and the latter going on to Concord. Revere, later to be celebrated as the hero of the tale, was detained by the redcoats and sent packing back to Lexington on foot. The poem has him reaching Concord about two in the morning, whereas, in fact, Prescott was the only one who got there at all.

It's not clear why Longfellow, almost ninety years after the event, chose to eulogize Revere and forget his companions. Perhaps the survival of his silverwork made him a more natural hero than the doctor and shoemaker, whose work had died with them. Or perhaps it was that business about the lights in the tower ("one if by land and two if by sea") that caught the poet's imagination. Revere did set up that signal, so it may not be entirely without justice that the tale revolves around him. Had he not done so, we might now better remember the "midnight ride of Billy Dawes." David Wallechinsky and Irving Wallace, *The People's Almanac* (Bantam, 1975).

WHERE WAS MARY PICKFORD, "AMERICA'S SWEETHEART," FROM?

One of the most remarkable of American actresses, Mary Pickford ruled Hollywood as "America's Sweetheart," as "Little Mary," as the eternal Rebecca of Sunnybrook Farm, from her early days with D. W. Griffith to the advent of sound. With Griffith, her husband Douglas Fairbanks, and Charlie Chaplin, she founded United Artists in 1919 as a way of ensuring greater artist control over "product"; in doing so, she anticipated Bette Davis's independent streak by a generation, and in the process helped create the Star System. Enthroned with Doug at Pickfair, their lavish mansion, she was this democracy's own princess throughout the wild 1920s.

As a paragon of American innocence, however, she had one curious blemish. It was a blemish that her fans either forgave or forgot, realizing perhaps that it was soul and not birth that made royalty: She was born as simple Gladys Smith not in America but in Toronto, Ontario. It was the legendary stage producer David Belasco who, after seeing her promise, changed her name and her destiny. Mary Pickford, *Sunshine and Shadow* (Doubleday, 1955); Robert Windeler, *Sweetheart: The Story of Mary Pickford* (Praeger, 1974).

EPICURUS WAS NO EPICURE.

"Epicure" has a faint stench about it, like the odor of too-sweet jasmine. The common picture of the epicure, or epicurean, is of a voracious but fastidious gourmet, indulging his overripe appetite in an orgy of haute cuisine. No hot dogs or candy bars for him—only the most refined dishes will do.

This is quite an irony, for Epicurus himself, who lived in the third century B.C., was most abstemious in his tastes. Pleasure, it is true, he considered the only reasonable aim in life, but he was not thinking of sensual delights, as is commonly believed. To the pleasures of the body he preferred those of a disciplined mind: *Ataraxia,* or serenity, was his ideal. In all things he counseled moderation, since in the long run that afforded one greater delight than the frenzies of bed and board. So it is erroneous to think of the epicurean as a hedonist in the extreme. As Radoslav Tsanoff observes, "There are pleasures more lasting, more reliable, more fruitful than those of sensual indulgence. The good hedonist avoids profligacy, not because it is unworthy, but because its pleasures betray him in the end and bring him to grief."

A sensual life, but a plain one, that was the philosopher's goal. Epicurus himself existed on water and bread; cheese he considered a luxury. As for sexual delight, that other great hedonistic interest, he avoided it entirely. "Sexual intercourse," he wrote, "has never done a man good and he is lucky if it has not harmed him." His goal was the absence of pain, and he must have understood well the pains that indulgence can bring. For this reason he preached a simple life, and for the same reason he fervently opposed religion. In his view it instilled rather than banished fear, and fear was the most grievous pain.   Bertrand Russell, *A History of Western Philosophy* (Simon & Schuster, 1965); Radoslav A. Tsanoff, *The Great Philosophers* (Harper & Row, 1964).

LUCREZIA BORGIA WAS A) CRUEL, B) DEVIOUS, OR C) GENEROUS?

Poor Lucrezia Borgia. People who know nothing of Renaissance Italy are still convinced that she was just about the baddest lady alive. Because her family name is about as popular as "Dracula" or "Hitler," and no doubt also because she was a woman, she had been branded for centuries as a sadistic, unfeeling monster. Victor Hugo wrote a play, and Gaetano Donizetti an opera, devoted to her reputation as a paragon of vice.

Contemporary historians dispute this conventional view. It is true that the lady was much married, and that one of her husbands, the Duke of Bisceglie, was murdered. But the villains of the piece seem to have been not Lucrezia herself, but her designing father and brother. She herself, it is now thought, was more pliable than passionate, and the evil deeds that surround her name seem to have been less her personal doing than the way of the Renaissance world—a way she was too weak to divert. Her problem, according to Bergen Evans, was "an insipid, almost bovine, good nature. She was famed in her own time for a sort of lady-bountiful piety." Generous to a bloody fault. Bergen Evans, *The Spoor of Spooks and Other Nonsense* (Knopf, 1954).

WHO RODE NAKED THROUGH COVENTRY?

Her name was Godgifu, she was the wife of Leofric of Mercia, and there is no doubt that they were real figures in eleventh-century England. Contemporary chroniclers agree that the husband was a harsh tax-master, and that Godgifu (Latinized as Godiva) was more bending in her treatment of the peasants. So there is a basis for the tale that, to dramatically protest her husband's tax policies, she rode through Coventry nude, covered only by her hair.

But it wasn't a contemporary tale. No eleventh-century chronicle makes any mention of it, and it first appears in the literature a century and a half after the supposed protest, in a St. Albans abbey manuscript written by the monk Matthew Paris. There we read that the good lady, failing to soften Leofric by logic, is told by him that if she rides through the marketplace nude, he will grant the town a charter. She does so, he keeps his word, and she goes down in history as a paragon of sacrifice.

Can we believe the tale, or was it a clerical fancy? At this point we will never know, though the story seems certain to last. It has the exotic lubriciousness, coupled with a virtuous moral, that is guaranteed to ensure its popularity among puritans and peepers alike. Ashley Montagu and Edward Darling say it has "survival value." Ashley Montagu and Edward Darling, *The Ignorance of Certainty* (Harper & Row, 1970).

WHO FIRST BROUGHT TOBACCO TO ENGLAND?

Considering Sir Walter Raleigh's many accomplishments, it's a pity he should be remembered for the cloak-and-puddle story (which, though fanciful, may be true) and for importing a noxious weed to Great Britain. Raleigh was one of tobacco's principal champions in England, and he contributed greatly to its Elizabethan vogue, but he was not responsible for its introduction.

The plant had been known in Europe since the late fifteenth century, when Columbus's sailors brought it back from Cuba; the people of Ayamonte, Spain, claim their kinsman Rodrigo de Xeres, a seaman in Columbus's party, was the first to smoke in Europe. By the middle of the sixteenth century, tobacco was known in France, where it was thought to have medicinal properties. This misconception can be laid at the door of the French ambassador to Portugal, Jean Nicot, who sent his queen samples of the "curative" leaves around 1560: It is from his name that we get "nicotine." From France, smoking crossed the channel to England, and it was probably from the French connection that Raleigh picked it up. It was not imported directly to England until 1565, when the privateer Sir John Hawkins brought back leaves from Florida.

Raleigh's championship of smoking was abetted when Thomas Hariot, author of a *Briefe and True Report of the New Found Land of Virginia* (and England's first lung cancer victim), brought to England some of the clay pipes which the Virginia Indians used for smoking. When Raleigh picked up the habit, it soon became fashionable in court, and remained so until the turn of the century, when James I denounced it.

For James, part of the problem was that Raleigh, now considered a blackguard, had been the English "father" of the weed. "It seems a miracle to me," the king wrote in his *Counterblast to Tobacco* (1604), "how a custom springing from so vile a ground, and brought in by a father so generally hated, should be welcomed." In addition to that, however, the king had sounder objections. Smoking he called "a custom Lothsome to the eye, hatefull to the Nose, harmefull to the braine, daungerous to the Lungs, and in the black stinking fume thereof, neerest resembling the horrible Stigian smoke of the pit that is bottomless." Ironically, two years later, he chartered the James River plantations, whose principal crop became tobacco.   Robert Lacey, *Sir Walter Raleigh* (Atheneum, 1974); Joseph C. Robert, *The Story of Tobacco in America* (Knopf, 1949).

THOREAU NEVER LIVED AS A RECLUSE AT WALDEN POND.

Iconoclastic, nettlesome, unkempt by bourgeois standards, Henry David Thoreau was as much a gadfly to nineteenth-century American society as Socrates had been to Athens. It was not for nothing that when a stamp commemorating him appeared in the late 1960s, many said the Concord sage looked like a goddamned hippie. Yet as innovative as he was in both dress and thought, he was not nearly so much an outlaw as his later admirers have led us to believe. On the two episodes which established his popular reputation—the sojourn at Walden and his incarceration for refusing to pay his poll tax—the facts are slightly less exciting than the legend.

He stayed at Walden, all right, and he even built the cabin in which he lived with his own transcendentalist hands. But a recluse he was not. During the two years he lived there (that's right, two years, not a lifetime), he took the brief brisk walk to Concord with great regularity to chat with friends and to sample his mother's home cooking. In addition, he entertained frequent visitors, including Emerson (who owned the property), Bronson Alcott, and Hawthorne. "Hardly a day went by that Thoreau did not visit the village or was not visited at the pond," and occasionally, entire groups of visitors made their way to the "recluse's" cabin "to hold picnics on his front doorstep." Obviously, although the Walden digs were relatively isolated, Thoreau was anything but an anchorite.

As for the poll tax story, that, too, has been a bit embellished by late-generation radicals. He did go to jail for refusing to pay the tax to a government which supported slavery. But what is commonly forgotten is that he spent only one night there, being sprung the following morning by a party unknown—some say Emerson paid the bill, others say it was Thoreau's Aunt Maria. Thoreau was outraged at being let off the hook so early, and argued vociferously with his jailer to be allowed to stay, but to no avail. At least he got a lot of mileage out of the incident in *Civil*

Disobedience. Walter Harding, *The Days of Henry Thoreau* (Knopf, 1965).

WHAT WAS SAMUEL F. B. MORSE'S CLAIM TO FAME?

It depends on whether you mean his fame before the telegraph or after it. Certainly after his invention of the long-distance transmission system in the 1830s, he was known principally as an inventor, and it is as the father of the telegraph that he is remembered today. But he was well over forty when the instrument was perfected. For the first half of his life, he had shown little more than a casual interest in electricity; only after an 1832 discussion with Dr. Charles Jackson, a student of electricity, did he begin the experiments which were to bring him fortune and lasting fame.

Before 1832 he was a painter, and an extremely successful one. Had he died in that year, he would still be remembered today as a seminal influence in American art, for he not only painted many notable figures of the day, but was principally responsible for the foundation of the organization that was to become the National Academy of Design; he acted as its first president from 1826 to 1845. A student of Washington Allston, Morse won numerous awards for his work, and as a young man had been touted as one of the heirs to the aging greats Copley, Trumbull, and West. His landscapes have been called derivative, but his portraits of such dignitaries as Noah Webster, Benjamin Silliman, William Cullen Bryant, and Lafayette are penetrating and vivid accomplishments. Carleton Mabee, *The American Leonardo* (Knopf, 1943).

JOHN HARVARD DID NOT FOUND HARVARD COLLEGE.

Though scholastic justice might dictate that a college be named for its founder, this has not always been the case in our history. The idea of founding an institution of higher learning, after all, is one that requires imagination but not necessarily funds; then as now, it has been the funder rather than the founder who most frequently gets the nod when names are being considered.

John Harvard, a young Charlestown minister, was dying of

tuberculosis when, in 1637, the General Court of Massachusetts ordered a school to be established at "Newetowne," later Cambridge, Massachusetts. Harvard bequeathed a four-hundred-volume library to the school, and since the books were worth nearly twice as much as the colony itself had pledged, the Court saw fit, after the benefactor's death in 1638, to name the new institution after him.

The same thing happened elsewhere. Yale, originally called the Collegiate School, was renamed in 1716 after receiving substantial gifts from one Elihu Yale. Rutgers University, originally Queens College, was renamed in 1825 after the philanthropist Henry Rutgers. Dartmouth, founded in 1754 by Eleazar Wheelock to educate the local Indians, was renamed in 1816 in honor of the second earl of Dartmouth, who had been Wheelock's chief backer. The lesson of all this is clear: Posterity remembers the purse. "Harvard," "Yale," "Rutgers," and "Dartmouth" in *Encyclopedia Americana* (1980).

WHO WAS HIAWATHA?

To schoolchildren the hero of Henry Wadsworth Longfellow's "Indian Edda," *The Song of Hiawatha,* is an actual historical figure, and his exploits are as real to them as those of Sacajawea or Daniel Boone. Adults, thinking they know better, consign the colorful character to the realm of poetic fancy, ridiculing Longfellow for having riddled his doggerel epic with such trochaic improbabilities as Minnehaha, Chibiabos, and Laughing Water.

But the children have the last laugh. Hiawatha may not have lived by the shores of Lake Superior, where Longfellow set his poem, but he was an actual person, and quite as notable in his way as the poet's romantic invention. He lived in upstate New York at the end of the sixteenth century, and it was largely because of his influence that the five tribes whom the whites called the League of the Iroquois were able to put aside their factional differences and forge a centuries-long peace.

Around 1570 a Huron mystic called Deganawidah preached a message of community and goodwill to the warring tribes of the northern woodlands. Within five years after the beginning of his ministry, his first convert and disciple, Hiawatha, had succeeded in uniting the Cayuga, Onondaga, Seneca, Mohawk, and Oneida peoples into what they called the Great Peace. The confederacy endured for two centuries, controlling the northeast of the continent as firmly as Rome had once controlled Europe—and with more of the democratic spirit than Rome was ever able to muster. Because the five member tribes (or the Five Nations, as they came to be called) constituted a real confederation, the League of the Iroquois has often been identified as the first democratic government on the continent. This would make Hiawatha not only his people's St. Paul, but a woodland John Adams as well.

Longfellow knew some of the Hiawatha legends from reading the anthropologist Henry Schoolcraft, whom he thanked in his notes to the poem. Why he moved Hiawatha from New York to the Great Lakes is a mystery, although it's clear that he was not especially meticulous about keeping his legends unmixed: The word Minnehaha, he admitted, came from the even more distant Dakota. *The American Heritage Book of Indians* (American Heritage Publishing, 1961).

WHO SHOT AN APPLE FROM HIS SON'S HEAD?

William Tell is one of those heroes, like Robin Hood or Billy the Kid, in whom populist zeal and macho bravado join to produce the stuff of democratic legend. As the champion of Swiss independence against the incursions of Austrian bailiffs, he is a luminous example of the Good Peasant, striving with yeomanly dignity against Tyranny's yoke. That he nearly kills his heir to accomplish this only seems to enhance his attractiveness: We recall not so much the chance he takes with the boy's life as the fact that he has reserved a second arrow for Gessler in the event the child is killed. It's no wonder the tale has been retold many times—notably by Schiller and Rossini—since its medieval Swiss appearance.

But the Swiss version, which comes to us from the sixteeth-century chronicler Aegidius Tschudi, is anything but original. Stories with identical motifs appeared hundreds of years before Tschudi among the Danes and Norse, and a similar tale was told as early as the twelfth century in Persia. To make matters even worse for the Swiss, although the Tell legend clearly grew out of an actual thirteenth-century event—the formation of a Swiss league against Hapsburg hegemony—no contemporary source notes either Gessler or Tell. The whole thing is a patriot's "Tell tale." Bergen Evans, *The Spoor of Spooks and Other Nonsense* (Knopf, 1954).

GALILEO DID NOT DROP WEIGHTS FROM THE LEANING TOWER OF PISA.

It's such a charming story. The young Galileo, the sole rationalist in all of sixteenth-century Italy, demonstrates the uniformity of acceleration by dropping unequal weights from his native city's most famous landmark, thus impressing the entire assembled faculty of the university and earning himself a reputation as an experimentalist without equal. The only trouble with it is that it was the invention of the Italian scientist's first biographer, one Vincenzio Viviani, who in accord with the "fashionable hagiographical style of his day," idealistically misrepresented Galileo's early interests. According to William Shea, the famous Pisan's approach was fundamentally mathematical—he was, in fact, a professor of mathematics—and was "not derived from detailed observation of natural phenomena." The same thing goes for the idea that Galileo discovered the isochronism, or regularity, of the pendulum by observing a swinging lamp; Shea says there is no evidence, outside of Viviani, that he knew how to count a pendulum's pulse. William R. Shea, *Galileo's Intellectual Revolution* (Macmillan, 1972).

WHO HOLDS THE WORLD'S HOME RUN RECORD?

When Hank Aaron broke Babe Ruth's record of 714 lifetime homers on April 8, 1974, he became not only the new major-league champion, but a household name. By the time he retired two years later, he had tallied up a total of 755 home runs in a twenty-two-year career. That remains the *major league* record, but equally impressive records are held by two men whose names remain obscure.

The first one plays for the Giants. Not the New York Giants, the Yomiuri Giants. His name is Sadaharu Oh, and he broke

Aaron's record on September 3, 1977, by hitting his 756th homer. The Japanese player was then thirty-six years old. On June 12, 1980, he hit his 850th home run.

The other is our own Josh Gibson, who in 1972 was elected to the Baseball Hall of Fame. If you've never heard of Gibson, it's because he was black, and in the 1930s, when he was in his prime, blacks could not play in the majors. As a catcher for the Negro League team the Homestead Grays, he once hit 84 homers in one season. His lifetime record was a solid 800. He lived just long enough (1911–1947) to see Jackie Robinson break the majors' color ban. *Guinness Book of World Records* (Sterling Publishing, 1980).

WHO KILLED LIZZIE BORDEN'S PARENTS?

For nearly a century now, the name "Lizzie Borden" has been synonymous with cold-hearted stealth. When her parents were hacked to death with a hatchet on August 4, 1892, she became the prime suspect, and the sensational trial that followed the murders made her name a household word. Even before the trial was over, children in the streets of Fall River, Massachusetts, were, with the innocent cruelty of the young, chanting the now familiar refrain:

> Lizzie Borden took an ax
> And gave her father forty whacks
> When she saw what she had done
> She gave her mother forty-one.

Not surprisingly, by the time the verdict came in, much of the nation was convinced that the prim New England spinster was a reincarnated Lady Macbeth.

That verdict, though, was not guilty, and there is every reason to believe that it was soundly arrived at. Only circumstantial evidence linked her to the killings, and as Edward Radin suggests, the Bordens' maid, Bridget Sullivan, was, even on the circumstantial evidence, a more likely suspect than Lizzie. The acquittal did her little good. The jingle stuck, the press continued its lurid speculations, and the good people of Fall River alternately hounded and snubbed the "murderess." A pretty hard lot for someone who was known for charity work and donations and who, in her will, gave the town a hefty stipend to maintain her family's graves. Edward Radin, *Lizzie Borden: The Untold Story* (Simon & Schuster, 1961).

WHO KILLED ABRAHAM LINCOLN?

There seems to be no doubt that the bullet which ended the life of the "American Christ," Abe Lincoln, was fired by John Wilkes Booth. It is often forgotten, however, that Booth did not act alone, but was part of a large conspiracy that had determined to bring down the government of the United States by killing not only the president, but the vice-president and secretary of state as well. Secretary of State William Seward, in fact, was attacked and wounded by Booth's accomplice Lewis Paine at the same time as the Ford's Theater incident. So it might be said that although Booth did the actual shooting, responsibility for Lincoln's death lay on several shoulders.

That is the way the government saw it, and after the assassination it rounded up several conspirators, hanging four of them, including one woman, three months after the killing. After a military tribunal had found them guilty of conspiring with, among others, Jefferson Davis, the four—Paine, David Herold, George Atzerodt, and Mary Surratt—were executed on July 7, 1865, over the protests of many who felt the trial had been unfair and that Mrs. Surratt, being a woman, should not be hanged in any case. She was the first woman in our history to have been so honored.

By this time Booth had been dead for ten weeks. Cornered on a Virginia farm twelve days after the assassination, he either took his own life or was shot by Boston Corbett, who claimed he was following God's orders. Whether or not God also directed Corbett to castrate himself and shoot pistols into the Kansas legislature the record does not show. He was committed, escaped, and disappeared.

There have been many attempts to implicate others, beside the several indicted, for participation in the murder; among the most recent is that of David Balsiger and Charles Sellier, who in *The Lincoln Conspiracy* (1977) suggest that Secretary of War Edwin Stanton may have been behind an attempt to kidnap the president to thwart his moderate reconstruction policy. It is likely that as in the case of the Kennedy assassination, we will never know who was truly responsible. John Cottrell, *Anatomy of an Assassination* (Frederick Muller, 1966); Lloyd Lewis, *Myths After Lincoln* (The Readers Club, 1941); Theodore Roscoe, *The Web of Conspiracy* (Prentice-Hall, 1959).

SANTA CLAUS WAS A TURK.

The jolly old elf of Christmas fame, the bringer of presents and good cheer, is a recent European invention; the figure on whom the red-suited benefactor is based came from the ancient Near East. He arose, the historical Saint Nicholas, in Asia Minor in the fourth Christian century. Born at Patara, in Lycia, he was bishop of nearby Myra during Diocletian's purges of Christians and in the more congenial days of Constantine. St. Methodius, who wrote his biography, called him a worker of miracles and a defender of the faith against the Arians. His popularity among early Christians probably stems less from this antiheretical zeal than from his legendary kindness to the oppressed.

Among the tales that celebrate this kindness, two may be singled out. In the first he salvages three girls from prostitution by paying dowries from his own pocket. In the second he intercedes with a governor on behalf of three innocents condemned to death. The latter story appears in two forms: In one the governor is Eustathius, in the other Constantine himself—and in this one the saint appears to the emperor in a miraculous dream, urging him to spare the condemned.

In the East, where "St. Nick" appears frequently on Byzantine seals, he is revered as the patron of sailors; in the West his special charges are children. In Russia before the revolution he ranked with St. Andrew the Apostle as the patron saint of the nation. The "Santa Claus" tradition came later, when northern Europeans (Swiss, Dutch, and Germans) started the custom of giving presents in his name. The custom was brought to America by settlers of New Amsterdam, who according to Alban Butler "had converted the popish saint into a nordic magician." He had come a long way from Turkey. *Butler's Lives of the Saints* (Christian Classics, 1956).

AMERICANA:

THIRTEEN ORIGINAL CALUMNIES

WHERE WAS THE NEW WORLD'S FIRST "LOST COLONY"?

So much romance surrounds the disappearance of the Roanoke colony in the 1580s that it is seldom realized that nearly a century before the Virginia disaster occurred, a colony of European settlers was established, and soon after "lost," a few hundred miles to the south.

The founder was Columbus himself. On Christmas Day 1492, as he was preparing to return to Spain, his flagship, the *Santa Maria,* foundered on a coral reef in Caracol Bay, and it soon became apparent that it would not be able to make the return voyage. Making a virtue of necessity, the admiral had the ship dismantled, and out of its timbers constructed the first European fort in the New World. He called it, after the day of its founding, La Navidad, and to guard it he left forty volunteers while he took the rest of his crew back to Spain.

A year later, when he returned to the Caribbean on his second voyage, nothing remained of the settlement, and not a man of its complement was alive. Friendly Indians, who had helped the Spaniards erect the fort, told a tale of avarice and lust that, they said, had led to the colony's demise barely a month from its establishment. Evidently, the Europeans left behind had tested the patience of the Indians by numerous robberies and rapes, until the natives had reacted and killed them. Thus the first lost settlement set a pattern that would be much imitated, until numbers outweighed scruples and the losses all ran red. Samuel Eliot Morison, *Admiral of the Ocean Sea* (Little, Brown, 1946).

WHERE DID THE PILGRIMS LAND?

The story of the Pilgrims landing at Plymouth Rock that chilly day in 1620 has been told so many times in so many schoolrooms that it has become a patriotic treasure. The picture of those tall-hatted folk stepping off the *Mayflower* and being greeted at the Rock by friendly Indians has adorned almost as many history books as the view of Washington crossing the Delaware. As a result the famous boulder has become a national touchstone: As the current residents of Plymouth, Massachusetts, can tell you, thousands of tourists still come each year to stand near it in awe.

It's a great tale, but unfortunately as much legend as fact. The Pilgrims did disembark at Plymouth, but only after members of their party had already tried several other, now forgotten, places. They had sighted the highlands of Cape Cod on November 19, and two days later pulled in to what is now Provincetown harbor. On November 25 the first of them went ashore—sixteen stalwarts under the command of Miles Standish. This party explored the area, scared away a couple of Indians and a dog, appropriated some hidden Indian corn, and returned to the ship. A second exploration convinced the *Mayflower*'s master that the harbor here was unsuitable, and so Standish took another scouting party in a shallop (a small open boat) to the south. This time they landed near present-day Eastham, built a barricade, repulsed an Indian attack in what came to be known as the First Encounter, and again headed back to the ship.

Continuing to search for a hospitable harbor, the scouts circled Cape Cod Bay until deciding, finally, on Plymouth. On December 19 first mate Clark stepped ashore, giving his name to Clark's Island, and two days later they decided on Plymouth proper. The famous December 21 landing thus took place while the *Mayflower* was still moored at Provincetown. The ship made it to Plymouth a few days later, when the passengers began to disembark. No Indians greeted them (for which they heartily thanked God); nor is there any contemporary evidence that they set foot on Plymouth Rock.

The Rock story got started in 1741 by John Faunce, who was born twenty-six years after the landing, and who presumably had heard tales of it from his elders. The Rock *may* have been the place, but it may, like another rock, have been blarney.   William Bradford, *Of Plymouth Plantation,* Samuel Eliot Morison, ed. (Knopf, 1952).

THE PURITANS DID NOT DESPISE SEXUALITY.

Today Puritanism implies social stiffness, an obsession with sin, and above all, an abhorrence of the body. Most of us would agree with H. L. Mencken's characterization of it as "the haunting fear that someone, somewhere, may be happy."

To historian Carl Degler this is an unfair view of seventeenth-century attitudes. While the Puritans were indeed conscious of the depravity of the world and the ubiquity of temptation, they took this, he says, as a spur to moral activity rather than an excuse to retreat from social life. Indeed, since God had made the world, it was incumbent upon the good Puritan to enjoy its many delights as well as to guard against excessive pleasure. Even Calvin had observed that God had made "many things worthy of our estimation independent of any necessary use." The Puritan was thus enjoined to moderation, but also cautioned not to belittle the senses.

This went for sexuality, too. "Though it would certainly be false," Degler says, "to suggest that the Puritans did not subscribe to the canon of simple chastity, it is equally erroneous to think that their sexual lives were crabbed or that sex was abhorrent to them." That notion was a nineteenth-century accretion, added to the "moderate and essentially wholesome view of life's evils held by the early settlers of New England."

Loveless though their lives may look to us, there is considerable evidence that the Puritans encouraged love in marriage, and that, even outside of marriage, sexual relations were not uncommon. Such lapses were to be confessed, of course; but their presence in Puritan communities suggests that daily life in the seventeenth century may not have been as bloodless as is often supposed. Hester Prynne, evidently, had company.   Carl Degler, "Were the Puritans 'Puritanical'?" in *Myth and the American Experience,* Nicholas Cords and Patrick Gerster, eds. (Glencoe, 1978).

NO WITCHES WERE BURNED TO DEATH AT SALEM.

During the McCarthy era, one of the liberals' favorite complaints was that they were being subjected to a "witch hunt"—the obvious allusion being to those dark days in seventeenth-century

Salem, Massachusetts, when the village was purged of its "witches." It is a sign of Salem's importance in the popular imagination that two and a half centuries after the executions there, mention of it could still evoke feelings of disgust. "Salem" is as much a blot on the national escutcheon as McCarthyism itself.

Things were bad there, all right, but not quite as bad as most people believe. For the hundreds of innocents many think were executed, substitute the actual twenty, and you get an idea of how rumor has swelled the infamy over the years. Of the twenty, nineteen were hanged and one, the male "witch" Giles Corey, was pressed to death under heavy weights for refusing to enter a plea. Nobody in Salem was burned: That method of execution had been perfected in Europe, and continued to be practiced there on supposed witches deep into the "enlightened" eighteenth century.

To the question of the witches' guilt or innocence, one can only shrug in stupefaction. Certainly it was true that the girls who started the craze were afflicted by *something:* You do not experience convulsions, choking, deafness, blindness, and hallucinations without cause. But whether that cause was supernatural or psychosomatic is something that must be left up to the psychologist or theologian to decide. It is an oversimplification to suggest that they were "possessed" by demons, but it is no less incautious to see the episode as merely an opportunistic purge, whipped up by the church elders to consolidate their authority. "He who believes in the devil," said Thomas Mann, "already belongs to him." Perhaps that's a fair way of suggesting who was really possessed at Salem. Chadwick Hansen, *Witchcraft at Salem* (Brazillier, 1974); Marion L. Starkey, *The Devil in Massachusetts* (Anchor, 1969).

THE AMERICAN REVOLUTION WAS NOT A REBELLION AGAINST ROYAL TYRANNY.

It's fairly well recognized by now that the colonial American populace was not united in its opposition to England; Tories were not a small minority in the 1770s. What is not as commonly understood is that even after rebellion was under way—after the 1774 Intolerable Acts had made resistance inevitable—the rebels, even the most radical among them, did not identify George III as the tyrannical ruler he was later seen to be. The second Continental Congress, meeting in 1775, saw Parliament, not the king, as its enemy. As late as July of that year, the Congress issued an "Olive Branch Petition," reiterating American resentment at parliamentary dominion but professing loyalty to George himself. According to historian Darrell Rutman, the rebels' original goal was not independence, but "home rule under the king."

George, though, refused the branch. His rejection of the petition in August preceded a proclamation in which he said that the Americans, their avowals of loyalty notwithstanding, were in revolt against him personally. This crushed the last hope of reconciliation, and in January 1776 the first attack on George himself appeared. This was Thomas Paine's *Common Sense,* which, "sold in record numbers, passed from hand to hand and from tavern to tavern," was immediately effective in creating the image of a tyrant king. With the war in progress, of course, George started taking plenty of abuse, and by the end of the conflict he had replaced his ministers in the popular mind as the arch symbol of tyrannical rule.   Darrell B. Rutman, "George III: The Myth of a Tyrannical King," in *Myth and the American Experience,* Nicholas Cords and Patrick Gerster, eds. (Glencoe, 1978).

WHAT HAPPENED ON JULY 4, 1776?

The most famous date in American history is generally taken to be the day on which the Declaration of Independence was signed. This is off by almost a month. What happened on July 4 was that the declaration, which had been drafted the previous month by Thomas Jefferson, John Adams, and Ben Franklin, was formally adopted by the Second Continental Congress, then meeting at the Pennsylvania State House (now Independence Hall) in Philadelphia. The only signers that day were the congressional secretary Charles Thomson and the body's wealthy, flamboyant president, John Hancock. And all they signed was a draft.

After this official approval, the document went to printer John Dunlop, who published it as a broadside for distribution to the colonies. Within days it was proclaimed publicly in Philadelphia, and on July 9 New York, the only colony which had not so far ratified it, did so; this made the declaration unanimous. It wasn't until July 15, though, that Congress ordered it "engrossed" on parchment, in the form Americans now know it. The parchment copy was made, and on August 2, almost a month after its adoption, it was finally signed by fifty assembled delegates. Straggling signers were still coming in the fall.   Jack P. Greene, "Declaration of Independence," in *Encyclopedia Americana* (1980).

THE MOUNTAIN MAN WAS A GOOD BOURGEOIS.

Popular fiction, abetted by the Hollywood dream machine, has portrayed the mountain man as a virtual recluse, unwilling to bear the restraints of bourgeois community life and comfortable only in the wild, among savages and mountain winds. Historian William Goetzmann has shown that this is an inaccurate picture. His study of the Rocky Mountain fur trade in the beginning of the nineteenth century yields a view of the mountain man that is far more in keeping with the enterprising spirit of the Jacksonian age: The fur trade, he notes, was a business venture, and most of the frontiersmen engaged in it were attracted at least as much to the possibility of riches as they were to life in the wild. As the trapper Louis Vasquez noted as he set off on an 1842 trek, "I leave to make money or die."

The most fascinating revelation in Professor Goetzmann's article is that many of the over four hundred mountain men whose lives he studied had more than one occupation. Few were simply trappers. Some were miners, some scouts, some traders. A large number were ranchers or farmers, and others worked in a variety of respectable trades. Of the primary occupations listed in his survey, two of his "reclusive wild men" were bankers, one was a lawyer, one a newspaper editor, and one a superintendent of schools! Obviously, life in the raw held at best a limited attraction to these kings of the wild frontier.

Statistically, Goetzmann concludes, "the Mountain Man was hardly the simple-minded primitive that mythology has made him out to be. Indeed it appears that whenever he had the chance, he exchanged the joys of the rendezvous and the wilderness life for the more civilized excitement of 'getting ahead.' " The image of the roughhewn recluse, he suggests, was primarily a literary convention.   William H. Goetzmann, "The Mountain Man as Jacksonian Man," in *Myth and the American Experience,* Nicholas Cords and Patrick Gerster, eds. (Glencoe, 1978).

WHAT ETHNIC GROUP INSTITUTED THE AMERICAN PRACTICE OF SCALPING?

Scalping was not an American Indian custom. Not originally, that is. It's true that many Indian tribes, from the Iroquois of New York State to the Dakota of the high plains, practiced the custom with grisly abandon, both on whites and on neighboring tribes. But it didn't start in North America; like smallpox and gunpowder, it was imported from Europe.

An English ballad reveals that Godwin, Earl of Wessex, was scalping his enemies as early as the eleventh century A.D. This fine old Anglo-Saxon tradition was brought to America first by the Dutch and then by the English, in the seventeenth century. By the time of the French and Indian War, most of the American colonies had at one time or another paid their settlers "scalp bounties" to discourage Indian resistance to their presence. The colonial governments, that is, would pay you so much per hairpiece (Massachusetts paid £100 per scalp in 1722) as a way of cutting down on hostiles.

Colonists hungry for these rewards sometimes dispatched actual warriors, sometimes women and children. Few colonial governors were picky about the size of the scalp, as long as the skin was red.

When the Indians picked up on this custom and began to turn it against the whites, the settlers became curiously outraged. Although bounties continued to be paid well into the nineteenth century for the tops of Apache heads, popular prejudice gradually reassigned responsibility for the custom to those who had been its first victims, and the misconception remains common today. *The American Heritage Book of Indians* (American Heritage Publishing, 1961).

IN WHAT PART OF AMERICA DID COWBOYS ORIGINATE?

Nearly a century before it was applied to the cattle-driving bravos of the Western plains, the term "cowboy" was used to describe Tory irregulars in the Hudson River valley of New York. During the Revolutionary War, bands of these intrepid but treacherous guerrillas inhabited the no-man's-land between British and American lines, where they lured gullible colonists to their deaths by an ingenious deception: Tinkling cowbells to simulate the sound of lost cattle, they would "beguile the patriots into the brush" and there ambush them—just like in the Old West.

It should be pointed out that both sides in the Revolution had "cowboys"—the patriots just called theirs "skinners." According to Washington Irving, both groups were "arrant marauders" as well as soldiers—probably like Quantrill a short time later. Neither took the time, he wrote, "to ascertain the politics of a horse or cow which they were driving off into captivity, nor when they wrung the neck of a rooster did they trouble their heads whether he crowed for Congress or King George." Evidently, the line between "liberation" of goods and mere theft was no clearer in the 1770s than it has been in any war since.

The original cowboys were also accused of treason: of having, like cattle rustlers later, no fixed allegiance. Even the three stalwarts who captured the famous Major Andre in 1780 were assailed, when he had been hanged as a spy, as being mere opportunists themselves: *Niles Register* in 1817 was still taking up for their cause, claiming that, though some had called the three "cowboys . . . as often in the enemy's camp as in our own," the charge was frivolous and false. Its appearance, however, a generation after the event, suggests it was not uncommon. Sir William Craigie and James Hulbert, *A Dictionary of American English on Historical Principles* (University of Chicago Press, 1940; repr. 1968); William Henry Phyfe, *5000 Facts and Fancies* (1901; repr. Gale Research, 1966).

WHAT DID THE EMANCIPATION PROCLAMATION DO?

The Emancipation Proclamation freed no slaves. Lincoln's famous proclamation, issued on January 1, 1863, is still seen as evidence for Old Abe's high moral fiber. It was, however, far more a political than an ethical event, and had no immediate effect on the slaves. By defining the Union cause as an anti-slavery crusade, Lincoln immediately muted opposition to the war and ensured that France and England, who had been supplying the rebels, would henceforth keep out of the fray.

There is little evidence that the Great Emancipator's motives were primarily humanitarian. In August 1862 he had admitted to abolitionist Horace Greeley that his aim was not the curtailing of slavery but the preservation of the Union. "If I could save the Union without freeing any slave," he said, "I would do it."

As it turned out, the famous document freed nobody. Its promise was freedom for the slaves in rebellious states only (Union slaves remained property until the Thirteenth Amendment was passed in December 1865), and, in fact, even these Confederate slaves remained unemancipated for another two years. Since the South had seceded from the Union, Lincoln's flourish had no effect in law until the Appomatox surrender. Francis Butler Simkins, *A History of the South* (Knopf, 1953).

FEW AMERICAN SLAVES WENT "NORTH TO FREEDOM."

Slavery was such a volatile issue in American history that partisans on both sides of it have tended to see it as the fulcrum in the War Between the States. In spite of the varied economic and political factors in the emergence of hostilities, the dichotomy set up by slavery allows us to believe today that in the years preceding the war, the South was uniformly in its favor and the North was uniformly abolitionist. Tales of the Underground Railroad, and of what C. Vann Woodward calls the "North Star Legend," contributed to the idea that blacks escaping the South, as soon as they got over the Mason-Dixon Line, entered an earthly paradise where ancient shackles were dissolved.

As both Woodward and Carl Degler have shown, though, the differences between North and South were somewhat less clear than this. The South before the war was anything but solidly proslavery. John Calhoun's position seems today to have dominated the region's thinking, but that does not mean that debate on the subject was lacking. Among the notable Southerners who argued against the "peculiar institution," Degler mentions Hinton Rowan Helper, who blamed slavery for the South's economic backwardness; and Cassius Marcellus Clay, namesake of Muhammad Ali, who gained a large Southern abolitionist following and freed his own slaves in 1833.

The other side of the "North to freedom" image—the notion that the North was free of oppression—has also been discredited.

Not only were "free" Negroes denied the vote in many Union states, both during and after the war, but economic opportunities in the North, especially job and housing opportunities, were extremely restricted for them. "Custom, extralegal codes, and sometimes mob law," in Professor Woodward's phrasing, "served to relegate the Negro to a position of social inferiority and impose a harsh rule of segregation" in both North and South.

This is not to suggest that slavery was the congenial institution its defenders depicted—only that Northern "freedom" was less a corrective to it than has been commonly supposed. American racism, unfortunately, has always transcended regional lines. Carl N. Degler, "There Was Another South," and C. Vann Woodward, "The Antislavery Myth," in *Myth and the American Experience,* Nicholas Cords and Patrick Gerster, eds. (Glencoe, 1978).

WHAT STARTED THE GREAT CHICAGO FIRE?

Mrs. O'Leary's cow, like Lizzie Borden's hatchet, is an icon of American popular culture. "Everybody knows" that the fire which devastated Chicago in October 1871 was started in the small O'Leary cowshed when a cow kicked over a lantern, setting fire to its straw, then the building, then the town. Years later Michael Ahern, a reporter, admitted he had made up the story because he thought it would make colorful copy. Nevertheless it has persisted, fired no doubt by a quite understandable human need to lay the blame on brute accident, rather than on the conditions which made such a blaze inevitable.

For days before the fire, Chicago had been visited by premonitions, as small fire after small fire dotted the rainless and windswept town, leaving everything in so dessicated a condition that, as the *Chicago Tribune* noted, "a spark might set a fire which would sweep from end to end of the city." That fire came on Sunday the eighth, and by the following day it had destroyed virtually the entire downtown area of the Midwest giant. Its cost in people killed or missing was about five hundred. The financial loss was an estimated two hundred million dollars. In the three and a half square miles it burned, more than seventeen thousand buildings, none of them fireproof, succumbed.

In the aftermath of the disaster, Chicago took a new look at its construction, and for the recent tragedy looked for scapegoats, or rather scapecows. The O'Leary story gained wide currency in spite of the fact (or maybe because of the fact) that it was obviously merely a circulation-booster for the yellow press. The same papers that blamed Mrs. O'Leary's negligence also "ran eyewitness accounts of mass lynchings of incendiaries after the fire, asserted solemnly that 2,500 babies were born and died within two days after the fire, and warned of a mass invasion of the city by out-of-town safe-crackers, even mentioning a couple by name." So much for journalistic integrity.

We will never know what really happened in that cowshed, but the most likely explanation is that friends of Patrick and Catherine O'Leary, playing cards there, knocked over a lantern or were careless with cigars, then denied their part when the damage was known. The cow story, in any case, was bull. Robert Cromie, *The Great Chicago Fire* (McGraw-Hill, 1958); James Sheahan and George Upton, *The Great Conflagration* (Union Publishing, 1871).

WHAT DID PROHIBITION PROHIBIT?

With the passage on January 16, 1920, of the Eighteenth Amendment, America became one big dry country. Between then and 1933, when the government finally realized it was easier to collect liquor duties than sweep up tommy-gunned gangsters, the only drinks in town were illegal. Or were they?

Actually, it was perfectly legal to get drunk throughout the Roaring Twenties. What was prohibited, according to the Amendment, was the "manufacture, sale, or transportation" of the demon rum or any of his lesser angels. Technically, that meant that if you chanced upon a bottle of hooch on the sidewalk outside your home, you could guzzle all you wanted on the spot, and the long arm of the law couldn't touch you. As long as you hadn't made, sold, or moved the stuff, you were in the clear. In fact, you might even plead innocent if you were caught in a speakeasy raid. The owner who sold you your drink could be busted, to be sure, but the law said nothing about buying, though it's doubtful the cops would have been amused if you'd offered them that defense. U.S. Constitution.

WAR:

MAN'S FAVORITE SPORT

WHERE DID THE BATTLE OF BUNKER HILL TAKE PLACE?

It was the first major engagement of the Revolution, and for the British, who lost nearly half their men, it proved to be the costliest one as well. Pitting sixteen hundred American irregulars against twenty-five hundred redcoats, it showed that embattled American farmers were a match for England's finest, and almost singlehandedly created the legend of the citizen soldier. After June 17, 1775, the British survivors of "Bunker Hill" knew the war would not end in a month.

They had learned that lesson, however, not on Bunker Hill but on nearby Breeds Hill, the rise from which the Americans had twice repulsed their attacks before making an orderly retreat. The American commander William Prescott had been ordered to defend Bunker Hill but fortified Breeds instead. Why the misnomer survived, and indeed became a rallying call, is unknown. My guess is that Prescott's superiors had already put "Bunker Hill" into their reports by the time the battle was joined, and never bothered to correct it. Maurice Matloff, ed., *American Military History* (Office of the Chief of Military History, U.S. Army, 1969).

WHERE DID NAPOLEON "MEET HIS WATERLOO"?

Ever since that long bloody day in June 1815, when Britain's Duke of Wellington ended Napoleon's imperial ambitions forever, the name "Waterloo" has been a symbol for unmitigated defeat. For Napoleon that's just what it was, but the battle did not transpire at Waterloo; it took place in a small valley to Waterloo's south, dotted with towns whose names only generals remember.

If you were among the approximately one hundred thousand soldiers who survived the engagement (nearly forty thousand did not), the places you would have told your grandchildren about are Mont St. Jean and La Haie, Belle Alliance and Plancenoit, Château de Hougoument and Papellotte, and—most important of all—the hamlet of La Haie Sainte.

For it was at La Haie Sainte (which in French means "holy hedgerow") that the hitherto invincible French Guard made its last catastrophic charge. When it began to retreat at seven-thirty that June evening, the fate of the French empire was sealed. The town of Waterloo seems to have captured its glory because Wellington slept there before the battle, or perhaps because, shortly after the victory, he went there to write the news home. David Chandler, *The Campaigns of Napoleon* (Macmillan, 1966).

THERE WERE NO "WARS OF THE ROSES."

Oh, there were wars between the houses of Lancaster and York, but they were not called the Wars of the Roses until long after the last battle had ended. To most English people, the thirty-odd years of civil strife that agitated the country in the late fifteenth century were not as clearly defined as later tradition made them: The years between the battle of St. Albans (1455) and the battle of Stoke (1487) constituted not a single conflict of flowers, but a nameless time of troubles.

The red rose is generally seen as the principal badge of the Lancastrians, the white rose as the main Yorkist symbol. In fact, the white rose was only one of several Yorkist badges (Richard III's white boar being a better-known one, at least toward the end of the wars), and the red, or Tudor rose, was made popular by Richard's rival Henry VII only after his victory at Bosworth Field (1485). (Henry VI, the chief Lancastrian, had not used the symbol at all.)

Henry VII quickly made the red rose a popular image not only of the Tudor line, but, retrospectively, of all the anti-York forces. By Shakespeare's time, a century later, the red and white roses had become firmly identified as symbols, respectively, of Lancaster and York. The first written use of the term "Wars of the Roses," however, did not come until 1762, when David Hume introduced it into his *History of England.* Many modern scholars, therefore, see its use as anachronistic and unhistorical. Even

Charles Ross, who considers this basically a pedantic quibble, admits that the idea of warring roses may have been "the product of clever Tudor propaganda," instituted after Richard III's defeat at Bosworth.   Charles Ross, *The Wars of the Roses* (Thames & Hudson, 1976).

WHAT LONG-HAIRED GENERAL WAS KILLED AT LITTLE BIG HORN?

Often portrayed by Hollywood as one of the nation's great tragic heroes, George Armstrong Custer was, in fact, an intemperate and ambitious egotist who started his career leading madcap charges in the Civil War and ended it, less than a dozen years later, by leading his men, contrary to orders, against a vastly superior force of Cheyenne and Sioux. In between he was once court-martialed for disobeying orders, and then put in charge of the army's Seventh Cavalry, whom he led first in a massacre of Black Kettle's camp on the Washita River in Oklahoma, then on a gold-seeking expedition into the Sioux's sacred Black Hills. He was thus a central figure in both the avarice and the brutality of the Westward expansion.

His defeat—and the death of his entire command—was a direct result of arrogance. Disregarding the battle plan of his superior, Brigadier General Alfred Terry, he determined to wipe out Sitting Bull's hidden encampment by himself, and to that end split his forces in three columns and led his own column to their deaths. It was the greatest Indian victory of the Plains wars, but it turned out to be a tragedy in disguise, for soon after news of Custer's death reached the East, an outraged populace demanded a final solution, and within a few years after the battle, the Indians had lost the war.

The man whose foolishness had inadvertently brought this about was not, as is popularly supposed, a general at the time of the battle. He had reached the rank of major general during the Civil War but, as with many wartime promotions, this was removed after the war, and he rode to the Little Big Horn (which the Indians, by the way, called the Greasy Grass River) as a lieutenant colonel. As for his famous golden locks, here are the words of the Hunkpapa chief Crow King: "No warrior knew Custer in the fight. We did not know him, dead or alive. When the fight was over, the chiefs gave orders to look for the long-haired chief among the dead, but no chief with long hair could be found." Perhaps, as with Samson, Custer's strength had been in his hair, for just before that day in June 1876, he had had it cut short. *The American Heritage Book of Indians* (McGraw-Hill, 1961); David Wallechinsky and Irving Wallace, *The People's Almanac #2* (Bantam, 1978).

WHAT WERE THE DEFENDERS OF THE ALAMO FIGHTING FOR?

The more chauvinist Texans, asked this question, will say "freedom" or "independence" or "honor." Actually this most famous battle of the Texan Revolution, like the Revolution itself, was fought because American colonists in the Mexican state of Texas preferred American to Mexican rule, largely because under it they could continue to own slaves.

The Mexican government, as rigid and cruel as it could be, had always frowned on the institution of slavery. Since most of the Americans who had accepted its invitation to colonize Texas in the 1820s had come from slave-owning states, friction on this point was inevitable, and various injunctions against the peculiar institution had brought matters to a head late in the decade. The law of April 6, 1830, which outlawed slavery in the province, became known as the revolution's "Stamp Act," because it precipitated the crisis that erupted in war five years later. The grievances of the ensuing revolution included customs regulations, the enforced use of Spanish, and the lack of trial by jury, but the slavery issue remained a focus of popular resentment. The Texans were all for freedom, as long as you were the right shade of white.

The battle, in which less than two hundred defenders killed more than fifteen hundred Mexican soldiers before succumbing, might have been avoided if William Travis had obeyed Sam Houston's orders and abandoned the fortress instead of defending it. Like Custer's Last Stand, the Alamo battle was an exercise in military futility which became useful after the fact, as a rallying cry. *Dictionary of American History* (Scribner's, 1976).

DISEASE, NOT FIREARMS, WAS THE AMERICAN INDIANS' WORST ENEMY.

Now that revisionist historians have made it clear that it was the whites, not the Indians, who were the real villains in the frontier wars, those wars are sometimes depicted as a series of massacres of red people by bellicose, racist whites. The Indians, so goes the modern liberal version of Western history, were wiped out by bastards with bigger guns.

I would be the last to deny that Europeans were ruthless in their extermination of native peoples, but it is important to remember that in that long nightmare known as Manifest Destiny, the white intruders' principal ally was not the bullet but the bacillus: It was epidemics rather than intermittent massacres that really decimated the Indian populations. Killer diseases such as smallpox, cholera, and syphillis took an enormous toll on native populations, and among peoples who had not developed European immunities, even "minor" disturbances such as measles sometimes had grave results.

According to historian Wilcomb Washburn, "The effect of epidemics brought by the white man . . . was catastrophic and nearly universal." New England's coastal areas were "providentially cleared by epidemics, and in the 1630s and 1640s the Iroquois confederacy lost half its numbers to disease. A 1781 smallpox epidemic among the Blackfeet also cut the population in half, while in 1837 over two-thirds of that people succumbed. In 1849, when white prospectors traveled West in search of California gold, they brought with them not only trading beads and steel knives, but the seeds of a cholera epidemic that in that same year took away twelve hundred of the Pawnee people alone. Compared to these figures the massacre toll—such as the several hundred Indians slaughtered by John Chivington at Sand Creek or by George Custer on the Washita—seems a drop in the racist bucket.

Though it is hardly a defense of their institutionalized barbarity, it is interesting to note that the white settlers' most effective ammunition was something they themselves barely understood. In Washburn's unnerving summation, "Disease literally destroyed much of the native population of America and altered and shaped the customs of the survivors. Unwittingly, disease was the white man's strongest ally in the New World." Wilcomb E. Washburn, *The Indian in America* (Harper & Row, 1975).

WHAT WERE THE NAMES OF THE U.S. CIVIL WAR IRONCLADS?

Two misconceptions surround the famous "battle of the ironclads" that took place off Hampton Roads, Virginia, on March 9, 1862. One is that the names of the ships involved were *Monitor* and *Merrimack*. The other is that the two queer-looking behemoths were the first armor-clad ships the world had ever seen.

The Union ship—that "tin can on top of a shingle"—was, in fact, named *Monitor,* but its Confederate counterpart had not been called *Merrimack* for a year. Originally a federal warship, it had been scuttled the previous spring at Norfolk, to prevent it from falling into the hands of the rebels when the naval station there was abandoned. Raised and armored by the South, it was renamed C.S.S. *Virginia,* and under that name it fought at Hampton Roads, spreading devastation throughout the Union fleet before being stalemated by *Monitor.* The battle was a fitting emblem, in Bruce Catton's words, of "a war that destroyed one age and introduced another."

The *Monitor-Virginia* confrontation was the world's first battle between ironclads, but the idea that the two ships were the world's original armored vessels was laid to rest fifteen years ago by Ashley Montagu and Edward Darling. Quoting Albert Trevor's *History of Ancient Civilization* (1937), they described a Hellenistic wonder named *Syracusa,* built by Hiero II of Sicily as a passenger, merchant, and military vessel. "It was covered with plates of lead, and had eight towers equipped with catapults which could hurl against an enemy stones . . . or long arrows." Apparently, it was even clumsier than the nearly unnavigable *Merrimack,* for Hiero ended up giving it away to one of the Ptolemies as a curiosity. Bruce Catton, *Terrible Swift Sword* (Doubleday, 1963); Ashley Montagu and Edward Darling, *The Prevalence of Nonsense* (Harper & Row, 1967).

WHERE WAS THE BATTLE OF SHILOH FOUGHT?

The so-called Battle of Shiloh, fought on April 6 and 7, 1862, was notable for two reasons. One was that it was, up to that time, the bloodiest battle ever fought in North America: Union casualties exceeded thirteen thousand men, and Confederate losses eleven thousand. The other was that it gave rise to Lincoln's famous defense of General Grant. Surprised by the Southern general, Albert Johnston, Grant nearly lost the battle on the morning of April 6 because, flushed with recent successes, he had failed to reconnoiter properly and was evidently unaware of the presence of the large Confederate force only two miles from his own position. His counterattack carried the day, but he was severely criticized afterward, which led Lincoln to comment, "I can't spare this man; he fights."

Where he fought was not Shiloh but Pittsburg Landing, Tennessee. The battle became known as Shiloh because of the presence of Shiloh Church near the center of the costly battlefield. The church had been named for the original Shiloh, a Biblical site north of Jerusalem which had been destroyed around 1000 B.C. by the Philistines.   Maurice Matloff, ed., *American Military History* (Office of the Chief of Military History, U. S. Army, 1969).

HOW LONG DID THE HUNDRED YEARS' WAR LAST?

The Thirty Years' War lasted thirty years (1618–1648), and the Seven Years' War lasted seven years (1756–1763), and "one hundred" has such a nice round ring to it that we may be forgiven for assuming that here, too, the designation is apt as well as euphonious. Alas, history tells us otherwise.

Consensus gives May 24, 1337, as the opening date of the war, because on that day the French king Philip VI confiscated the English duchy of Guienne, forcing Edward III five months later to issue him a formal challenge. Armies were promptly outfitted, and for the next one hundred sixteen years, apart from intermittent truces, the flower of English and French manhood debated their monarchs' claims to land and dignity in such memorable spots as Crecy, Poitiers, and Agincourt. Edward the Black Prince became the Audie Murphy of his day. Richard III cried for a horse. Joan of Arc died at the stake. And early in 1453 the British were once more expelled, this time for good, from Guienne. This event is often taken as marking the end of the war.

A generation later, however, French and English armies again faced each other at Calais, and were saved from renewing the hostilities only because their sovereigns Edward IV and Louis XI, in a rare mutual burst of intelligence, decided to negotiate in-

stead. The truce they signed on August 29, 1475, is the only document which might reasonably be seen as officially ending the
conflict—since a peace treaty was never approved.

So you can take your choice. If a ceasefire will satisfy you, the
war lasted one hundred sixteen years. If you put your faith in
papers, it's one hundred thirty-eight. If you consider territory the
decisive factor, you'll have to add on another seventy-eight years,
since it wasn't until 1553 that British troops withdrew completely
from French soil. As for the English claim to the French throne—
a principal factor in the conflict—that was not officially with-
drawn until 1801. *Encyclopaedia Britannica* (1970).

DURING WHAT WAR WAS THE BATTLE OF NEW ORLEANS FOUGHT?

Among the principal attractions of Andrew "Old Hickory"
Jackson, when he came to run for the presidency in 1828, was
that he had been the hero of New Orleans thirteen years before.
His victory over the British in that city had, in the popular imagination, effectively ended the War of 1812 and brought the nation
"peace with honor." The surge of patriotic sentiment which swept
the country after the war helped to fix the Battle of New Orleans
in the popular mind as a symbol of American might and resolve.

It's easy to see why, looking back on an ineptly managed and
ultimately inconclusive conflict, Americans would want to remember its major triumph rather than its many reverses. But, in
fact, the Battle of New Orleans occurred not *during* that botched
panorama, but two weeks after it ended. Intimidated by Captain
Thomas Macdonough's defeat on September 14, 1814, of their
naval forces on Lake Champlain, British negotiators had signed
the Treaty of Ghent, officially ending the hostilities, on Christmas
Eve 1814. The mails being somewhat sluggish in those days, the
news of this agreement did not reach Washington until almost
two months later. It was not until mid-January 1815 that Jackson's intrepid crew met their British adversaries, killing more
than two thousand of them, including the commander, Edward
Pakenham. In February they discovered that they had earned
their laurels in "peacetime." Robert Leckie, *The Wars of America* (Harper & Row, 1968).

ETHAN ALLEN'S GREEN MOUNTAIN BOYS PREDATED THE REVOLUTIONARY WAR.

Since Ethan Allen's most notable achievement was the capture of the British forts at Ticonderoga and Crown Point in 1775, his Green Mountain Boys are usually considered offsprings of the American Revolutionary War. In fact, the famous contingent of Vermont irregulars was formed five years before the Revolution in response to what Allen and his fellow New Englanders saw as New Yorkers' intrusion on their land.

The anti-Yorker body was the most noted fighting group to grow out of a colonial land dispute that started in the mid-eighteenth century, when the British crown granted the area that is now Vermont to both New York and New Hampshire, under conflicting patents. Allen, one of New Hampshire's staunchest partisans, formed the Green Mountain Boys in 1770, and was so successful in keeping would-be Yorker settlers out of the disputed area that New York governor William Tryon soon put a price on his head. Only after the outbreak of the Revolution was Allen's partisanship absorbed by a wider patriotism; ironically, when the Boys became part of the American army, it was under New York officers that they served.

A contentious and determined character, Allen led an eventful life. As a continental officer, he proposed an invasion of Canada which was rejected, undertook one which was unsuccessful, and was a prisoner of the British for almost three years in England. In 1779 he published a narrative of his capture and a defense of his stand against New York. He died in 1789, two years too soon to see his dream of Vermont statehood become reality.   "Ethan Allen" in *Encyclopedia Americana* (1980); Tom Burnam, *Dictionary of Misinformation* (Crowell, 1975).

IN WHAT MONTH IS RUSSIA'S OCTOBER REVOLUTION CELEBRATED?

October is not just another month in the Soviet Union. Late in that month of 1917, the Bolsheviks made their move, overthrowing the provisional government of Alexander Kerensky and establishing themselves as the dominant faction in Soviet politics. As a result revisionism became, at least for the moment, a thing of the past, and the Soviet Union became the first viable communist power in history. No wonder filmmaker Sergei Eisenstein celebrated the events of October in his small epic *Oktiabr* (1928), or that "Oktobriana," a leather sex goddess of the underground, is a favorite cult heroine in contemporary Soviet comics.

Unfortunately for the coherence of this mythos, however, the October Revolution is no longer celebrated—indeed, has never been celebrated—in the month of October. One of the first revolutionary acts of the new Bolshevik government—along with nationalizing the banks and setting up revolutionary tribunals—was to abolish the Old Style dating system which the czarist government had kept on well after Pope Gregory XIII had instituted his reforms in the sixteenth century. The Soviet Union, as opposed to Russia, was to be a modern nation, in step with the "new" Gregorian calendar. As a result the October revolution has always been celebrated according to the New Style dates: in the first week of November. *Encyclopaedia Britannica* (1979).

WHAT WAR GAVE US "YANKEE DOODLE"?

"Yankee Doodle" is the quintessential Revolutionary war tune, and has for centuries been our ultimate patriotic air, a kind of national anthem in mufti. It's disconcerting, therefore, to discover that the song predates the Revolution by at least twenty years, and probably longer than that. One authority claims the words first appeared in 1745, after the British capture of Louisburg; a more widely accepted view is that they were written by a Dr. Shackburg (some authorities give Shuckburgh) in 1755, just before the joint British and colonial attack on Fort Niagara; he composed them, according to Charles Bombaugh, "in derision of the motley clothes, the antiquated equipments, and the lack of military training of the militia from the Eastern provinces, all in broad contrast with the neat and orderly appointments of the regulars." In either case the song came out of the French and Indian Wars, not the Revolution.

Considering its origin as a chide to colonial disarray, it's comforting to recall how "Yankee Doodle" came to be used *against* the British. On the way to the battle of Concord, the redcoats apparently marched to it, as a way of demoralizing the colonials; after the battle, with the regulars high-tailing it to Boston, the "embattled farmers" picked it up, and it has been an American refrain ever since.   Charles C. Bombaugh, *Facts and Fancies for the Curious* (Lippincott, 1934); James J. Fuld, *The Book of World-Famous Music* (Crown, 1966).

WHEN WAS NAPALM INTRODUCED?

Napalm is an aluminum soap which, when mixed with gasoline, produces a flammable gel that burns furiously and sticks to its target until burned out. The word comes from the two components naphthenic acid and palmitic acid. Encased in incendiary bombs and in flamethrowers, it makes what the military calls an excellent "antipersonnel" weapon, because it both demoralizes and defunctionalizes the target. In English that means it scares the hell out of you unless you like the idea of being burned alive.

Because of its wide use in Vietnam, napalm became a horrid symbol of that war's senseless rapacity; many antiwar protestors denounced the chemical companies as vociferously as they did the army itself, since their manufacture of napalm was seen as a vivid example of the military-industrial complex's insensitivity to suffering.

But napalm was already over a decade old when President Eisenhower committed our first advisers to Vietnam. It had been developed during World War II by a Harvard University research team, and was first used extensively in the Pacific theater. In the television series *Victory at Sea* there was a sequence in which a Japanese soldier is flushed out of an island hideout by a flamethrower. Running through the jungle with his clothes aflame, he seems now an awful premonition of things to come.

The first major use of the new weapon was in March 1945, when American bombers under General Curtis LeMay dropped nearly two thousand tons of napalm bombs on Tokyo, creating a firestorm that lasted for days. LeMay was the chap who thought we should end the Vietnam war quickly by "bombing them back into the Stone Age."   Col. Trevor N. Dupuy, *The Evolution of Weapons and Warfare* (Bobbs-Merrill, 1980); David Wallechinsky and Irving Wallace, *The People's Almanac #2* (Bantam, 1978).

WHO SAID "WAR IS HELL"?

It seems oddly fitting that William Tecumseh Sherman, the sacker of Atlanta and author of Sherman's march to the sea, should be remembered for the pithy disclaimer "War is hell." It both sums up his career and gives a good sense of the jaundice with which he apparently came to view it. The remark is a little too well turned, however, and that is because it was edited after he said it.

The place was Columbus, Ohio, the date was August 11, 1880, and the audience was a group of Union veterans. What the old general actually said was this: "There is many a boy here today who looks on war as all glory, but, boys, it is all hell. You can bear this warning voice to generations yet to come. I look upon war with horror, but if it has to come I am here."

His remarks at this point were interrupted, according to the *Ohio State Journal,* by "long applause and a hurrah." Evidently the assembled old soldiers had somewhat less jaundice than Old Billy. Years later he forgot that he had said it, but by that time the phrase-mongers had got ahold of it, and shortened it to "War is hell," and it had entered the national storehouse of Famous People's Famous Lost Words. A phrase he had actually written down, during the war that made his reputation, had less pith but more point: "War is cruelty and you cannot refine it."   Lloyd Lewis, *Sherman: Fighting Prophet* (Harcourt, Brace, 1932).

RELIGION:

BIBLE LESIONS

WHAT FRUIT LED TO ADAM AND EVE'S EXPULSION FROM THE GARDEN?

Eve, the Serpent, and the apple form one of the most popular iconographic triads in Western culture. As a snapshot of the Fall, the legendary scene of Adam accepting the apple has inspired artists and writers for centuries. But the idea that Eden's forbidden fruit was an apple is just applesauce. In Gen. 2:17 God forbids Adam to eat of "the tree of the knowledge of good and evil," mentioning no fruit at all. Gen. 3:3, where the fruit is first mentioned, calls it only "the fruit of the tree which is in the midst of the garden." It could have been a pomegranate, a fig, or an olive.

The apple interpretation seems to have been started by Aquila Ponticus, who translated the Old Testament into Greek in the second century. In his version of the Song of Solomon he gives, "I raised thee up under the apple tree; there thy mother brought thee forth" as "I raised thee up under the apple tree; there wast thou corrupted." Since "corruption" suggested the Genesis fruit, the apple soon became the culprit in the popular imagination. It was a case of hearsay following mistranslation to a frame-up. David Wallechinskey and Irving Wallace, *The People's Almanac #2* (Bantam, 1978).

HOW MANY CHILDREN DID ADAM AND EVE HAVE?

Everyone remembers the original nuclear family: Adam, Eve, and their two sons, Abel and Cain. Everyone remembers, too, that it was no model of familial bliss, what with the parents starting out as renegades and the firstborn following in their footsteps after murdering his younger brother. Few people recall, though, that Cain was not their only survivor. In Gen. 4:25–26, we read that Eve bore a third son, called Seth, and it is from Seth (since

Abel was dead and Cain was banished to Nod) that the tribes of Israel descended. As if this were not enough to ensure his significance, the so-called P-document, one of the two chief Old Testament sources, says that Seth is Adam's firstborn: Cain and Abel are not even mentioned.

So much for the three named sons. In addition, Gen. 5:4 tells us that after begetting Seth, Adam lived another eight hundred years, during which he busily "begat sons and daughters." Eve is not mentioned in this enterprise; nor is the number of unnamed children. It's understandable, though, that the Bible gives them short shrift, since their heirs were later doomed: In spite of his lesser repute, only Seth's line survived the Flood.   Isaac Asimov, *In the Beginning: Science Faces God in the Book of Genesis* (Crown, 1981).

WHAT WAS THE MARK OF CAIN?

It's often assumed that after Cain slew Abel, God put a mark on his brow so that he would be identified as an outlaw, and could with impunity be killed. In fact the mark was meant to serve precisely the opposite purpose: to protect Cain "lest any finding him should kill him" (Gen. 4:15). Evidently God wanted the murderer to suffer a good long time for his sin, and chose neither to kill him outright nor allow anyone else to do so.

And so Cain set out toward Nod, condemned like the Flying Dutchman of a later tradition to be "a fugitive and a vagabond in the earth." (Nod, in Hebrew, means "wandering.") The Bible says nothing about where on his body the mark was set, or what it looked like. Nor does it explain how Cain managed (in Gen. 4:17) to find a wife—since the account up to that point had mentioned only Adam, Eve, and two sons. This remains one of those scriptural conundrums that delight the cynics and that even the religious find puzzling.   *The Holy Bible* (Gen. 4).

HOW MANY OF EACH ANIMAL DID NOAH TAKE INTO THE ARK?

The obvious answer, two, is supported by centuries of paintings and stories. But in the text which gives us the story—Gen. 6 and 7—there is a contradiction which makes it unclear whether or not, for certain animals, God did not mean fourteen rather than two.

It's true that in 6:19 He commands Noah to bring "two of every sort" to the Ark: one male and one female "of every living thing of all flesh." This injunction, however, finds its way into the Word through the so-called P-document, one of the two principal sources of the Scriptures, written down in the sixth century B.C. If we look ahead a few verses, we find a passage that derives from the other major Genesis source, the so-called J-document. And what does the J-document say? It says that Noah should take in a pair of every *unclean* beast only; of *clean* beasts he is instructed to gather them in "by sevens," that is to say, seven pair. This is 7:2.

Since "clean" at the time meant "fit to be sacrificed," we may assume that God, as Isaac Asimov suggests, either wanted to be sure he would be paid for his trouble at the end of the journey or wanted "to ensure their survival." Asimov favors the former, others the latter interpretation, but in any event the conclusion is the same: The Bible as it now stands does not give us an unequivocal, consistent inventory of the zoo.   Isaac Asimov, *In the Beginning: Science Faces God in the Book of Genesis* (Crown, 1981).

WHERE DID NOAH'S ARK COME TO REST?

A longstanding tradition identifies Mount Ararat, in eastern Turkey, as the peak where the ark came to rest, but in spite of numerous scourings of the site, no conclusive evidence has been found to suggest a historical basis for the conjecture. Perhaps this is because the Mount Ararat story was invented after the Scriptures were written. What the Bible (Gen. 8:4) says is that the ship settled somewhere "upon the mountains of Ararat." Just where the Book doesn't say.

"Ararat" itself is neither Turkish nor Hebrew in origin. It's the Hebrew form for "Urartu," the Assyrian name for a kingdom that flourished at the headwaters of the Tigris and Euphrates rivers in the ninth to seventh centuries B.C. The Urartian domain was, and is, exceptionally mountainous, so that it would have afforded the Ark any number of above-water moorings. Mount Ararat, at 16,804 feet, is the highest of these, but that does not make it the most likely. *Academic American Encyclopedia* (1981).

DELILAH DID NOT CUT SAMSON'S HAIR.

Few Biblical stories illustrate better than that of Samson the profound distrust of women implicit in scriptural writing. In the space of three brief chapters, Samson, the slayer of Philistines and lions, is betrayed by not one but two perfidious females. Judg. 14–16 might almost be taken as an object lesson in why you shouldn't trust girls.

First it's Samson's own wife, who is a Philistine. After killing the lion and eating the honey he finds inexplicably in its carcass, he bets her people "thirty sheets and thirty change of garments" that they cannot solve this riddle: "Out of the eater came forth meat, and out of the strong came forth sweetness." They persuade her to wheedle the answer out of him, she tells them, and as a result he loses the bet. This vexes him so sorely that he goes out and kills thirty Philistines.

Then along comes Delilah, with whom Samson proves as gullible as ever. Even after he's given her false answers and found himself set upon by her friends as a result, he still somehow manages to maintain the illusion that she is on his side. On the fourth, fatal, questioning he tells her the truth—and ends up eyeless in Gaza.

Though it is not Delilah who actually wields the scissors. This is done by "a man" she calls for the purpose, while Samson is lying in her lap and she is beginning to "afflict" him. Indeed. *The Holy Bible* (Judg. 14–16).

WHO IS "LUCIFER" IN THE BIBLE?

It was St. Jerome and other early Church fathers who started the idea that "Lucifer" and the devil were one. The only Biblical appearance of the name is in Isa. 14, where it refers not to the devil, but to the king of Babylon, whose overweening pride led to the association with Satan. The king here thinks to himself, "I will ascend to heaven; above the stars of God I will set my throne on high. . . . I will make myself like the Most High." For this blasphemy he is spoken of as "fallen from Heaven," just as Satan in Luke 17:18 is seen to "fall like lightning from Heaven."

"Lightning" was evidently Jerome's key, for the epithet in Isaiah is "day star" or "star of the morning," and Lucifer in Latin means "light-bearer." Interestingly enough, the same kind of light imagery is applied elsewhere in the Bible to the arch adversary's arch adversary, Jesus. Peter's second letter, 1:19, calls for the "morning star" to rise in the hearts of the faithful, and in Rev. 22:16 Jesus (so says John) calls himself by the same name. It's an irony that would have pleased William Blake: a brilliant metaphorical marriage of the captains of heaven and hell. *The Oxford Dictionary of the Christian Church* (Oxford, 1974).

THE STAR OF DAVID WAS NOT ORIGINALLY JEWISH.

The Star of David, also known as the Seal of Solomon, the six-pointed star, and the hexagram, became a specifically "Jewish" symbol only in the nineteenth century, when European Jews, wanting a figure that would suggest their faith as succinctly as the cross suggested Christianity, began to display it on synagogues and ritual objects. From Europe it spread worldwide, and was adopted by the Zionist Theodor Herzl as the emblem of the first issue of *Die Welt*.

But the star, which has been the national emblem of Israel since 1931, predates Zionism by thousands of years. As a magical or decorative device, it was in use in India and the Iberian peninsula before the Roman conquest, and it appeared in Britain and the Near East as far back as the Bronze Age. Jews did use it, but only as one symbol among many: The second- or third-century synagogue at Capernum displayed it on a frieze alongside the pentagram and the swastika. "There is no reason to assume," the *Encyclopaedia Judaica* comments, that at that time "it was used for any purposes other than decorative."

Jews today call the sign *magen David,* or the "shield of David," signifying that it has a protective quality, but this notion is not of Jewish origin either. Some scholars say it arose out of Jewish mystical traditions, but others see an Arabic influence, since the Koran identifies David as a source of "protective arms." As a magical device the star enjoyed a vogue throughout the Middle Ages, when it was even more popular among Christian princes than among the Jews whom they periodically persecuted.

In the seventeenth century alchemists used the symbol frequently to denote the harmony between fire and water, and Rudolf Koch, interpreting it as an intersection of a male and female triangle calls it an image of perfect marriage. Eighteenth-century kabbalists incorporated it into their rituals as a symbol of messianic optimism, but only in this century has it become a purely sectarian image. *Encyclopaedia Judaica* (Keter Publishing, 1971); Rudolf Koch, *The Book of Signs* (Dover, 1955).

WHO TRUMPETED DOWN THE WALLS OF JERICHO?

Joshua was a pretty solid leader—perhaps the only man in Israel who could succeed the patriarch Moses. But even he was not so phenomenal that he could raze the city of Jericho all by himself. Many illustrations of that noted event have him raising the ram's horn to his own mouth, but in fact he delegated the authority for the destruction of the city to seven of his priests. They walked before the ark of the Lord, circling the city until the walls finally fell. That was on the seventh day, after the priests had blown their seven trumpets once each on the first six days and seven on the seventh—thirteen times before the fall. What really brought the walls tumbling down, moreover, was a communal shout of the people (which Joshua also commanded). "It came to pass," says the Book of Joshua, "when the people heard the sound of the trumpet, and the people shouted with a great shout, that the wall fell down flat." *The Holy Bible* (Josh. 6:1–20).

THE CROSS WAS NOT ORIGINALLY A CHRISTIAN SYMBOL.

Centuries before the death of Jesus made it the principal Christian symbol, the cross had religious and mystical connotations among pagan peoples. The ancient Egyptians combined the *tau*, or T, cross with a superimposed circle to create the ankh; similar symbols were used by numerous other peoples, including the Aztecs and Phoenicians. Crosses composed of four equal arms were common in ancient cultures as diverse as those of the Persians, Indians, Chinese, Babylonians, Druids, and Incas.

Although Christianity has been responsible for making the cross, especially the Latin variety, universally recognized, early Christians took to the symbol slowly and with misgivings. Out of fear of persecution or of profanation, the symbol was rarely displayed in the first Christian centuries, and because of the general horror attached to crucifixion (which was used to dispatch only foreigners and slaves), even the crosses that were displayed contained no Savior's form. According to the *New Catholic Encyclopedia,* "Christians showed an unwillingness to contemplate the Savior's ignominy on the cross, particularly His nudity. They preferred to see in the cross a symbol of His victory, a source of life."

Diffidence about viewing the crucified Christ started to wane in the fourth century, when the rumor began that the True Cross, the one on which Jesus had died, was "in the Church's possession in Jerusalem," and that pieces of it were already showing up "throughout the land." This naturally generated a great interest in the symbol, which has survived to the present day.   *New Catholic Encyclopedia* (McGraw-Hill, 1967); Edward West, "Cross," in *Encyclopedia Americana* (1980).

WHEN WAS JESUS' BIRTHDAY?

Nobody knows for sure on what day Jesus was born. Late December, a cold and rainy time in Judea, seems an unlikely choice, since in such weather shepherds would normally have sought shelter rather than keep watch over their flocks outside, as the Bible tells us they were. Speculation over a possible date only started in the third century, after Clement of Alexandria suggested May 20. The first mention of December 25 does not come until the year 336, and this only in the Western Church; in the Eastern Church, the Feast of the Epiphany, January 6, was commonly identified with the child's birth as well as his baptism. In the Armenian Church January 6 is still Christmas Day.

Why this time of year at all? Apparently, because placing the Savior's birth in late December was a way both of acknowledging and of transcending existing pagan rituals. For centuries non-Christians had celebrated the winter solstice, a late December event, as a death-and-resurrection of the sun. In the Roman calendar, in fact, December 25 was the Natalis Solis Invicti, or "birthday of the unconquerable sun," on which the Persian sun god Mithras was widely honored. The Church, threatened in its infancy by this rival cult, ended up defeating it by absorption: In the words of Robert Myers, "the pagan symbolism was taken over and, in the Christian view, elevated. Jesus became the "Sun of Justice" and the "Sun of Righteousness."

Early Christmas observances also owed a great deal to the Roman feast of the Saturnalia, a combination fertility rite, carnival, and feast of fools in which a mock king ruled Rome in an atmosphere of merrymaking and permissiveness. The Saturnalia thus set the stage for a similarly revolutionary rule, that of the child thought divine.

The year of Jesus' birth is also in question. The commonly accepted idea that he was born in "the year One" derives from the reckoning of the sixth-century monk Dionysius Exiguus, whose interpretation most scholars now reject. Bible experts have placed the birth as far back as 20 B.C. and as far forward as A.D. 6. The most respected view today is that Jesus was born toward the end of Herod's reign—probably around 6 "B.C." James Hastings, ed., *Dictionary of the Bible* (Scribner's, 1963), *The Oxford Dictionary of the Christian Church* (Oxford, 1974); Robert J. Myers, *Celebrations: The Complete Book of American Holidays* (Doubleday, 1972).

HOW MANY KINGS VISITED THE BABY JESUS?

Unless you came from a very pious family, you probably recall the irreverent version of the Christmas hymn that began "We three kings of Orient are/trying to smoke a loaded cigar." The cigar allusion was, of course, ridiculous, but something was loaded, all right: the story of the three kings itself.

The second chapter of Matthew, where the story of the visit first appears, mentions only "wise men from the East," specifying neither kingship nor the number three. The Greek original for "wise men" is *magoi (magi),* which means "sorcerer" or "sage," and the idea that they were kings arose only in the second century, when the African church father Tertullian called them *fere regis,* or "almost kings." The number three, which, of course, has ancient "magi-cal" significance, was also a patristic invention: Origen (185–154) suggested it first, probably inspired by the fact that Matthew does mention three gifts—gold, frankincense, and myrrh. The visitors' names—Gaspar, Melchior, and Balthasar—do not arise until the sixth century, in the obscure collection

Excerpta Latina Barberi. F. L. Cross and E. A. Livingstone, eds., *The Oxford Dictionary of the Christian Church* (Oxford, 1974).

WHEN WERE THE GOSPELS WRITTEN?

Fundamentalist Christians sometimes assert, in what they believe to be evidence of authenticity, that we know of Jesus' life from men who knew him personally, and who wrote their impressions down not long after he died. This stretches the facts somewhat. The earliest gospel, that of Mark, was written no earlier than A.D. 65, and possibly as late as 70. Mark is supposed to have gotten his information from Peter, who of course did know Jesus, and it is the Petrine connection, as much as the early date, which gives Mark's gospel such weight among Biblical scholars. The other three evangelists followed Mark by many years. Matthew wrote sometime between 65 and 115; Luke probably after 80; and John not until the second century.

None of this, of course, says anything about the veracity of the four, or about their common belief that they were writing about the Son of God. It merely deflates the notion that any of the evangelists was an eyewitness to the events he was reporting; even Mark's account is secondhand. James Hastings, *Dictionary of the Bible,* rev. ed. by Frederick Grant and H. H. Rowley (Scribner's, 1962).

IN THE BIBLE, WHAT IS THE ROOT OF ALL EVIL?

Not money, as is often supposed, but the *love* of money. St. Paul made the famous, but generally misquoted, observation in his first epistle to Timothy (6:10): "For the love of money is the root of all evil: which while some coveted after, they have erred from the faith, and pierced themselves through with many sorrows."

In specifying covetousness, rather than wealth itself, as the source of our woe, Paul struck an Oriental note; compare Buddhism, which counsels that *attachment* to materiality is the human curse, because the material is itself an illusion. This makes sense when you recall that Paul's teachers in Tarsus were the

most rigorous of all world despisers, those curmudgeonly icon-
oclasts the Cynics. The grand old man of their tradition was the
Sinopian Greek Diogenes; his observation, "The love of money is
the marketplace of every evil," was made three centuries before
Paul was born. *Herakleitos and Diogenes* (translated by Guy
Davenport, Grey Fox Press, 1979).

IN JESUS' WARNING AGAINST WEALTH, WHAT IS THE "EYE OF A NEEDLE"?

In all the Synoptic Gospels (Matthew, Mark, and Luke), Jesus
says it would be easier for a camel to pass through the eye of a
needle than for a rich man to enter the kingdom of Heaven. This
denunciation of wealth is compatible with the Gospels' overall
approval of poverty, but throughout Christian history it has been
a needle in the side of those who wanted it both ways: In the
nineteenth century, when great fortunes were being made by
Christians, the need for a rereading of the text became particularly acute.

That need was fulfilled by two revisionist glosses. The first took
the Greek *kamelos*, or "camel," as a scribal error for *kamilos*, or
"rope," thus reducing from impossibility to mere difficulty the
idea of threading it through a needle. The second took "Eye of
the Needle" as a small, low gate in the wall of the city of Jerusalem, which a camel, stripped of its baggage and pushed by help-
ful hands, could just barely squeeze through. You can imagine
how this reading, which is still popularly accepted today, must
have pleased the Andrew Carnegies of the time: No matter how
much money they made, they could divest themselves of their
worldly baggage at the end and still be admitted to the Presence.

But the tendentious revisions are unjustified. The word is
clearly *kamelos* in all but a few late manuscripts, and the image
of a large animal passing through a needle's eye was a common
ancient metaphor for impossibility: In the Babylonian Talmud
the animal is an elephant, and in the Koran, Mohammed says of
those who reject his teachings, "They shall not enter Paradise
until a camel passes through the eye of a needle." As for the
small Jerusalem gate, virtually all modern scholars agree that
the only gate which could possibly be meant was *so* small that,

baggage or no baggage, a camel would have to be chopped into tiny pieces first in order to get squeezed through. Some deny there was such a gate at all.

The inescapable fact is that, allowing for hyperbole, Jesus meant just what he said. Reading gates and ropes into the text is like grasping at a straw to break the camel's back. It's an unnecessary exercise, too, for Jesus himself provides the real salvific "straw" immediately after the metaphor, when he notes that in God all things are possible. *The Interpreter's Dictionary of the Bible* (Abingdon Press, 1962); J. D. Douglas, *The New Bible Dictionary* (Eerdmans, 1973); James Hastings, *Dictionary of the Bible* (Scribner's, 1962).

WHAT'S THE WEATHER LIKE IN HELL?

Although the Christian tradition of hell as a region of burning torment has activated the popular imagination for hundreds of years, there has frequently been disagreement among theologians as to whether we should take the "fire and brimstone" picture literally or figuratively. The Bible has plenty of references to fire as a method of divine punishment (from Sodom and Gomorrah to Revelation's lake of fire), but only the inveterately literal take it today as an article of faith that if you die unsaved you will burn forever. Most Christians would agree with the *Catholic Dictionary*'s view that the "cataclysm with its trumpets, fire, worms and earthquakes is not a photographic record by anticipation of what will happen. The future is God's own mystery and is not to be captured by realistic description."

So, too, specifically, with Hell. Only a century ago the graphic visions of Gustave Doré, with their fumes and writhings, were seen as accurate representations of the nether regions. Today the fires of Hell are more often considered symbolic of anguish or remorse. This is especially interesting when you consider the etymology of the word. The Christian Hell was invented, by and large, around the steamy Mediterranean. The word Hell, though, comes from Hel, an ancient Norse term for their underworld, which was guarded by Hela, wife of Loki, and to which were sent those who did not die in battle. There are no fires here; to the ancient Scandinavians, Hel was miserably like every day—a place of darkness and cold. *Bulfinch's Mythology* (Crowell, 1970); *A Catholic Dictionary of Theology* (Thomas Nelson, 1967).

WHAT HAPPENS IN LIMBO?

The idea of limbo as a kind of waiting room for Heaven, a Purgatory without the flames, is a common one among people unfamiliar with the theological conundrums involved. To both modern and historical Catholics, Purgatory is a temporary state or place where the modestly sinful are made to suffer, and thus cleansed, before entering Heaven. Limbo is permanent, and even though it is thought to be free of suffering, it suffers by comparison to Heaven, for its denizens can never see God.

The invention of limbo was the outcome of an early Church riddle: If Heaven and Hell are the only choices after death, where does God put a) the Old Testament patriarchs, b) other adults who could not have heard the Christian message, yet might be spotless souls (such as ancient worthies and inhabitants of the New World), and c) unbaptized infants? Without some intermediate state to account for such anomalies, God would be in the untenable position of either "saving" those who had not been redeemed (a slap in the face for the Son) or condemning those who were personally innocent (a slap in the Father's own face, considering he is styled a God of mercy).

To get over this problem, the early Church fathers, beginning in the second century, posited a region of eternal gray delight for those who, through no fault of their own, died before Original Sin could be erased. Nobody was very pleased with the compromise, and debate on the issue has been intermittently resurrected. Augustine, arguing against the soft-hearted Pelagians (who denied the necessity of baptism), hinted that limbo may be one of the "many mansions" spoken of in John 14:2. Abelard called the pain of limbo "the lack of the vision of God" and, with exquisite casuistry, suggested that God would send there only *quem Deus pessimum futurum si viverit praevidebat:* those for whom the Lord had foreseen a wicked future if they had lived! Obviously this is a knotty question, and it's probably a relief to the Church today that at the present time the debate itself is in limbo. *A Catholic Dictionary of Theology* (Thomas Nelson, 1967).

WHAT IS THE IMMACULATE CONCEPTION?

Non-Catholics often assume that by Immaculate Conception Roman Catholics mean the conception of the baby Jesus—done without taint of Original Sin because that's the only way you could imagine God doing anything. That's a strange enough idea, speaking monotheistically, and yet the real meaning of the term Immaculate Conception is stranger still. It refers not to Jesus' conception by Mary but to that of Mary herself, by her parents, Saints Joachim and Anne. According to Church doctrine, Mary was preserved from Original Sin "thanks to a grace given in the first moment of her existence" by God the Father himself. Jesus, God's son, had curiously none of the same dispensation.

The doctrine is a relatively recent one. Feasts celebrating Mary's conception had begun in the Byzantine Church around 700, but for centuries the idea that the Mother of God was free of Original Sin remained merely a folk tradition, without scriptural authority or ecclesiastical support. Theologically, it was suspect because it seemed to make the Virgin independent of her son's own mediating grace—and that would never do in a religion that was as child-oriented as Christianity. If accepted, would not the concept have fatally flawed the doctrine of the Son's redemption, to mention nothing of the Father's "salvific will"?

The objection was not overcome until the thirteenth century, when the Oxford cleric Duns Scotus (from which we get, inappropriately, "dunce") pointed out that the objection could actually be read as a plus. "Complete preservation from sin would be the most perfect possible work of mediation, which is to be expected of Christ, the most perfect Mediator." Smart boy, that Duns.

Between the thirteenth and the nineteenth centuries the doctrine gradually gained credence among Church leaders, until in 1854 Pope Pius IX made it an article of faith. His proclamation, made on December 8 of that year, not only elided over the flimsy theological basis of the notion, but set the stage for another controversial papal fiat sixteen years later, when Pius decided that he himself was infallible. *A Catholic Dictionary of Theology* (Thomas Nelson, 1967).

PETER, THE FIRST POPE, WAS NOT INFALLIBLE.

Not Peter and not Linus (his successor) and not Cletus (Linus's successor) and not any of the hundreds of pontiffs who led the Church up to 1870. The doctrine of papal infallibility, far from being contemporaneous with the founding of the Church, came into being only at the end of the nineteenth century, when Pius IX (that's only nine popes ago) pushed the idea through the First Vatican Council against the horrified objections of many non-Italian cardinals who favored the idea of a decentralized Church.

Papal infallibility as an article of faith had been proposed as early as the thirteenth century by the Franciscan Peter Olivi, but Pope John XXII found the notion so offensive that in 1324 he condemned it as a work of the Devil. Rome pushed on, however, and by the mid-nineteenth century, with the accession of Pius IX, the stage was set for the codification of the eccentric doctrine into ecclesiastical law. Using Jesus' statement to Peter in Luke 22:32 ("I have prayed for thee, that thy faith fail not") as proof, Pius opened with the gambit of Immaculate Conception, then forged on to the overall idea that anything he said on faith and morals, at any time in the future, must be taken as divinely inspired. Over largely German opposition, this ingeniously centralizing fiat was passed by the Council, and has been Church law ever since.

However, as historian August Hasler points out, the doctrine was politically motivated, and had very little connection, in terms of Scripture, with Jesus' original intention. In the words of Hasler's colleague Hans Küng, "Jesus does not promise Peter freedom from error but the grace to persevere in the faith till the end." Seeing Luke 22:32 as a sanction for papal infallibility he sees as "an innovation with no textual basis."

The real reason for the success of the doctrine in 1870, according to Hasler, was political. Pius and his conservative Roman buddies, concerned with the rise of populist sentiment in both France (the Commune) and Italy (Garibaldi), endeavored to reduce the attractions of democratized religion by proclaiming, simply and without qualifications, that truth would henceforth come from Rome. They did not succeed, of course, but they did throw a powerful new contender into the hopper of religious debate. August Bernhard Hasler, *How the Pope Became Infallible* (Doubleday, 1981).

CATHOLIC PRIESTS WERE NOT ALWAYS CELIBATE.

Contemporary arguments over the Roman Catholic position that priests may not be married have led some to suppose that the Church's servants have always been celibate. So firm have been papal pronouncements on this score that enforced sexual continence has taken on an aura of ancient tradition. One is given the impression, to judge from papal opinion, that the custom was enjoined on priests by Jesus himself.

Actually, it's a more recent policy. For the first three centuries of the Church's existence, sexual conduct was left up to the individual, and no one expected a priest to be celibate unless he so desired. In the fourth century church councils began recommending (though not commanding) that clerics abstain from sex, and the Council of Nicea in 325 forbade priests to marry *after* ordination; it left the sex lives of already married priests up to them and their wives—and, in not a few cases, concubines.

It wasn't until around the fifth century that celibacy was enjoined on all priests as a law of the Western church. This did not mean, however, that all priests thereafter obeyed it. Throughout the Middle Ages, the law of celibacy was regularly debated and disregarded. It was a recurrent issue of the councils, and in England, for example, it was not until after the Fourth Lateran Council (1215)—which gave the Church transubstantiation and annual confession—that priestly marriage really began to decline.

Part of the reason for this was that "the married clergy had long ensured the succession of the priesthood, since they seem commonly to have been succeeded by their sons; in this way they ensured the essential religious needs of the people."

Even after the Reformation had made celibacy one bone of contention with Rome, the Council of Trent (1545–1563), in *De Matrimonio,* failed to settle the question of whether holy orders was an impediment to marriage (and therefore sex) because of ecclesiastical law or because of a "tacit or implicit vow of celibacy taken by the ordained." Not until 1920 did a pope, Benedict XV, state the hard line against clerical marriage in final, unwavering terms. *A Catholic Dictionary of Theology* (Thomas Nelson, 1967).

WHAT DO THE LETTERS "IHS" STAND FOR?

This common Catholic monogram has been variously misinterpreted over the centuries as an acronym. Some have said it stands for *In Hoc Signo,* or "In this sign," referring to the vision Constantine was supposed to have had before the battle at Mulvian Bridge, when the sky lit up with a cross and the words *"In hoc signo vinces"*—"In this sign you will conquer." Medieval Franciscans and later the Jesuits said it meant *Iesus Habemus Socium,* or "We have Jesus as an ally." The most common reading is *Iesus Hominum Salvator,* or "Jesus the savior of humanity." My personal favorite is the one given to me as a child by a Protestant friend who thought Catholics made too much of pain: He was convinced it stood for "I have suffered."

All of these interpretations derive from taking the monogram's *H* as an "h," the seventh letter of the Latin alphabet. Actually the *H* is the capital form of the Greek letter η sounded as "ē." When we read the whole thing as Greek, we see that *I, H,* and *S* are simply the first three letters of the name Iησοῦς, or Jesus.   F. L. Cross and E. A. Livingstone, eds., *The Oxford Dictionary of the Christian Church* (Oxford, 1974).

WHAT GOD DO BUDDHISTS WORSHIP?

Because most of us are heirs to the Judeo-Christian tradition, we tend to view all religions with that tradition's monotheistic bias, and assume that the principal figure in a given religion must be that religion's "god." Thus Buddha is commonly understood to be the deity Buddhists worship.

This would probably have amused the Indian teacher Gautama Sakyamuni, the first though not the only "Buddha." His way to enlightenment (the word Buddha means "enlightened one") was less a religion than a self-directed psychology, by the use of which a devotee could come to understand his or her own "Buddha nature," or oneness with the God-in-all-being. Strictly speaking, there *is* no Buddhist god, any more than there is a Taoist or a Confucian god. The point of all three "religions" is to bring the seeker in contact with an inner, rather than external, peace. S. G. F. Brandon says that basic to these Eastern pathways is the belief in "an underlying unitary, spiritual Reality," but that "it is doubtless incorrect to use the term 'God,' with its Christian, Jewish, and Islamic connotations," to describe this reality.

This nontheistic approach to self-mastery was converted into a theistic religion soon after the original Buddha died. Like Jesus he was quickly deified in the popular mind, and came to be seen not as one who had glimpsed the truth, but as a manifestation of the transcendent itself. Since popular religion, East or West, seems to need its avatars, the enlightened ones were translated into deities even though they consistently proclaimed that God is within. Throughout the East today the Buddha of Infinite Light, Amitabha, is widely revered as a kind of supreme deity, both creator and preserver of the universe. This takes the responsibility for enlightenment off one's personal shoulders, and that is a comfortable development, but it is one that is clearly at variance with the ideas of the religion's founder. S. G. F. Brandon, *A Dictionary of Buddhism* (Scribner's, 1972).

CLEANLINESS IS NOT NEXT TO GODLINESS.

Although the pithy comment that "Cleanliness is next to Godliness" was favorably quoted by John Wesley, and by many methodical soul-scrubbers after him, there is no evidence that the notion was common in Christian history, and a good deal of evidence that for most of the Church's two-thousand-year history dirt enveloped more souls than lye.

To judge from the yogic exercises in which Indian holy men are said to be able to wash not only the conventional bodily parts but also their entrails, an obsession with cleaning up one's act has long been popular in the East. In the West, the equation of cleanliness with God appears first in the Talmud, and it does not seem that the rabbis who invented it were very successful in passing it on as part of the Judeo-Christian heritage. For most of the Christian era, holiness has been pretty high.

As Vilhjalmur Stefansson wryly observes, the soap companies have done more in a couple of centuries than the Church did in ten times that long to inspire us with the fear of dirt. You have only to recall the saints who avoided bathing entirely (as a penance for themselves—and for others?) to see that he is right. The most committed bathers of Western history were, after all, the pagan Romans, and those least inclined to wash were those who lived in the Age of Faith. "Tristram," as Stefansson points out, "liked the smell of his sweetheart, and she liked his, both being used to it, and . . . the sinners as well as the saints of the Middle Ages really enjoyed what we would call the stink of foul linen." Henry Frederic Reddall, *Fact, Fancy, and Fable* (A. C. McClurg, repr. Gale, 1968); Vilhjalmur Stefansson, *Adventures in Error* (Robert McBride, 1936).

ARTS:

BEAUX ARTS, FAUX ARTS

WHO CREATED MICKEY MOUSE?

In 1919 Walter Elias Disney and Ubbe Ert Iwerks were Kansas City teen-agers intent on careers in commercial art. They formed a short-lived partnership and worked briefly for the Kansas City Film Ad Company until, in 1923, the enterprising Walt packed his bags for Hollywood. The following year, needing an accurate and facile draftsman to execute his designs, he sent for his old friend, and it was Iwerks who subsequently did the actual drawing for Mickey Mouse's first cartoon shorts, *Plane Crazy, Gallopin' Gaucho* (both 1927), and *Steamboat Willie* (1928). On all of these, Ub got the "drawn by" credit.

His relationship with the new Disney studio lasted until 1930, when he was lured away by distributor Pat Powers with the promise of his own company. This concern, which produced such forgettable characters as Willie Whopper and Flip the Frog, lasted until 1940, when Ub returned to the Disney fold. He stayed there until his death in 1971, lending his considerable talents to such gems of animation as *Song of the South* (1946) and *Mary Poppins* (1964).

Champions of obscure genius sometimes claim that Disney was a mediocre draftsman and that without Iwerks, animation's forgotten man, Mickey would have remained an unsung, indeed unborn Mortimer (Disney's original name for the rodent). This probably overstates the case. Certainly Ub was astonishingly deft with a pen—he did all of *Plane Crazy,* for example, in two weeks—but without Disney's creative drive (not to mention his entrepreneurial zeal) Iwerks might well have lived out his days in Kansas City.

It's true that Disney never could draw Mickey right—a source of some embarrassment to him—but just as true that Iwerks lacked the narrative imagination to transform his own Flip and

Willie into memorable characters. The two men were a superb combination: The pen that won the world was Ub's, but the gleam in the eye was Walt's. Leonard Maltin, *Of Mice and Magic: A History of American Animated Cartoons* (McGraw-Hill, 1980); Richard Schickel, *The Disney Version* (Simon & Schuster, 1968).

WHAT IS THE PROPER NAME OF LEONARDO DA VINCI'S MOST FAMOUS SITTER —THE LADY WITH THE "MYSTIC SMILE"?

When we were kids, we all went along with Nat King Cole and called her "Mona Lisa." In high school a few of us discovered that the "correct" name of the famous painting was "La Gioconda," since the lady who sat for it was married to one Francesco del Giocondo, an aging Florentine merchant. Those of us who had found this out thought ourselves very superior indeed to our friends who still believed Cole's song. Actually, although the painting is frequently called "La Gioconda" as a way of identifying the sitter, to contemporaries she was known as Madonna (or, more briefly, Mona) Lisa: That's the name used by one of Leonardo's earliest biographers, Giorgio Vasari. Our sophomoric wisdom, it turns out, was as fleeting as the sad lady's smile. Richard Friedenthal, *Leonardo da Vinci: A Pictorial Biography* (Viking, 1959); Antonina Vallentin, *Leonardo da Vinci: The Tragic Pursuit of Perfection* (Viking, 1938).

WHERE DID "AS TIME GOES BY" MAKE ITS APPEARANCE?

Casablanca is the quintessential American movie, and its theme song has become a late-show addict's national anthem. Even people who have seen the movie only six or seven times can hum its lush tune in their sleep, and nearly forty years after Rick commanded Dooley Wilson to "Play it," every piano player in the world still considers it a standard. I have requested it, with success, in piano bars from New Jersey to Japan.

But it did not start with the movie. Its original appearance was in the 1931 Broadway stage show *Everybody's Welcome,* a frothy comedy about a young mystery writer whose wife works "as a Roxyette or something so that he can have the leisure required for his literary labors." That's from the *New York Times,* whose reviewer also observed that the Irving Kahal lyrics "made some familiar statements on the subject of love" and that the interpolated songs "were—well, the interpolated songs."

The principal songs for *Everybody's Welcome* were written by Sammy Fain, who later gave us "Love Is a Many-Splendored Thing" and "April Love." "As Time Goes By," written by the far less successful Herman Hupfeld, was one of the maligned interpolated songs—hardly worth a mention. The play ran for one hundred thirty-seven performances, anyway, nothing close to the season's winner *The Cat and the Fiddle,* but lengths ahead of *The Singing Rabbi,* which closed after only four nights. Hupfeld went on to write his big hit "When Yuba Plays the Rumba on the Tuba" and to entertain in piano bars until his death in 1951.

The line that everyone remembers *about* the song, incidentally, is almost always misquoted. "Play It Again, Sam" is the title of Woody Allen's spoof; what Ilsa says in the movie is simply, "Play it, Sam." What Rick says, a few too many drinks later, is "If she can stand it, I can. Play it!"   *New York Times* theater reviews (1931); Roger D. Kinkle, *The Complete Encyclopedia of Popular Music and Jazz* (Arlington House, 1974).

IN THE 1930 FILM, WHO WAS THE "BLUE ANGEL"?

Because the moody, decadent Josef von Sternberg film *Der Blaue Engel* was the vehicle by which Marlene Dietrich achieved stardom, it's sometimes thought that her character, the dancehall singer Lola Fröhlich, is the Blue Angel of the title. Actually "Der Blaue Engel" is the name of the cabaret in which she works, and in which the stodgy pedagogue played by Emil Jannings is reduced to a love-maddened clown.

The film was a turning point for both principal players. Dietrich, who had been an obscure German actress, soon became, under Sternberg's direction, the femme fatale of the century; Jannings, who had enjoyed a distinguished career in the silents, faded from the public view as sound eclipsed his mimetic ingenuity. Ironically, the story line of the film—in which the aging professor is seduced and abandoned by the singer—presaged their subsequent achievements. Dietrich's career took a *fröhlich* (happy) turn, while Jannings became, eponymously, *Unrat,* or refuse.

The novel on which the film was based was published in 1905 under the title *Professor Unrat.* Its author was Heinrich Mann, elder brother of the more famous Thomas. *The Oxford Companion to Film* (Oxford, 1976); Georges Sadoul, *Dictionary of Films* (University of California Press, 1972).

WHAT NATIONALITY WAS GEORGE BERNARD SHAW?

The plays of George Bernard Shaw, or G.B.S., as his hierophants like to call him, are among the most durable dramatic creations in the history of the English theater. Because few writers have ever surpassed Shaw in acerbity or wit, plays like *Pygmalion* and *Arms and the Man* are as fresh today as they were when they were first produced. Shaw is a pillar of the English stage, and because of this many playgoers think of him as British. He was, however, Irish; born in Dublin in 1856, he did not leave his native land for London until he was twenty years old. Although he often spoke of the Irish as addled dreamers, he never completely disavowed his heritage, and in the preface to *John Bull's Other Island,* produced by Dublin's Abbey Theatre in 1916, he mentions his "instinctual pity for those of my fellow creatures who are only English." Thaddeus F. Tuleja, "Horsemen Passing: Yeats, Shaw, and the Uses of Drama." Unpublished dissertation (Cornell, 1968).

ROBERT BURNS DID NOT WRITE "AULD LANG SYNE."

It's charming to think of Bobbie Burns, Scotland's favorite poetic laddie, as the author of the country's most famous popular air, but, in fact, Burns did not write "Auld Lang Syne," and there is no indisputable evidence that the tune is even Scottish. A very similar tune appears in the 1783 opera *Rosima,* by the English composer William Shields (1748-1829)—although, to give the Scots their due, it should be noted that Shields grew up near the

Scottish border, was fond of incorporating traditional airs into his compositions, and noted that the *Rosima* tune was composed in imitation of bagpipe music.

The song first appeared with Burns's lyrics in the 1796 *Scots Musical Museum,* a collection of traditional tunes on which the poet worked in the last decade of his life. The version which appeared there, according to Burns, was a recasting of an old song which he had taken down from an old man singing it. Probably, though not certainly, that song was of Scottish origin: Burns's lyrics, in any case, were in a Scottish dialect. However, according to a Manchester *Guardian* correspondent, the melody's origin is unclear: He heard it in a religious procession in Corsica, and was told it was "a very old Corsican tune." Percy A. Scholes, *The Oxford Companion to Music* (Oxford, 1970).

HANDEL'S MESSIAH *IS NOT A CHRISTMAS ORATORIO.*

When I was a teen-ager, a predictable high point of the Christmas season was the performance in the high school auditorium of that massively exuberant oratorio, George Frederick Handel's *Messiah* (commonly miscalled "the" *Messiah).* My high school, I later discovered, was not alone in its fondness for this superb piece of "Christmas" music; I have since heard it sung in several cities, and it seems to appear nearly always as Santas jingle schoolbells outside. Probably because of its memorable chorus "For unto Us a Child Is Born," *Messiah* is as closely associated with Christmas as "Jingle Bells" or "Frosty the Snowman."

But it was composed not for this season, or indeed for any specific holiday. Handel was asked to write it by Dublin's Lord Lieutenant, who wanted an oratorio to boost the fortunes of the city's charities. That was in 1741, the year in which Handel's opera *Deidamia* had rung an embarrassing close to his waning stage career. He tackled his appointed task, therefore, with an energy born as much of professional desperation as of that divine intoxication which he later claimed had visited him as he worked.

The result was a phenomenal success. The Dublin premiere audience was overwhelmed, and in London the following spring (1743), King George II was so moved during the "Hallelujah Chorus" that he involuntarily rose to his feet—initiating a tradition that persists to the present day. Two and a half centuries later, *Messiah,* an "unbirthday present" for the Lord, remains "the most frequently performed oratorio ever written, as well as the most highly esteemed." David Ewen, ed., *The Complete Book of Classical Music* (Prentice-Hall, 1965).

HORATIO ALGER WAS NOT A PROPHET OF CAPITALIST ENTERPRISE.

The Horatio Alger myth is one of the most well-worn, most frequently fondled icons of American popular culture—so much so that today it's much quicker quoted than understood. The "rags to riches" dream is so much a part of the general American dream, and Alger is so firmly identified with it, that we no longer feel compelled, when speaking of the myth, to check our assertions against the text: "Everybody knows" that Alger's heroes worked their way from poverty to success, and "everybody knows" that they have therefore always stood as paragons of nineteenth-century industry.

If the Rotary Club speakers and Sunday morning lesson mongers who eulogize Alger would bother to read his books, though, they would find that matters there are a little less simple than they suppose. Alger was a Harvard-educated Unitarian minister, and according to his biographer, John Tebbel, he seems to have viewed the rise of rugged individualism with a good deal of outrage and misgiving. It's true that his heroes—all those Ragged Dicks and Tattered Toms—end up better than they begin; but what is generally forgotten is that their virtue and industry are seldom the decisive factors in their rise. In Tebbel's words Alger "constantly preached that success was to be won through virtue and hard work, but his stories tell us just as constantly that success is actually the result of fortuitous circumstance." Generally, what brings his boys success is meeting a wealthy businessman who gives them a first big chance.

That success, moreover, is always modest, and this, Tebbel and Gary Scharnhorst agree, is because Alger had a deeply divided attitude toward wealth. He saw himself as a moral reformer, and would have been horrified to think that a generation after his death, his stories would be taken as guidebooks for mere business enterprise. He was uneasy in the Gilded Age, and often painted rich boys as villains.

The transformation of the minister into the moguls' mouth-piece, says Scharnhorst, happened in the 1920s, when a new wave of individualism was sweeping the country and cheap, badly edited reprints of the Alger juveniles were popular. "It may be," he says, "that the success story of the Alger hero was misconstrued during the period at least partly because the modest success of the Alger hero came to be confused with the astounding sales success of the books. If true, this would also account for the persistent, mistaken belief that Horatio Alger was not an author but a character in success stories." Gary Scharnhorst, *Horatio Alger, Jr.* (Twayne, 1980); John Tebbel, *From Rags to Riches: Horatio Alger, Jr., and the American Dream* (Macmillan, 1963).

WHAT IS THE TITLE OF WHISTLER'S MOST FAMOUS PAINTING?

In his day the American artist James MacNeill Whistler (1834–1903) was a celebrated dandy and wit, though you'd hardly suspect a colorful personality from looking at the noted picture of his mother. It suggests a famous conversationalist about as clearly as "American Gothic" suggests a stand-up comic.

The title was not "Whistler's Mother," or "My Mother," or "Mom in an Uncomfortable Chair." The artist, fond of abstraction in words as well as oils, called it "Arrangement in Grey and Black #1." This is not to be confused with "Arrangement in Grey and Black #2" (a portrait of Thomas Carlyle) or with "Arrangement in Black and White" (a study of a young girl) or with "Arrangement in Grey" (a self-portrait). These three works are arranged in lesser museums, while Mom goes on sitting in the Louvre. *McGraw-Hill Dictionary of Art* (McGraw-Hill, 1969).

WHEN DID THE "STAR-SPANGLED BANNER" BECOME THE NATIONAL ANTHEM?

Francis Scott Key's masterpiece was written, according to a reliable legend, during the 1814 siege of Fort McHenry, when the Washington, D.C., lawyer was being detained by the British lest he relay advance information about the attack to his fellow Americans at the fort. His delight at seeing Old Glory still aloft after a night of bombardment inspired the famous lines, which he promptly wrote down and, upon his release, had distributed throughout Baltimore. The poem was an instant success locally, but more than a century would pass before it was made the national anthem. That happened on March 3, 1931, when Congress officially adopted it.

Ironically, the tune to which Key's poem was later set was a staunchly British product. Written around 1780 by the English composer John Stafford Smith, it was originally intended to accompany the words of "To Anacreon in Heaven" as the official song of a London musical society. Ralph Tomlinson, the lyricist, was, like Key, a lawyer. By the 1790s the tune had become popular in America, and Key himself, a decade before Fort McHenry, had set to it a poem honoring Stephen Decatur.

The anthem, originally entitled "The Defense of Fort McHenry," has four verses in all, only one of which is generally sung. Considering that the latter stanzas contain phrases like "foul footsteps' pollution" (in reference to the British) and "heaven rescued land" (in reference to the home of the brave), perhaps that's just as well. "Star-Spangled Banner" in *Encyclopedia Americana* (1979).

WHO WROTE GRIMMS' FAIRY TALES?

Few collections of fairy tales have been as influential, among children and adults alike, as Jacob and Wilhelm Grimm's 1812 *Kinder und Hausmärchen* (Tales of Home and Children). Translated into English as *Grimms' Fairy Tales,* they have puzzled scholars and astonished readers for decades because of their haunting magic, narrative invention, and intermittent sadism. Modern readers complain of a Teutonic "Grimmness" in the tales, while others see them as the epitome of literate folklore.

Because their name has so long been associated with them, it's often thought that the brothers invented the stories themselves. This is not so, and the Grimms—good folklorists that they were—would have been the first to acknowledge it. What they did was to gather together traditional tales, both from earlier collections and by word of mouth from peasant storytellers, and then to write them down in a more-or-less "definitive" form. "The novelty of their approach," says Richard Dorson in his foreword to *Folk-*

tales of Germany, "lay in the principle of obtaining tales directly from the lips of storytellers, and seeking in print other tales secured in a similar way." They were really compilers, then, rather than authors.

In this they were part of a rich reevaluation of literature which animated Germany, and ultimately the rest of Europe, at the turn of the nineteenth century. Beginning in the 1760s with Johann Gottfried Herder, who "exhorted his countrymen to collect folk poetry and himself edited a volume of *Volkslieder,*" Germans especially were anxious to recapture what they saw as the simple, pure soul of the *volk.* Nationalism and primitivism combined to produce what Wilhelm called *Naturpoesie,* and this "nature poetry" soon transformed European thought: German literary romanticism, already implicit in the late eighteenth-century writing of Goethe and Friedrich Hölderlin, received an enormous boost in the first decade of the new century when writers Achim von Arnim, Clemens Brentano, and the Grimms collected and published folktales.

The Grimms, not content to present their tales unadorned, also published companion volumes on ancient sagas and mythology. To the "household tales" they amended copious notes and essays, so that what had started as a country pastime became "a majestic five-volume work of reference." It is this full dimension of their work, says Mr. Dorson, "which won for them recognition as creators of a folklore science."   Kurt Ranke, ed., *Folktales of Germany* (University of Chicago Press, 1966).

FRANKENSTEIN WAS NOT A MONSTER.

The most famous monster story of our time was written as a kind of contest entry by the eighteen-year-old Mary Shelley (1797–1851). She, Percy Shelley, Lord Byron, and Byron's friend John Polidori were staying at Byron's Villa Diotadi in Geneva when the host suggested that to while away a rainy evening each of the four compose a "ghost story." The results were three forgotten fantasies and *Frankenstein, or the Modern Prometheus.*

Since its appearance in print in 1818, volumes have been written analyzing Shelley's odd masterpiece, and numerous films, beginning with the 1931 Boris Karloff version, have made the name Frankenstein a byword for terror. The name, however, does not refer to the monster, but to his creator, the ambitious scientist Victor Frankenstein, whose lust for the "secret of life" brings ruin to all around him.

It has been suggested that the young author's fear, so evident in the eerie tenseness of the book, was not simply the theological fear of peeking into things that human beings "ought to leave alone," but the biological fear—common enough for a young bride—of the dangers of sex and birth. Mary's own mother had died shortly after giving birth to her, and some critics consequently see *Frankenstein* as a nervous, guilty meditation. "It comes down to this," says Leonard Wolf, "that lovers risk babies, and babies can kill." The monster, then, becomes a grotesque stand-in for the abstract child that Mary Shelley feared—and perhaps the actual child, William Shelley, that she had borne only five months before. But it is the child's creator (Percy or herself, take your pick), as much as the creature itself, on which she really lavishes censure. Mary Shelley, *The Annotated Frankenstein,* with an introduction and notes by Leonard Wolf (Clarkson Potter, 1977).

HARPO MARX WAS NOT MUTE.

Harpo's peculiar charm was always his ability to communicate perfectly without ever uttering a syllable: With his toy horns, coat full of props, and wonderfully plastic expressions, he created a language of silence which, in its own way, was every bit as precise and provocative as the wisecracking lingo of his brothers. It's a tribute to his inventiveness as a mime that many Marx Brothers' fans take his muteness as a constitutional given rather than a theatrical ploy.

But Harpo was no more mute than, say, Marcel Marceau or any of the other wordless chatterers who, in an ancient clown's tradition, make actions speak louder than words. He tipped his hand to the general public only in 1961, with the appearance of his autobiography, *Harpo Speaks!* But his friends had known for decades that off the screen he was as voluble as Groucho or Chico. One of his closest friends was the essayist and radio personality Alexander Woollcott, a noted conversationalist who would hardly have been satisfied with toy horns. According to the *Current Biography* description that appeared toward the end of the Marx Brothers' film career, Harpo was "said to be the most garrulous of the Marxes." "Marx Brothers" in *Current Biography* (1948).

THE JEW'S HARP IS NOT JEWISH.

The Jew's harp, or Jew's trump, as it was first called in England, arose in many parts of the ancient world independently. It was known throughout aboriginal Europe and Asia, samples having been associated by musicologists with such widely diverse culture areas as China, Japan, the Philippines, Siberia, Borneo, and Scotland. It was a popular dance instrument in seventeenth-century Scotland, while on the Continent two centuries later, the traveling German player Charles Eulenstein made it a virtuoso instrument. In the Austrian Tyrol peasants used to play two Jew's harps simultaneously, thus producing a harmonic chord, and at least one Yorkshire village had an entire band of Jew's harp players.

The instrument is simply a vibrating metal "tongue" set in an iron frame: By holding the frame between the teeth, plucking the tongue, and varying the shape of the mouth cavity, a player can produce numerous harmonic notes and even melodies. Why the "harp" was named after the Jews is not known. The association is at least four centuries old, for sixteenth-century English sailors speak of using "Iewes-harpes" in trade with American Indians. It has been suggested that the name arose because the instrument was introduced to England by Jewish merchants, or because it was "a good commercial name, suggesting the trumps and harps mentioned in the Bible." This is ingenious but unlikely, since the Jew's harp is neither a harp nor a trump (trumpet).

Wary of embarrassing Jewish customers, some sellers of musical instruments in this century began referring to "jaws harps," while others hinted that the name may have derived from the French word *jeu,* for "game." The *Oxford English Dictionary* calls both these explanations "baseless and inept." Percy Scholes, acknowledging defeat more graciously, says that the Jewish connection is an unfathomable "mystery of ancient false etymology." *Oxford English Dictionary* (Oxford, 1970); Percy A. Scholes, *Oxford Companion to Music* (Oxford, 1972).

WHAT WERE CINDERELLA'S SLIPPERS MADE OF?

Cinderella never wore a glass slipper. The Cinderella story, which is ancient and international, was popularized in the West by the French writer Charles Perrault (1628–1703). His version, which appeared in his famous *Tales of Mother Goose* (1697), has the young lady wearing *pantouffles en verre,* or slippers made of glass, and it's from this rendition that most subsequent versions derive.

But *verre* was a mistranslation. The old French versions which Perrault used as his sources gave the girl *pantouffles en vair,* and *vair* is white squirrel fur. Confusing the two words, Perrault introduced an error which has stood to this day. As if the poor child didn't already have enough problems, she has ever since been condemned, because of Perrault's verre-sion, to mince around in breakable shoes. David Wallechinsky and Irving Wallace, *The People's Almanac #2* (Bantam, 1978); Leo Rosten, *The Power of Positive Nonsense* (McGraw-Hill, 1977).

WHO WERE TOM AND JERRY?

The violence-prone cat and mouse duo featured in the MGM cartoons has been applauded now by three generations of children. The cartoons, drawn by William Hanna and Joseph Barbera, were produced by Fred Quimby between 1937 and 1965, when he died; they included such Academy Award winners as *Yankee Doodle Mouse* (1943), *Cat Concerto* (1946), and *The Two Mousketeers* (1951).

It's not commonly known, though, that the animated Tom and Jerry had been preceded a century before by a literary duo of the same name that, in its day, was every bit as popular as the cartoons. The original Tom and Jerry were created by the English sportswriter Pierce Egan (1772–1849), whose 1821 novel, *Life in London,* recounted the urban adventures of Jerry Hawthorn, Corinthian Tom, and their Oxford pal Bob Logic in a series of "Rambles and Sprees through the Metropolis."

An armchair voyeur's guide to London, the book enjoyed an enormous vogue in the 1820s, giving rise to numerous imitations both literary and dramatic. According to the *Dictionary of Na-*

tional Biography, "The alternate scenes of high life and low life, the contrasted characters, and revelations of misery side by side with prodigal waste and folly, attracted attention, while the vivacity of dialogue and description never flagged." You can hardly credit the MGM Tom and Jerry with vivacious dialogue, but the "prodigal waste and folly" strikes a familiar note.

Life in London was so frequently pirated and plagiarized that in 1828 Egan issued a debunking sequel in which the consequences of the original trio's high living were seen to be sickness and degradation. This *Finish to the Adventures of Tom, Jerry, and Logic* is said to have suggested to Charles Dickens the idea for *The Pickwick Papers.* Leslie Halliwell, *The Filmgoer's Companion* (Hill and Wang, 1977); "Pierce Egan" in *Dictionary of National Biography* (Oxford, 1973).

WHAT WAS LEWIS CARROLL'S OCCUPATION?

It's widely recognized by now that the author of *Alice in Wonderland* (originally "Alice's Adventures Underground") was not primarily a writer of children's books. People who know him only through his fiction are aware that he was an Oxford professor, and a few even recall that his fields were mathematics and logic. Anyone who has reveled in the Red Queen's sublime illogic can appreciate to what good use Carroll put his expertise.

It's less commonly known that Carroll—or Charles Lutwidge Dodgson, as he was baptized—was also a clergyman and a photographer. His clerical ambitions were limited: He was ordained an Anglican deacon in 1861, but never took priest's orders. As a photographer he was more adventurous, and after Julia Margaret Cameron is considered one of England's best amateurs.

His photographic reputation may be explained, however, less by the exactness of his technique than by the oddity of his subject. For the most part he photographed little girls, among them Alice Liddell, for whom he wrote his masterpiece. He had an unbridled, if apparently platonic, passion for girls, and once confessed wryly that he was "fond of children, except boys." In the 1860s and 1870s, in his rooms at Oxford, he entertained many young guests, photographing them in romantic costumes and occasionally in the nude.

He was also fond of kissing his charges, and this raised eye-

brows at least once, when he underestimated the age of a sev-
enteen-year-old friend and gave her what he thought was an
innocent peck; her mother was not amused. Apparently, the author of *Euclid and His Modern Rivals* had his own problems with
numbers. Lewis Carroll, *The Annotated Alice,* Martin Gardner,
ed. (Clarkson Potter, 1960); Derek Hudson, *Lewis Carroll* (Constable, 1976).

WHERE WAS THE WOODSTOCK CONCERT?

Ever since those "three days of peace and music" happened in
August 1969, the name "Woodstock" has evoked dreams of a lost
millennium. More than the marches on Washington, more than
the Beatles on Sullivan, more even than the "summer of love" on
the Haight, the Woodstock festival symbolizes the glorious possibility of the sixties: the decade's happily addled conviction that
the revolution was at hand.

The concert which gave the name its power, though, did not
take place in Woodstock. Since that New York State hamlet was
a lodestone for musicians (among them Bob Dylan and The
Band), the festival's promoters initially had it in mind when they
considered sites, and they even named their production company
Woodstock Ventures in its honor. However, as the summer of
1969 approached, they shifted their sights elsewhere, and settled
on the town of Wallkill. The fete would have taken place there,
except that early in the summer, its residents got cold feet. Realizing that they didn't really want several thousand spaced-out
hippies camping on their doorstep, the town fathers proposed
ground rules that were simply impossible to abide by, and the
boys of Woodstock Ventures had to renew their search.

At that point, nervously watching the calendar, they met a man
by the name of Max Yasgur. He owned a farm, he said, about
forty miles southwest of Woodstock, at a place which was part of
the town of Bethel. It might be just right for their shindig. It was,
and the rest is history—but not the history of Woodstock. The
papers did not record what, if anything, went on that weekend in
Woodstock, New York, although a reasonable guess would be
that most of its inhabitants were in Bethel. Joel Rosenman,
John Roberts, and Robert Pilpel, *Young Men with Unlimited
Capital* (Harcourt, Brace, Jovanovich, 1974).

WHAT WAS THE LAST TUNE THE
TITANIC *BAND PLAYED?*

The gravest fallacy associated with the *Titanic* disaster, of course, was the notion that the ship was unsinkable. In thrall to this dim idea, the owners and captain of the vessel steamed it much too fast through waters that were known to be ice-infested. The result was not the record time they had hoped for, but the loss of nearly fifteen hundred lives. Naturally, in an "unsinkable" ship, a short complement of lifeboats had been thought sufficient.

In the wake of the tragedy, several subsidiary fallacies were born, among them the notions that the crew had kept perfect discipline, that most male passengers had given up their lifeboat seats to women, and that icebergs had never been seen that far south before. All nonsense, and all fervently believed by the public for years after the disaster.

One of the most tenacious myths about that chill April night in 1912 is that as the great ship went down, the band was playing Sarah Adams's noted hymn "Nearer, My God, to Thee." Actually, as Tom Burnam discovered in Walter Lord's *A Night to Remember,* the last thing the band played, before the tilt of the deck sent the musicians tumbling, was the Episcopalian hymn "Autumn." Lord's book appeared back in the 1950s, but his debunking of the myth had no effect: Both the American and the British films which followed it included the Adams strains.

Adams was an Englishwoman, while the composer of "Autumn," François Barthelemon, was French. That may partially explain the reluctance of the public to accept the fact over the fancy. A more compelling factor, though, was surely the sense of appropriateness that was suggested by the "Nearer" ending. Geoffrey Marcus notes that when the "news" reached England, the *Daily Chronicle* called the mythical hymn playing "a fitting ending to a solemn and terrible tragedy." *Lloyd's Weekly News* printed the text in full, with the score. When the fact becomes legend, print the legend. Tom Burnam, *More Misinformation* (Lippincott & Crowell, 1980); Geoffrey Marcus, *The Maiden Voyage* (Viking, 1969).

INVENTIONS:

PATENTS PENDING

WHO INVENTED THE ELECTRIC LIGHT?

Although it was the wizard of Menlo Park who perfected a marketable filament for the incandescent lamp, Thomas Edison had had some precursors. Edison's triumph came in 1879. A generation earlier, the English inventor Joseph Swan had made several impractical lamps, and as early as 1845 the American J. W. Starr had patented an experimental illumination device which, like Swan's and Edison's, utilized a vacuum bulb.

But the real father of the electric light was probably the English chemist Sir Humphrey Davy (1778–1829). In 1802, before Edison's parents were born, he caused a platinum wire to glow by passing an electric current through it. Although he received little credit for the feat, we need not feel sorry for him. As one of the most brilliant scientists of his time, he achieved international fame, considerable wealth, and a presidency of the Royal Society. Chemists remember him today as the discoverer of several new metals: calcium, sodium, barium, potassium, magnesium, and strontium.   Gordon Friedlander, "Incandescent Lamp," in *Encyclopedia Americana* (1979).

WHO INVENTED THE TELEPHONE?

In February 1876 a Boston speech teacher named Alexander Graham Bell took out what was to prove the most valuable patent ever granted for a device that he said would transmit the human voice over a wire. His "telephone," which a month later carried the famous message "Mr. Watson, come here, I want you," was to make its inventor rich and also embroil him in numerous lawsuits brought by people who debated the priority of his invention.

Bell's chief rival for the title of "Father of the Telephone" was a Frankfurt physicist named John Philip Reis, who in 1861 had developed an apparatus for carrying sound impulses by wire. Constructed of such homey parts as a beer barrel cork (for a mouthpiece) and a sausage skin (for a diaphragm), it successfully transmitted the human voice, though so indistinctly that individual words were incomprehensible. Bell apparently knew of Reis's work, and credited him, but that did not get him off the hook. In 1900, twenty-five years after the German inventor's death, the United States government was still harassing Bell, saying he had concealed his knowledge of the sausage-skin speaker from its patent officers.

If by "telephone" you mean simply an instrument that can carry the human voice, then Reis was clearly its inventor; if you mean an instrument that can carry intelligible, not just audible, speech, the nod should go to Bell. Modern improvements on the Reis model have transmitted articulate speech, though, and this argues in his behalf. At least one student of the issue, Edward Hyde, thinks that "from a purely technical standpoint, the telephone was born at the instant Reis threw the first switch." I wonder if Ma Reis's rates would have been any better than Ma Bell's.   David Wallechinsky and Irving Wallace, *The People's Almanac #2* (Bantam, 1978).

WHO INVENTED THE SEWING MACHINE?

Elias Howe (1819–1867) is usually given the credit, and there is poetic justice in that, for the Massachusetts inventor endured extreme trials before achieving his success. He received a patent for a lockstitching machine in 1846, but finding no interest in the United States, had to go to England to sell it. His English partner, William Thomas, ignored their royalty agreement, and Howe returned to America nearly destitute, having to borrow money from his father to afford a fare to Boston, where his wife was dying of consumption. Only after her death drove home to him how shabbily he had been treated did he begin to take on those who had deprived him of his fortune. In the 1850s the courts vindicated his claims against Thomas and other patent infringers (including Isaac Singer), and he died rich and widely honored.

His lockstitch machine, however, was not the first such device.

A decade before Howe's patent, a versatile New Yorker named Walter Hunt developed a machine which, like Howe's, set a locked stitch in fabric. Thinking that it might put seamstresses out of work, he decided not to apply for a patent, and had to content himself with being the developer of, among other things, the paper collar, a repeating rifle, and the paper clip.

A decade before Hunt's invention, a French tailor named Barthelemy Thimmonier had developed a machine to sew chain stitches. This was inferior to the Hunt and Howe models, since a chain stitch, once broken, quickly pulls out entirely. But the device was clearly a sewing machine, and a pretty popular one too. The French army bought eighty of Thimmonier's invention in 1831, and he prospered until his fellow tailors, with a concern similar to Hunt's, raided his shop, smashed his apparatus, and forced him to flee for his life. For years he sold handmade machines at ten dollars apiece. Mitchell Wilson says he was defeated "not by lack of ingenuity, inventiveness, or persistence, but by the time and place in which he lived."   Mitchell Wilson, *American Science and Invention* (Bonanza Books, 1960).

JAMES WATT DID NOT INVENT THE STEAM ENGINE.

The Scottish engineer James Watt (1763–1819) made so many improvements on the steam engines of his day that he is frequently credited with having invented the device himself. This attribution is erroneous. The power of steam had been understood since ancient times, and various European designers in the seventeenth century had developed steam-driven machines to raise and propel water, as, for example, in Solomon de Caus's 1615 "steam fountain." At the end of that century, in 1698, the Englishman Thomas Savery used a steam-driven engine to pump out flooded mines in Cornwall, and in 1712 his countryman Thomas Newcomen patented "the first steam engine really worthy of the designation."

The Newcomen engine was widely used in the first half of the eighteenth century. The problem with it was that, like Savery's engine, it was technically inefficient: It wasted enormous amounts of steam because vaporization and condensation took place in the same chamber. In 1763 Watt was repairing a Newcomen engine when he hit upon the innovation that was to make his reputation. His introduction of a separate condensing vessel greatly increased the work efficiency of the machine; the 1769 patent in which he described this innovation also called for insulation of the steam cylinder to guard against heat loss, and the use of pumps to remove noncondensable gas.

From 1775 to 1800 Watt was a partner in the Soho Engineering Works, run by Matthew Boulton, which produced many of England's steam engines. While there he continued to improve the machines, inventing such devices as a speed governor, the sun-and-planet gear wheel (to convert reciprocating into rotary motion), and the throttle valve. He also coined the term "horse-power," and quite justly lent his name to our most common measure of power.   Kenneth J. Moser, "Steam Engine," and "James Watt" in *Encyclopedia Americana* (1979).

WHO INVENTED THE FRANKLIN STOVE?

Benjamin Franklin invented something he *thought* was a stove, but as Tom Burnam points out, the device he called the "Pennsylvanian Fireplace," and which in later years bore his name, was functionally a dud. Misunderstanding the laws of heat convection, Franklin designed his stove so that it would draw smoke out of the bottom instead of the top. This, he thought, would make it more heat-efficient; in fact, it made it inoperable.

Since you could not expect inoperable stoves to be successful items commercially, it's hardly surprising that in twenty years of marketing the invention, Ben's brother, Peter, succeeded in selling only two to the public. It was left to a man named Rittenhouse—possibly Franklin's American Philosophical Society colleague David Rittenhouse—to improve on Ben's design and make the thing a success. The familiar cast-iron device we now call a Franklin stove was, when originally sold widely in the 1790s, called a Rittenhouse stove.   Tom Burnam, *More Misinformation* (Lippincott & Crowell, 1980).

WHO INVENTED MOTION PICTURES?

In spite of the fact that Thomas Edison usually gets the credit, a lot of people invented motion pictures. It was Edison's peculiar genius not only to be able to coordinate the work of others but also to market his contributions in such a way that it seemed he had done all the work himself. This is not a slap at his brilliance (which is unassailable), but only a plea for a more balanced appraisal, now that the master is gone.

Motion pictures grew out of the work of an Englishman, an American, and a Frenchman. The Englishman, William George Horner, in 1833 invented the zoetrope, or "wheel of life," a rotating slotted cylinder which made pictures appear to move when the device was turned. This "persistence of vision" toy was a major inspiration to Edison. The American was the San Francisco photographer Eadweard Muybridge, who in 1879 patented "a method and apparatus for photographing objects in motion"; he used his setup initially to win a bet for California governor Leland Stanford, who was convinced that a running horse lifts all four of its feet off the ground simultaneously, but could not prove it. Muybridge's mechanism, by which a horse tripped a wire and thus took its own picture, won the governor $25,000 and Muybridge a place in history. The Frenchman was Etienne Jules Marey, who devised a photographic "gun" in 1882 to record the flights of birds.

Aware of the work of these three men, Edison in 1887 directed his assistant William Kennedy Dickson to develop a device "which should do for the eye what the phonograph does for the ear." Two years later Dickson came up with the first "peep show" model; they called it the kinetoscope, and an accompanying camera the kinetograph.

Meanwhile, across the big water, many others were also at work. In France the ingenious Lumière brothers were developing their own motion-picture camera and projector; they began showing short films in Paris in 1895. In England Robert Paul began selling Edison cameras, and then developed a smaller, portable one of his own. In Berlin Max Skladanowski demonstrated his "bioscope" projector, also in 1895. By the end of the century "Edison's" idea had led to strings of movie houses throughout Europe and America. Many people had contributed to this, although Edison's entrepreneurial genius made him the chief beneficiary. A. R. Fulton, *Motion Pictures: The Development of an Art from Silent Films to the Age of Television* (University of Oklahoma Press, 1960).

WHO INVENTED THE MORRIS CHAIR?

A man of prodigious energy and unflagging imagination, William Morris (1834–1896) was an accomplished poet, novelist, social reformer, painter, designer, and craftsman. His luxurious painting and poetry made him one of the most significant Pre-Raphaelite artists, while his championship of medieval-style handwork made him a pioneer in the Arts and Crafts movement: In the late nineteenth century, largely under Morris's direction, this movement infused all English crafts—from bookmaking to wallpaper design, from cabinetry to architecture—with a new decorative charm.

In 1861 Morris and several friends formed the crafts firm of Morris, Marshall, Faulkner and Company, devoted to "fine art" work in "painting, carving, furniture, and the metals." Their areas of expertise included muralism, decorative woodwork, stained glass, tapestry, jewelry, leatherwork, and furniture; in most of these areas Morris was personally engaged. But although he did design numerous items of furniture, the adjustable-back chair for which he is best remembered was not his doing. It was adapted by his architect partner Philip Webb from an old Sussex design, and made by the Morris firm from about 1866 on. Philip Henderson, *William Morris: His Life, Work, and Friends* (McGraw-Hill, 1967).

WHO INVENTED BASEBALL?

The British game of rounders is played on a field with four stones or posts, twelve to twenty feet apart, forming a square. A "pecker" or "feeder" throws a ball to a "striker," who tries to hit it and, if successful, "round" the square by touching the four corner markers in succession. He is out if he misses the ball three times, hits a foul ball, is hit by a thrown ball, or hits a fly which is caught. When his whole team is out, the sides switch.

Sound familiar? It ought to because rounders, with a few obvious differences, was the basis of the game that, in the mid nineteenth century, would become America's pastime. As early as 1834, the American form of rounders, called "Base, or Goal Ball," was being played by American youngsters. A decade later, a New York City bank clerk named Alexander Cartwright and several friends formed the Knickerbocker Base Ball Club and devised rules that, with few changes, are still observed today. It was Cartwright who specified that the ball diamond should be ninety feet on a side, that each team should have nine players, and that three outs should constitute an inning. It was also Cartwright who, on an 1849 journey to California, familiarized the rest of the country with the game.

What about Abner Doubleday? Well in 1839, when Doubleday was supposed to have invented baseball in Cooperstown, New York, he was a West Point cadet, unable to get home for the summer. The Doubleday legend got started just after the turn of the century, when the sports equipment manufacturer Albert Spaulding, miffed at a British friend's suggestion that baseball had come from rounders, set up a commission to investigate the game's origins. Its chairman, former National League president Abraham Mills, came up with the Doubleday story on the basis of hearsay alone: Abner Graves, a Cooperstown schoolboy in 1839, cited the other Abner's "invention," and Mills swallowed the tale with patriotic glee. Baseball was on its way to becoming known, erroneously, as the "national game."

Doubleday's actual career was quite impressive. He fired the first Union shot at Fort Sumter, distinguished himself at Gettysburg, and in 1867 attained the rank of full colonel. On duty in San Francisco two years later, he obtained the charter for the city's first cable car. He also studied French, Spanish, and Sanskrit. The *Dictionary of American Biography* called him "a man of wide interests and varied attainments." It's ironic that he should be remembered for a tall tale.   Ralph Hickok, *New Encyclopedia of Sports* (McGraw-Hill, 1977); Allen Johnson and Dumas Malone, "Abner Doubleday," in *Dictionary of American Biography* (Scribner's, 1930).

THE EARL OF SANDWICH DID NOT INVENT THE SANDWICH.

England's high-living John Montagu, the fourth Earl of Sandwich (1718–1792), has long been thought to have invented the meal that bears his name as a gambling-table expedient: Not wanting either to leave the table or go hungry, he hit upon the meat-between-bread slices as a way of keeping his hands "grease-and fork-free during his card-playing binges."

The good earl did give the item a name, but the idea that he actually constructed the first sandwich is about as substantial as American white bread. The Arabs had been stuffing pita bread with meat centuries before Montagu was born. In medieval Europe peasants consumed field lunches of bread and cheese, while the open-faced sandwich enjoyed a vogue among "trenchermen" who ate meat piled on top of a slab of bread—and then consumed this impromptu plate, or "trencher," as well.

Moreover, among the ancient Jews, a common Passover repast was a sandwich of nuts and fruit between matzohs—with the filling meant to represent the mortar used by their ancestors in Egypt to hold together those strawless bricks. Anita Borghese calls this "probably the world's first recorded sandwich."   Anita Borghese, *The Great Sandwich Book* (Rawson Associates, 1978).

THE ARABIC NUMBER SYSTEM IS NOT ARABIC.

"Arabic" numerals created a revolution in Western mathematics, since they translated into a simple, easily learned system of figures that under the Romans had been cumbersome and complex. The new system introduced three extremely important concepts: decimal place-value, in which each place in a multidigited number was worth ten times that of the place to its right; the use of nine ciphers to count the possible members of a given place; and the use of the zero as a missing-position notation. With the adoption of these innovations in the early Middle Ages, European calculation was transformed.

Everybody knows that Europe got the new system from the Arabs. It is not so generally known that the Arabs had gotten it in turn from the Hindus, around the mid eighth century. The Hindu writer Aryabhata had described the ten-times place system back in 499, and the Syrian bishop Severus Sebokt in 662 praised the Hindus' "subtle discoveries in astronomy," especially their nine-sign notation. It wasn't until the 760s or 770s, when Baghdad caliphs started bringing Hindu works to their capital, that the Arabs' interest in the new number system was aroused.

That system became firmly identified with the Arabs in the

following century, when the Baghdad scholar Mohammed ibn-Musa al-Khowarizmi (whose famous treatise *Al-jebr wa'l-muqabalah* gives us our word "algebra") wrote an account of the Hindu system that was later translated into Latin as *De Numero Indorum* (On the Numbers of the Hindus). In this book al-Khowarizmi "gave so full an account of the Hindu numerals that he probably is responsible for the widespread but false impression that our system of numeration is Arabic in origin." He made no claim that he had invented the system, but later readers attributed it to him anyway. Carl B. Boyer, *A History of Mathematics* (Wiley, 1968).

WHO DISCOVERED NITROGLYCERIN?

The Swedish explosives king Alfred Nobel (1833–1896) was not the discoverer of nitroglycerin, as is often supposed. He worked extensively with the highly unstable substance, and in spite of numerous accidents (one of which killed his brother Emil) made several discoveries that facilitated its use. The most famous of these was that nitroglycerin could be used much more safely if first imbedded in an inert, protective matrix; in 1867 he patented such a combination, calling the new explosive "dynamite." His other contributions to mayhem included the percussive detonator, blasting gelatin, and a smokeless powder he called ballistite.

It is the supreme curiosity of Nobel's life that while he made a fortune from explosives, he constantly defended their production by saying that they would dissuade nations from war. (Apparently, the "More is less" philosophy of military preparedness is not peculiar to the nuclear age.) He may have had a cast-iron psyche, or he may have salved his conscience in his famous will, which stipulated large yearly grants for achievements in physics, chemistry, physiology or medicine, literature, and "fraternity among nations." The grant in this last category was to honor one whose efforts contributed to the reduction of standing armies and the promotion of peace conferences.

Who did discover nitroglycerin? An Italian named Ascanio Sobrero, who, although he was largely forgotten by his contemporaries, was another beneficiary of Nobel's largess. He engaged Sobrero as an adviser to his Swiss-Italian subsidiary, "a sinecure of a post," says Tony Gray, "in which the Italian scientist enjoyed a good salary until his death." Just before Nobel's own death, incidentally, he was forced to take nitroglycerin internally, to forestall the ravages of angina. In a letter to a friend he called this fact, wryly, "an irony of fate."   Tony Gray, *Champions of Peace* (Paddington, 1976).

WHO INVENTED THE STEAMBOAT?

Robert Fulton was one of the earliest American entrepreneurs to realize the importance of marketing. It was because of his skill at salesmanship, not his primacy as an inventor, that he became known, quite wrongly, as the creator of the steamboat. As John Morgan notes, when Fulton developed his model in 1807, "everything about the steamboat had already been invented—the boat, steam engine, paddle wheel, connecting devices." Fulton brought these elements together into a working boat, and "did something else essential for a technologist: he sold the public on his invention's utility and safety, an achievement in which all his steamboat predecessors had failed."

Those predecessors were numerous. Throughout the eighteenth century the idea of perfecting a steamboat had filled the reveries of inventors on both sides of the Atlantic, and there were as a result several half successful steamboats developed years before "Fulton's folly" triumphed. Among the British inventors who had made working steamboats before Fulton, Mr. Morgan mentions Robert Fourness and James Ashworth (1788), John Smith (1793), and William Symington (1788), whom the British still consider the boat's inventor. In America John Fitch and James Rumsey were the principal litigants in patent-infringement suits which attempted in the 1790s to determine which of them had invented the original steamboat: Both men ran regular, if brief, steamboat excursion lines on, respectively, the Delaware and Potomac rivers.

First honors, however, might well go to the French. In 1783 the Marquis Claude de Jouffroy d'Abbons ran a boat on the Saône which Morgan calls "the first documented real success in steamboat propulsion." And three quarters of a century earlier, in 1707, the engineer Denis Papin ran one on the river Fulda. Some historians deny that Papin's model was steam driven, but he did design an effective piston engine, and Morgan admits that his boat "may have been the first steamboat," even if its efficiency was poor.

Fulton's boat, which came a century after Papin's, was not called *The Clermont,* although that is what is commonly taught in school. It was named after the body of water on which it first ran, that portion of the Hudson known in 1807 as the North River. *The North River Steamboat* (also known simply as *The North River)* was dubbed *Clermont* by the popular press after the name of Fulton's partner's estate, where it sometimes landed. Fulton never called it that himself, but as early as 1810 it had become the standard nickname. The *Hudson Bee* in that year said, "The North River Steamboat is believed to be the first one built on the river and has lately been known by the name Clermont, that is in books"—which have perpetuated the misnomer. John S. Morgan, *Robert Fulton* (Mason/Charter, 1977).

WHO INVENTED PHOTOGRAPHY?

So significant was Louis Daguerre's contribution to the development of photography that the early days of the art are generally called the "daguerreotype era." When he announced his process in August 1839, he established France as the "home" of the infant technology, and himself as its founding father. It should not be assumed, however, that Daguerre's "invention" was solely his own, or that his claim to be its originator went unchallenged.

Photographic experimentation began in earnest a generation before Daguerre, when Thomas Wedgwood, aware of silver nitrate's sensitivity to light, produced images of leaves and other objects by laying them on silvered white leather and then exposing them to light. However, these early "heliographs" were impermanent, and the problem of "fixing" the image so that it would not fade became the principal interest of all the other pre-Daguerrean experimenters.

One of the most successful of these was Daguerre's countryman Nicephore Niépce, who in the 1820s produced what are believed to be the first permanent photographic images. One of these—a city view taken from a window of his home in Chalon-sur-Saône—is generally considered the world's earliest extant photograph; it was taken in 1826, thirteen years before Daguerre's announcement. Niépce was not forgotten for his pains; from 1829 until his death in 1833, he was the more famous inventor's partner.

Hippolyte Bayard was not so fortunate. In the late 1830s he had developed a negative-and-positive printing method similar to the one which was patented in England in 1841 by William Henry Fox Talbot. Daguerre's process produced only a single positive image, which meant replication was impossible, and should have given Bayard an edge. Not so. Just before Daguerre's announcement, the French government bought Bayard out, to avoid confusing the public and diverting attention from Daguerre.

Feeling quite rightly that he had been abused, Bayard published a famous self-portrait in which he is pictured as a drowned man; the semi-jocular caption explained that the subject had taken his own life in despair at the government's slight. As in so many other cases, it was not the earliest bird that had gotten the worm, but the one with the best connections.   Helmut and Alison Gernsheim, *The History of Photography from the Camera Obscura to the Beginning of the Modern Era* (McGraw-Hill, 1969); Oliver Mathews, *Early Photographs and Early Photographers* (Reedminster Publications, 1973).

DEFINITIONS:

FAMOUS LOST WORDS

THE BRIDE WALKS UP WHAT PART OF THE CHURCH?

Countless young American females still dream of that Day of Days when they will talk up the aisle to Prince Charming. This is good news for the wedding industry. Author Marcia Seligson, with felicitous sarcasm, has called this industry "the Great American Bliss Machine" (in a book of the same name) but strictly speaking, no bride ever walks up an aisle at all. In traditional architectural usage, it's the *nave* that is the central section of a church, and the side sections, separated by pillars from the center, that are properly called aisles. So unless she is married in a side chapel, the bride takes her last maiden voyage up the nave.

The extension of the word aisle to mean any interior passageway is, however, of fairly reputable vintage. As early as 1762 Horace Walpole spoke of the "middle isle" of a church, and by the 1830s this usage was evidently common enough to cause William Whewell, in his *Architectural Notes on German Churches,* to class it among notable "liberties taken with language." Today, of course, the extension has become the idiom—without noticeably affecting the marriage rate. *Oxford English Dictionary* (Oxford, 1961).

WHAT ARE "SALAD DAYS"?

"In my salad days" is often uttered as a brief invocation of the "good old days," those carefree, pleasure-filled hours when delight was ours for the asking, and romance a constant glow. What Shakespeare meant when he coined the phrase, though, was something quite different. It appears in *Antony and Cleopatra* (Act 1, scene 5), where the Serpent of the Nile is upbraiding her servant Charmian for comparing her current lover, Mark Antony, unfavorably to his predecessor, Julius Caesar. She loved Caesar, she says, in her "salad days, when I was green in judgment, cold in blood." When, in other words, she was too young to understand real passion.

Her metaphor here is a little better than her memory. When she bore Caesar's son, she was twenty-one, which was plenty of time for her blood to have gotten warm. What she means is that compared to her mature love for Antony, her tryst with Caesar was puppyish—as crisp and tasteless, perhaps, as an undressed salad. Not exactly the good old days.   Philip Ward, *A Dictionary of Common Fallacies* (Oleander Press, 1980).

WHEN DID "YANKEE" ARISE AS A TERM OF ABUSE?

Scarlett O'Hara notwithstanding, the term "Yankee" as a derisive epithet was not a Southern invention. Southerners were using it to describe rascally New Englanders at the end of the eighteenth century, true, but at the time it was also being applied to *all* American colonists by the British—and Americans are still Yanks "over there."

But the term is even older than that. Its first recorded appearance was in the seventeenth century, when it was a term of contempt for Dutch pirates (one of whom was named Yankey) and also for any Dutch person. Sometime around the end of the century, it was extended to include Dutch-born American colonists, and then North American colonists in general.

Thomas Anburey, a British colonial officer, claimed in 1789 that the word had come from *eankke,* a Cherokee Indian term for coward; others saw it as an Indian corruption of "English." A more plausible explanation than these is that it was a compressed version of *Jan Kees,* a German and Flemish nickname for a Dutchman.   *Oxford English Dictionary* (Oxford, 1961); Tristram Coffin, "Yankee," in *Encyclopedia Americana* (1979).

WHAT IS A JUGGERNAUT?

Popular usage has "juggernaut" as a massive, blind instrument of destruction, something that once impelled into motion, cannot be stopped. Modern prototypes include Hitler's Panzer divisions and the current Soviet and American war machines. This reading, while not entirely farfetched, does appear somewhat eccentric when you consider the fact that the original Juggernaut (also spelled Jagannath) was (and is) a Hindu deity, one of the incarnations of Vishnu, whose worship in southern India inspires far more reverence than fear.

The ritual that gave rise to the common Western conception of Juggernaut as a destructive force takes place at Puri, in Orissa. There devotees of the god mount a statue of him on a huge wheeled cart, which is then drawn slowly by worshippers to the god's nearby country house, while the religious prostrate themselves along the route. Years ago, when Europeans first witnessed this festival, an occasional careless worshipper was crushed by the cart, and the rumor got started that the god delighted in these mishaps. Some travelers even claimed that frenzied Indians frequently threw themselves under the wheels on purpose, in hopes of escaping the cycle of death and rebirth. Thus, the modern view was born.

That this view is biased now seems clear. No doubt a few devotees were unintentionally "sacrificed," but there is little chance that the festival was ever as bloody as the first travelers implied. In the words of the *New Century Cyclopedia of Names,* "The possibility of deliberate suicide is extremely unlikely, since all devotees know that such shedding of blood could defile the sacred event."

As for the "unstoppable" motion of the cart, that, too, seems to be fiction. The thing is forty-five feet high, and is supported by sixteen wheels seven feet across. Down a hill such a vehicle might well be unstoppable, but as it is the procession is a snail's pace affair. The route to the god's country house is a little less than a mile, but the journey takes several days. *Oxford English Dictionary* (Oxford, 1961); *New Century Cyclopedia of Names* (Appleton-Century-Crofts, 1954).

WHERE DO COOLIES, MANDARINS, AND PAGODAS COME FROM?

None of these three very Chinese terms originated in China. All three, in fact, came from South Asia, and were applied retrospectively to China by Europeans who had confounded their origins. "Coolie" is derived from the Tamil *kuri* or the western Indian *Koli*, the former meaning a menial worker, the latter the name of a tribe; Portuguese travelers in the sixteenth century brought the term into use in the West, and it was extended in the following century to cover workers in China as well. "Mandarin" is also a Portuguese corruption, having evolved around the same time as "coolie" from the Malay *mantri* and the Sanskrit *mantrin*, for "counselor." It was originally applied to all Asiatic officials, and only later limited to the Chinese. "Pagoda" is from the Portuguese and Italian *pagode*, which was a not very precise approximation of an Indian term for a temple: Tamil gives *pagavadi* for this, and Sanskrit *bhagavati*, meaning a place belonging to a deity. *Oxford English Dictionary* (Oxford, 1961); Eric Partridge, *Origins: A Short Etymological Dictionary of Modern English* (Routledge & Kegan Paul, 1959).

NO ONE EVER SLID DOWN A BANISTER.

At least no one ever did it and escaped serious injury. Properly speaking, the structure which prevents you from falling off a staircase is called a balustrade. It is composed of a handrail surmounting and connecting a series of upright posts, and it is these posts that are the structure's "banisters." The word "banister" is a corruption of the original "baluster," which comes from the Italian *balaustra*, meaning the blossom of the wild pomegranate; it was applied to the supports of Renaissance railings because their pear-shaped, bulging design suggested the swelling of that flower's calyx tube. When you slide down a balustrade, therefore, it's the railing that gives you the ride. Attempting to use the banisters for that purpose would only get you impaled. *Oxford English Dictionary* (Oxford, 1961).

WHAT DO YOU DO IN A BOUDOIR?

The request "Come into my boudoir" has such a lubricious tinge that it's often assumed a boudoir is a bedroom—one that is seldom used for sleeping. As Leo Rosten points out, though, the word originally had few such amorous connotations; a boudoir, among the old French gentry, was simply a small room to which petulant damsels would repair to get over a snit. *Bouder* is the French verb "to sulk" or "to pout," so a boudoir was, literally, "a place to sulk in." One could, of course, invite friends in for commiseration, and one thing might lead to another, and very soon you might be petting rather than pouting, and the precisions of the word would be lost. By such unintended modifications, no doubt, the word acquired its present reputation. *Oxford English Dictionary* (Oxford, 1961); Leo Rosten, *The Power of Positive Nonsense* (McGraw-Hill, 1977).

WHAT DOES "SOS" STAND FOR?

Because "SOS" has so long been a distress call for vessels in trouble, it's often thought that it stands for "Save Our Ship" or "Save Our Souls" or "Stop Other Signals." These explanations are speculative and inaccurate. The call letters SOS were adopted by international agreement in 1908 because, in Morse code, they were easy both to transmit and to understand. The letter *S* is sent as three short impulses, or "dits," and the letter *O* by three long impulses, or "dahs." This makes SOS a readily identifiable signal in any language: "dit-dit-dit, dah-dah-dah, dit-dit-dit."

This electrical message—which translated only by coincidence as the false acronym SOS—replaced the far more cumbersome signal CQD, which had been introduced by the Marconi Company around the turn of the century. CQ was an "Alert" signal and D stood for "Distress." Which was all right, except that these three letters, translated into Morse code, came out as "dah-dit-dah-dit, dah-dah-dit-dah, dah-dit-dit." Try sending that out a hundred times in succession and you'll see why the signal was changed. William and Mary Morris, *Dictionary of Word and Phrase Origins* (Harper & Row, 1962).

WHAT IS ONANISM?

The "sin of Onan," in the eighteenth and nineteenth centuries, was considered approximately equivalent to stealing money from poorboxes as a way of ensuring perdition. Onanism, it was thought, would not only cause God's eyes to glaze over in horror, but it would also almost certainly lead to insanity.

This was strange on a couple of counts. First, there was no scientific evidence (nor is there any today) that masturbation, euphemistically called onanism, was at all detrimental to health, either physical or mental. Second, the actual sin of Onan, according to the story in Gen. 38, was not masturbation at all, but coitus interruptus. Onan, the younger son of Judah, married his deceased brother's wife in accordance with the law of levirate (widow-brother marriage), but instead of trying to make her pregnant as that law demanded, he "spilled his seed on the ground" because he knew that any children conceived of the union would be taken not as his but as his brother's.

Apparently, it was a confusion about the "spilling" passage that led commentators to damn masturbation. But that was not Onan's crime. His mistake was the refusal to obey a law which would have ensured the survival of his brother's line at the expense of his own. "For this refusal, rather than for the supposed sexual perversion bearing his name, Yahweh slew him." *The Interpreter's Dictionary of the Bible* (Abingdon, 1962).

WHEN WERE POLICEMEN FIRST CALLED "PIGS"?

In the 1960s, when first the civil rights struggle and then the war in Vietnam made the United States a divided nation, embittered protesters came up with a pointed and provocative taunt to denounce the minions of those in command: "Pig" became the most commonly hurled epithet at the boys in blue who, under the pressure of fear and isolation, sometimes became brutally insensitive to the wishes of the self-proclaimed "people."

How the protesters came up with the term is not clear, though it was probably meant to evoke the picture of a grunting, mindless herd, swinish in its attitudes and behavior. Perhaps the cops' antagonists thought it was original with them. It was not. Among thieves in both England and the United States, "pig" had been a term of abuse for policemen as long ago as the early nineteenth century, and by the latter half of that century it had even acquired a quite specific connotation: It referred to a policeman's spy, an informer, or "stool pigeon." The London underworld called their nemeses "noses" as well, apparently in reference to both the animal and the human "pig's" habit of "nosing around" in search of usable finds.   Eric Partridge, *A Dictionary of Slang and Unconventional English* (Macmillan, 1970); Harold Wentworth and Stuart Flexner, eds., *Dictionary of American Slang* (Crowell, 1975).

A "BELLWETHER" HAS NOTHING TO DO WITH THE WEATHER.

In fact, "bellweather" is not even the correct spelling. A bellwether is a wether with a bell, and a wether is a castrated sheep. The bellwether wears a bell so that the shepherd can locate the flock by its sound: Sheep being the easily led creatures they are, he can be certain that wherever the wether has wandered, the other woolies have followed. Many people, reading wether as "weather," think the word is a synonym for harbinger, and refers to any advance signal of approaching "weather" or change. Actually, a bellwether causes rather than signals change; the best synonym would be "leader."   *Oxford English Dictionary* (Oxford, 1961); Tom Burnam, *The Dictionary of Misinformation* (Crowell, 1975).

WHO WALKS ON A WIDOW'S WALK?

Since you can see miles out to sea from them, and since they are built when shipwrecks were far commoner than they are today, the rooftop railed platforms that adorn many New England seaside houses are often called "widow's walks." The implication is that wives of sailors would spend hours up there in vain, searching for ships that never came. This touching story is of doubtful authenticity. The designation of these structures as observatories arose only in the twentieth century, and even then they were only occasionally called widow's walks. A more common designation was "captain's walk," indicating that they may have provided landbound seafarers with a fantasy "bridge," or a place from which to moon over the sea.

Tom Burnam notes, moreover, that architecturally, their function may have had nothing to do with observation. Chimney fires being common in the "olden days," the "walks" may have been simply convenient platforms from which to fight such blazes. Tom Burnam, *The Dictionary of Misinformation* (Crowell, 1975); Mitford Mathews, ed., *A Dictionary of Americanisms on Historical Principles* (University of Chicago Press, 1951).

WHAT DOES "THUMBS DOWN" MEAN?

"Thumbs down" is generally used as an expression of denial or rejection, and popular etymology gives it an origin in the old Roman arena: When the mob wished a bested gladiator to be spared, they turned their thumbs up, and when they wished him killed, they turned them down.

Ashley Montagu and Edward Darling point out that this interpretation depends on a mistranslation of the Latin phrase *Pollice Verso*, which was the title of a popular depiction of the presumed death gesture by the French painter Léon Gérôme. Gérôme, a specialist in classical scenes, evidently took *verso* to mean "turned down," and ever since 1873, when his picture was first shown, "thumbs down" has been seen as a condemnation. *Verso*, however, is ambiguous. It means simply "turned," and *pollice verso* could just as easily be translated as "with the thumb turned up" or "turned in" as "turned down."

Moreover, the weight of scholarship before Gérôme supports the view that "thumbs down," among the Romans, meant the hapless gladiator was to be spared, not slain: The gesture meant "Throw your sword down." A 1601 translation of Pliny equates the gesture with "assent" or "favor," and John Dryden's 1693 version of Juvenal's *Satires* gives the thumb being bent *back*, not down, as the death signal.

The general reversal of this view after Gérôme attests both to the popularity of his work and to the difficulties with which modern readers must contend when they are confronted by makers of images. Gérôme's interpretation, wrongheaded though it was, has by now taken the field; as Montagu and Darling observe, "There is nothing that can dam the flow of meaning from a certain direction when enough people begin to use a word for a certain purpose." So it looks like thumbs up on "thumbs down." Ashley Montagu and Edward Darling, *The Prevalence of Nonsense* (Harper & Row, 1967).

A MUGWUMP IS NOT A FENCE-SITTER.

"Mugwump" has a charming, though false, folk etymology. Ask a high school student what the word means, and he or she will tell you a mugwump is an indecisive or vacillating voter, sitting with his "mug" on one side of the political fence and his "wump" on the other. It's an amusing picture, but the implied suggestion that the word is a combination of two Yankee vulgarisms is, sad to say, totally wrong.

"Mugwump" is an Algonquin word for "chief," and it was used in print in that sense as long ago as 1663 by John Eliot in his Algonquin translation of the Bible. In 1884 the term was picked up by the American political press and given a meaning closer to, but not identical to, its current popular usage. In that year a number of Republican voters defected from their party to support the Democratic presidential candidate Grover Cleveland; these ad hoc independents were quickly labeled "mugwumps" by papers supporting James G. Blaine. Why this inappropriate term was chosen to chide the traitors is a mystery. In any case it became quickly popular as a derisive epithet for any independent voter, and in the twentieth century acquired the stamp of indecisiveness as well. That's a long way from the 1884 meaning, and even longer from the Algonquin. Mitford Mathews, ed., *A Dictionary of Americanisms on Historical Principles* (University of Chicago Press, 1951); William and Mary Morris, *Dictionary of Word and Phrase Origins* (Harper & Row, 1962).

WHAT IS A PAPAL BULL?

Since a papal bull is an official document setting forth a pontiff's views on a given matter, "bull" is often taken to be an abbreviation for "bulletin." Actually, it's an Anglicization of the Latin *bulla,* the leaden seal which from the sixth to the late nineteenth centuries was used to secure papal documents. Tie strings were embedded in the *bulla,* and this was then impressed on the generally parchment document with a stamping device. After the thirteenth century, the documents (for example, encyclicals) were themselves called bulls.

That is the official explanation. Two unofficial ones which I like much better surfaced a number of years ago in one of my father's Western Civilization classes. On an examination he had asked his students to define papal bull briefly. One student said it was a bull that was kept in the Vatican to trample on Protestants. Another claimed it was not a bull at all, but a cow, kept hidden somewhere in Rome to provide milk for the Pope's bastard children. Leaden seals, indeed. *New Catholic Encyclopedia* (McGraw-Hill, 1967).

SAYINGS:

TO CON A PHRASE

WHO SAID, "ALAS, POOR YORICK, I KNEW HIM WELL"?

The gravedigger scene in *Hamlet* is a classic example of "comic relief"—an episode of interpolated levity meant to distract the audience momentarily from the tragic motion of the play. Characteristically, Shakespeare uses the device to intensify rather than trivialize the drama's deepest meanings: The dialogue which follows the workmen's witticisms, in which Hamlet muses to his friend Horatio about the disinterred skull of the king's jester Yorick, obiquely attacks the same philosophical conundrums that hamstring the prince throughout the more "serious" parts of the play.

The scene's most famous line, though, is almost always misquoted. What Hamlet says to his friend, upon learning the identity of the skull, is "Alas, poor Yorick; I knew him, Horatio." It doesn't scan quite as well as "knew him well," but it does provide one of the play's rare instances in which the gloomy Dane actually addresses someone other than himself. William Shakespeare, *Hamlet* (Act 5, scene 1).

P. T. BARNUM DID NOT SAY, "THERE'S A SUCKER BORN EVERY MINUTE."

It's something that Phineas T. Barnum, dean of American hucksters, *should* have said, and it's hardly surprising that popular tradition (and *Bartlett's Quotations*) attributes it to him. It seems only right that the wryly cynical remark should have started with the man who once sewed a fish tail onto a monkey and displayed it as a mermaid. But there is no evidence that the phrase originated with Barnum—or that he ever actually said it.

The use of the word "sucker" to mean someone easily duped dates back at least to 1831, and the term was widely known by about 1850, the year in which Barnum raked in half a million dollars for promoting the "Swedish Nightingale" Jenny Lind. It is a nice coincidence that the popularity of the term increased at the same time as the showman's own notoriety. Certainly no entrepreneur, before or since, understood better than Barnum the ease with which humans can be gulled.

Many tales are told of his ingenuity. My favorite concerns the method by which he moved crowds quickly through his popular New York museum. Instead of hiring guards to hurry the gawkers along, he put up conspicuous signs announcing "This Way to the Egress." Expecting one of Barnum's fabulous beasts, viewers flocked eagerly to the door through which the Egress could be seen—and found themselves outside the museum. The Egress turned out to be the Exit.   Mitford Mathews, ed., *A Dictionary of Americanisms on Historical Principles* (University of Chicago Press, 1951); George Stimpson, *A Book About a Thousand Things* (Harper, 1946).

WHO SAID, "ELEMENTARY, MY DEAR WATSON"?

Those of us who have had the pleasure of hearing Basil Rathbone intone these famous words may make the assumption that their originator was the same person who originated the character Sherlock Holmes, the British dean of sleuthers, Sir Arthur Conan Doyle. This is not so. According to Philip Ward and other Baker Street aficionados, the literary Holmes never speaks this famous sentence in any of Doyle's many stories.

The closest he gets, as far as I can determine, is in the "The Crooked Man," published in *The Memoirs of Sherlock Holmes* (1894). Here Dr. Watson marvels that Holmes knows he has had a tiring day simply because his boots are clean—thus indicating he has had to use a hansom cab rather than walk, on his busy rounds. "Excellent!" says the good doctor. "Elementary," replies Holmes. The apostrophe "my dear Watson" was apparently Hollywood's addition.   Sir Arthur Conan Doyle, *The Complete Sherlock Holmes* (Doubleday, 1960); Philip Ward, *A Dictionary of Popular Fallacies* (Oleander Press, 1980).

WHO SAID, "BECAUSE IT IS THERE"?

In all the hooplah surrounding the Edmund Hillary–Tenzing Norkay conquest of Everest in 1953, the grand line about people climbing such a mountain "because it is there" was much bandied about, and somehow the idea got started that it was Hillary who had said it. Actually, it had been said over thirty years before, by another distinguished climber, George H. Leigh Mallory.

Mallory was one of the most adventurous and skilled mountaineers of his day. When Tibet opened the Himalayas to foreign exploration in 1921, Mallory led the reconnaissance party that first tackled the giant, and succeeded in reaching the North Col at nearly twenty-three thousand feet. Two subsequent expeditions, in 1922 and 1924, got over twenty-seven thousand feet, but on the 1924 ascent Mallory and his co-leader Andrew Irving were lost. Noel Odell, an expedition member, later said that he had seen them from about twenty-six thousand feet, "going strong for the top" just before they disappeared.

As for the famous line, Mallory said it sometime between the second and third attempt, in response to a questioner at one of his American lectures. What he meant by it has been endlessly debated, and perhaps its best gloss is something he himself wrote, in trying to come to terms with his obsession. "I suppose we go to Mount Everest, granted the opportunity, because—in a word—we can't help it. Or, to state the matter rather differently, because we are mountaineers. . . . To refuse the adventure is to run the risk of drying up like a pea in its shell."   David Robertson, *George Mallory* (Faber & Faber, 1969).

HORACE GREELEY DID NOT SAY, "GO WEST, YOUNG MAN, GO WEST."

The newspaper editor Horace Greeley is supposed to have said, in response to a youth who wanted to know how to make his fortune, "Go West, young man, go West," or (in some versions of the tale) "Go West, young man, and grow with the country." Greeley was an ardent champion of westward expansion, so it's not an uncharacteristic remark, but the fact is that neither

Greeley nor anyone closely associated with him ever claimed he had originated the slogan. That honor, as Greeley tried in vain to point out, belonged to one John Lane Soule, who had written it in the Terre Haute *Express* in 1851. Reprinted in Greeley's New York *Tribune,* it became known as the editor's own gem.

There was a queer justice in this, for as William Hale notes, Greeley had either written or spoken the sentence "in substance" to hundreds of people who had asked his advice. Many of them, taking that advice, were responsible for settling the West, and this enterprise was hastened, if not by the exact words of the slogan, certainly by Greeley's endorsements of its spirit. This could not have comforted Soule very much, but history has given him his due: Both Bartlett's and Bergen Evans's dictionaries of quotations now attribute the saying to him.   William Harlan Hale, *Horace Greeley: Voice of the People* (Harper, 1950); Glyndon G. Van Deusen, *Horace Greeley: Nineteenth-Century Crusader* (University of Pennsylvania Press, 1953).

WHAT DOES "TELL IT TO THE MARINES" MEAN?

This expression is sometimes construed as being a taunt or a challenge, since the marines have a reputation as a feisty and hardheaded lot. "If you think you're so smart," the interpretation goes, "try to get away with that with a marine, and you'll get what for." This implies that the marines are tough, skeptical, and unwilling to put up with nonsense.

This is pretty funny when you consider the original meaning of the phrase. In the early 1820s, marines were thought by sailors to be models of gullibility, not good sense. They might not *want* to put up with nonsense, but their natural foolishness (so said the sailors) would lead them to do so anyway. So the expression really meant, "What you're telling me is so patently ridiculous that only a marine would believe it." Interservice rivalry evidently got started early. One popular meaning of "marine," dating from about 1840, was "an ignorant or clumsy seaman"; another, from 1800, was "an empty bottle." It was a long way to the proud, the few.   Eric Partridge, *A Dictionary of Slang and Unconventional English* (Macmillan, 1956).

WHO COINED THE PHRASE "SURVIVAL OF THE FITTEST"?

Charles Darwin's most famous phrase was actually not his invention, but that of the popular philosopher Herbert Spencer, who was at least as influential as Darwin himself in making the theory of evolution familiar to a wide audience. His genius was popularization, and in its service he became the average person's Socrates: William James called him "the philosopher whom those who have no other philosopher can appreciate."

In spite of his dilettante's approach to the great ideas, Spencer's connection with evolution extended far beyond his fortuitous coining of the "Darwinian" phrase. According to Gertrude Himmelfarb, "He was a confirmed evolutionist at a time when his scientific knowledge consisted of little more than that of a schoolboy who collected stones and experimented with gases," and yet despite of (or because of) this amateurism, he was a significant force in making the idea of "progressive differentiation" widely known. He did not, however, have the scientific basis to found a specialist's as well as generalist's reputation, and Darwin himself, who admired him as a philosopher, felt that as a biologist he should have "observed more and thought less." The failing was not lost on him. In Himmelfarb's phrasing, it was "his lifelong regret that he had not thought to make the simple connection of ideas which would have produced the theory of natural selection." Gertrude Himmelfarb, *Darwin and the Darwinian Revolution* (Norton, 1968).

WHO SAID, "AFTER US, THE DELUGE"?

Or, as it is often misrepresented, "After me, the deluge." Singular or plural, it is usually attributed to France's King Louis XV, the not-so-enlightened despot who presided over the most sumptuous, and socially most atavistic, period of the *ancien régime*. Credited to him, *"Après moi, le déluge"* is not only an appropriate description of aristocratic extravagance, but a fitting personal motto for one of Europe's most out-of-touch rulers.

The consensus, though, gives the line not to the king but to his much-vilified mistress, Madame Pompadour. So said her near contemporary J. B. D. Depres, who introduced the *Memoirs* of the lady's lady-in-waiting; later writers have been divided between her and the king. But as Burton Stevenson notes, the quotation "was original with neither, for it is an old French proverb cited in many collections, and usually applied to spendthrifts." An appropriate designation for either the king or his mistress. Burton Stevenson, ed., *The Home Book of Quotations* (Dodd, Mead, 1967).

WHO SAID, "I DISAGREE WITH WHAT YOU SAY BUT WILL DEFEND TO THE DEATH YOUR RIGHT TO SAY IT"?

The sentiment is Voltaire, all right, and he may have said something like this many times in his long career. But the exact phrasing was not his. As Montagu and Darling point out, the splendidly pithy statement first appeared in its currently known form only in the twentieth century, as a paraphrase of something the French philosopher did say, in his *Essay on Tolerance*. The comment in the *Essay* was, "Think for yourselves and let others enjoy the privilege to do so too." Not bad, but hardly the gem it became in the hands of E. Beatrice Hall, in whose *Friends of Voltaire* (1907) the sentiment achieved its present form. In 1935 she admitted that she had not meant to attribute the phrasing to Voltaire, but only to suggest his attitude; confused herself by the confusion, she said she would be "much surprised" if the exact words were ever found in any of Voltaire's works.

Leo Rosten thinks he has found them, though not exactly in a "work." In a letter to the Abbe A. M. deRiche written in February of 1770, he finds the confession, "I detest what you write, but I would give my life to make it possible for you to continue to write." Again, not bad, but as Rosten admits, the Hall wording is far better. Ashley Montagu and Edward Darling, *The Prevalence of Nonsense* (Harper & Row, 1967); Leo Rosten, *The Power of Positive Nonsense* (McGraw-Hill, 1977).

WHAT WERE NATHAN HALE'S LAST WORDS?

Since my first grammar school was named after Nathan Hale, I have always had a soft spot in my heart for the boy martyr of the

Revolution; besides, even on objective judgment, "I only regret that I have but one life to give for my country" is one of the sublime curtain lines of history. I rank it next to Goethe's "More light" for appropriateness, and only a little behind Gertrude Stein's "What is the question?" for wit.

Because of this, I was much aggrieved to discover, in Tom Burnam's first miscellany, that Hale never said no such thing. Quoting a "recently discovered" diary of a British eyewitness to Hale's execution, Burnam gives the kid's last words as, "It is the duty of every good officer to obey any orders given him by his commander-in-chief." There's no indication which commander-in-chief he was referring to. If his own, then the line is a captive's pallid excuse; if his captors', it's a somewhat more noble absolution for his executioners—the kind of forgiveness medieval criminals used to speak to the headsman before he broke their necks.

In either case, it's hardly as quotable as the traditional line, and I don't think we Nathan Hale graduates need worry about popular history being rewritten: The traditional line, after all, echoes Joseph Addison's observation in *Cato* that it is a pity "that we can die but once to serve our country." On top of that, it has the ring of a hero's farewell. All the "commander-in-chief" quote has on its side is the facts. You can ask Madison Avenue which will win.   Tom Burnam, *The Dictionary of Misinformation* (Crowell, 1975).

W. C. FIELDS NEVER SAID, "ANYBODY WHO HATES DOGS AND BABIES CAN'T BE ALL BAD."

Although generations of his fans have attributed this piece of inspired biliousness to Hollywood's favorite misanthrope, W. C. Fields, there is no evidence that he originated it—or that he ever said it. He must have liked it enough to tacitly con people into believing that he had said it, but the truth of the matter is that this most famous of the great man's cantankerous apothegms was first said *about* him by a young and very nervous Leo Rosten, at a 1939 Hollywood "roast." Rosten says the press went into transports over his remark—and promptly credited it to Fields.   Leo Rosten, *The Power of Positive Nonsense* (McGraw-Hill, 1977).

WHO COINED THE PHRASE "LOST GENERATION"?

For reasons that escape me, many of the people to whom I put this question respond "Jack Kerouac" or "Allen Ginsberg"—suggesting some etymological affinity, perhaps, between "beat" and "off the beaten track." The more literary-minded recognize the flyleaf quote from *The Sun Also Rises* and remember that Hemingway attributes the phrase "in conversation" to Gertrude Stein. Alas, this answer, too, is wrong. Tom Burnam, citing Stein, notes that it was not she but a hotelier named Pernollet who first used the phrase—"in conversation," it is true, with her.

Monsieur Pernollet was referrring to a young mechanic who was fixing Stein's car; he represented to him all the *génération perdue* who, by going to war in 1914, had fatefully sidestepped the "civilizing process." Stein, adapting the epithet, used it in reference to the same generation, but because (according to Hemingway) it was "drinking itself to death." Hemingway's late-in-life explanation of the phrase's origin, in *A Moveable Feast*, mentions the mechanic but not Pernollet, and as a result, Stein has been stuck with it ever since. This probably would not have bothered her. Certainly, it would not have bothered Hemingway, to whom a pose was a pose was a pose. Tom Burnam, *The Dictionary of Misinformation* (Crowell, 1975).

WHO SAID, "YOU CAN FOOL ALL OF THE PEOPLE SOME OF THE TIME AND SOME OF THE PEOPLE ALL OF THE TIME, BUT YOU CAN'T FOOL ALL OF THE PEOPLE ALL OF THE TIME"?

Abraham Lincoln is supposed to have uttered this ringing defense of democracy in a speech at Clinton, Illinois, on September 8, 1858, during the famous Lincoln-Douglas debates. It's a wonderfully observant, quite characteristic sentiment, but there is no solid evidence that Abe said it then, or at any other time. In 1905 the Chicago *Tribune* and the Brooklyn *Eagle* gave a cachet of authenticity to the remark by citing several eyewitnesses to the speech, but the witnesses, all well into their seventies by that time, confirmed only that Lincoln "had said something generally of this nature." The Bloomington *Pantagraph,* which reported on the speech when it was delivered, did not mention the remark, and it is not found in any of the president's printed addresses. Evidence for its genuineness, according to Paul F. Boller, remains at best "quite shaky." Paul F. Boller, Jr., *Quotemanship* (Southern Methodist University Press, 1967).

WHO FIRST SAID, "ASK NOT WHAT YOUR COUNTRY CAN DO FOR YOU; ASK WHAT YOU CAN DO FOR YOUR COUNTRY"?

This is probably John Kennedy's most celebrated line; his use of it in his inaugural address set the tone of industrious optimism that was to characterize his presidency, and it is often thought of, even now, as a kind of Kennedy family motto—the American politicians' version of *noblesse oblige*. But it was not a JFK original. The sentiment appears, worded slightly differently, in speeches by Warren G. Harding and Oliver Wendell Holmes. It also appeared in Arabic around the time Kennedy was born: In a hortatory address to his country entitled, oddly enough, "The New Frontier," Kahlil Gibran asked, "Are you a politician asking what your country can do for you, or a zealous one asking what you can do for your country?" And, according to Leo Rosten, it also appeared in Latin, when Cicero used it in his first consular address, in 63 B.C. I have not been able to track this down, though the line certainly sounds Roman enough. Tom Burnam, *The Dictionary of Misinformation* (Crowell, 1975); Kahlil Gibran, *Mirrors of the Soul* (Philosophical Library, 1965); Leo Rosten, *The Power of Positive Nonsense* (McGraw-Hill, 1977).

WHO SAID, "ALL WE HAVE TO FEAR IS FEAR ITSELF"?

When Franklin Delano Roosevelt took over the reins of a tottering government in the spring of 1933, he knew his first job was to inspire confidence in a people that had been wracked by over three years of the Depression. He set about this with his characteristic gusto: His first inaugural address remains one of the most truly stirring calls to national unity that has been delivered in modern times.

But the address's most memorable line, it is not often realized, was a venerable hand-me-down. This is not to diminish its significance, but only to set the record straight. Four score and two years before the address, Henry David Thoreau had written in his *Journal,* "Nothing is so much to be feared as fear." Twenty years before that, the Duke of Wellington told the Earl of Stanhope, "The only thing I am afraid of is fear." In the seventeenth century Francis Bacon wrote, "Nothing is terrible except fear itself," and in the sixteenth, Michel de Montaigne said, "The thing I fear most is fear." As Roosevelt knew full well, borrowed wit doth often goodly wear.

As for the origin of the thought, that is earlier even than Montaigne. Where he got it—and where subsequent worthies did, too—was probably that grand chestnut stew, the Bible. Prov. 3:25 reads, "Be not afraid of sudden fear." *Bartlett's Familiar Quotations* (Little, Brown, 1980).

WHO SAID, "OLD SOLDIERS NEVER DIE; THEY JUST FADE AWAY"?

By all accounts one of the most headstrong and egotistical commanders in American military history, Douglas MacArthur is now remembered for having uttered two charmingly fulsome phrases. One of these—"I shall return"—he evidently originated in March 1942, when he left the Philippines for Australia. The other, however, was not his own; nor did he ever say it was. The remark about the fate of "old soldiers" like himself was part of his valedictory address to Congress, delivered on April 19, 1951, a week after President Truman had removed him from his Korean command. The memorable line, as he informed the legislators, was the refrain of "one of the most popular barrack ballads of that day"—"that day" being the turn of the century, when MacArthur was at West Point.

As Tom Burnam notes, both Bergen Evans and John Bartlett's collections of quotations identify the "old soldiers" refrain as being of World War I vintage. It is not unlikely that the ballad was still being sung then, but MacArthur's address makes it clear that the song was already over a decade old when the Great War began. Tom Burnam, *More Misinformation* (Lippincott & Crowell, 1980); Louis Morton, "Douglas MacArthur," in *Encyclopedia Americana* (1976).

WHO SAID, "LAFAYETTE, WE ARE HERE"?

The date was July 4, 1917, the location, the tomb of the Marquis de Lafayette in Paris. The United States had just entered the Great War, and General John (Black Jack) Pershing, head of the American Expeditionary Force, took a few moments out from making the world safe for democracy to say something that has stood for sixty-five years as an emblem of Franco-American unity. When he said, "Lafayette, we are here," a debt was officially paid, as the two once revolutionary nations congratulated each other on the perseverance of their commitments.

The only trouble with the story is that Pershing never spoke the words. The press attributed them to him, perhaps because it seemed only fitting that one international hero should eulogize another, but, in fact, they were spoken by Charles E. Stanton, the AEF's chief disbursing officer, whom Pershing had designated to speak for him at the tomb. In his book *My Experiences in the World War,* the general acknowledged that he wished he *had* spoken the line, but he gave the credit to Stanton.   Paul F. Boller, Jr., *Quotemanship* (Southern Methodist University Press, 1967).

WHOSE PHRASE WAS "OF THE PEOPLE, BY THE PEOPLE, AND FOR THE PEOPLE"?

Because of its appearance in the Gettysburg Address, the fine thumbnail definition of democracy as government of, by, and for the people has become, justly, a national catchphrase. Lincoln, though, did not originate it; he borrowed it from the Unitarian minister Theodore Parker, who throughout the 1850s was a tireless spokesman for the abolitionist cause. The phrase appeared in many of Parker's speeches and sermons, and on a copy of the printed text of one of them, the president is known to have underlined the sentence "Democracy is direct self-government, over all the people, by all the people, for all the people."

Both Lincoln and, in later speeches, Parker himself dropped the "all" because it retarded the flow of the phrase. That concession to euphony, memorable as it made the wording, at the same time muted its meaning: For the minister as well as the president, the "all," whether stated or implied, was a way of denouncing those "democrats" who felt the system could do without black participation.   Robert E. Collins, *Theodore Parker: American Transcendentalist* (Scarecrow, 1973).

MARIE ANTOINETTE DID NOT SAY, "LET THEM EAT CAKE."

Good democrats always like to believe the worst of royalty, and few royal figures have come in for as much plebeian censure as France's Marie Antoinette. She is the model of the useless sovereign, content to let the country go to the dogs as long as her tiara's on straight. It is difficult to imagine very many people shedding tears, even in retrospect, over her fate on the guillotine.

But the phrase by which she is best exemplified—the phrase which most succinctly suggests her aristocratic boorishness—was wrongly attributed to her. Told that the poor were complaining because they had no bread to eat, Marie is supposed to have said, "Why, then, let them eat cake." There is no evidence that she ever was so publicly callous. The myth apparently was started unwittingly by no less a figure than Jean-Jacques Rousseau, in whose *Confessions* the incident is sketched, but with an unnamed *"grande princesse"* as the speaker. Told of the lack of bread, she counsels her countrymen to eat *"brioche."* The *Confessions* were written around 1766, and the incident referred to happened around 1740—fifteen years before Marie was born.

Alphonse Kerr, writing in *Les Guepes* in 1843, noted that a 1760 book credits a certain "Duchess of Tuscany" with the remark. Apparently, the association with Marie was already known in 1843, for he feels obliged to discount it, saying that the comment was "put into circulation" not *by* her but *about* her, by enemies unknown—of which, of course, there were plenty.   A. S. C. Ackermann, *Popular Fallacies* (1950; repr. Gale Research, 1970).

WHO FIRST SAID, "HONEY, I FORGOT TO DUCK"?

President Ronald Reagan said it to his wife Nancy on March 31, 1981, after John Hinckley's bullet nearly ended his life, and it was taken at the time as an example not only of the wounded leader's pluck, but of his ready wit. As sportswriter Red Smith pointed out the day after the shooting, however, Reagan, a former sportscaster himself, had borrowed the line from boxer Jack Dempsey. Dempsey had said it to his wife, Estelle Taylor, back on September 26, 1926, just after Gene Tunney had taken the heavyweight crown away from him in Philadelphia. "Dutch" Reagan was then fifteen years old.   Red Smith, "Sports of the Times" column, *New York Times,* April 1, 1981.

BODY:

SENSE AND NONSENSE

WHAT COLOR IS BLOOD?

It depends on whether it's traveling away from or toward the heart. Blood which has just been pumped out of the heart, traveled through the pulmonary artery into the lungs, and left the lungs is red, because in the lungs the hemoglobin in the red blood cells combines with oxygen to produce the bloodstream's "characteristic" red color. Nonoxygenated blood, however—that is, blood which is traveling through veins back to the lungs and the heart—is a purplish, almost blue color. This does not mean that if you cut open a vein, you will release blue blood: Upon contact with the atmosphere, so rich in oxygen, even venous blood turns red. T. Pickering Pick and Robert Howden, eds., *Gray's Anatomy* (Running Press, 1974); Gerard Tortora and Nicholas Anagnostakos, *Principles of Anatomy and Physiology* (Canfield Press, 1978).

"HEART ATTACKS" DON'T KILL YOU.

Not directly, anyway. "Heart attack" is a rather imprecise term used to describe any number of cardiac traumas, including most commonly a "coronary occlusion" or "myocardial infarction" (MI), which happens when the coronary arteries are so restricted that they cannot get sufficient blood to the major heart muscle, the myocardium. When health professionals speak of a "heart attack," it's an MI they generally mean.

An MI is serious business, but it's seldom the immediate cause of death. The complications of this heart attack are what really concern cardiac care nurses, who monitor and care for patients who have survived myocardial infarctions. The main post-MI problem is that once the myocardium has been deprived of blood for long enough to cause an "attack," its tissues are dead and scarred, and these scarred tissues have a nasty tendency to generate irregular, confusing electrical impulses, or arrhythmias.

These arrhythmias can in turn lead to such potentially lethal complications as cardiogenic shock and congestive heart failure. That is why people who have had one heart attack are much more likely than the general population to have another one. And it is why arrhythmias, or irregular heartbeats, are considered the major danger signal in cardiac care units (CCUs).

CCUs, staffed by nurses expert in cardiovascular problems, have multiplied rapidly since the 1960s, and have been responsible for dramatically reducing the post-MI death rate. The main objective of these units, according to Brunner and Suddarth, is "to prevent, detect, and treat cardiac arrhythmias." These arrhythmias remain the leading cause of death following a so-called heart attack.   Lillian Brunner, R.N., and Doris Suddarth, R.N., *Textbook of Medical-Surgical Nursing* (Lippincott, 1980).

BONES ARE NOT BRITTLE OR DRY.

Them bones, them bones, them dry bones . . . are anything but dry. They'll get parched and brittle if they sit around in a desert, but as long as they're parts of a living body—that is, as long as they're inside of you—they're literally oozing with blood.

Your bones, like your skin or your lungs or your brain, are composed of living tissue, and like these other parts of your body, they are filled with hundreds of blood vessels which bring them the nutrients and oxygen without which they could not survive. As a result bones are blood-rich and extremely porous, never dry, in their living state. Far from being solid, they are actually spongy inside: Even the long, basically hard supportive bones 'ike the femur have a soft, mushy inside, or marrow, where red blood cells are produced. In the flatter, more irregularly shaped bones like the clavicle and sternum, spongy bone tissue composes an even greater percentage of the total structure. No part of the body's skeletal structure, therefore, is without a soft, living center.

This is a good thing for us all. One of the advantages of having porous bones—aside from the fact that we couldn't live without the blood cells they produce—is that they are lighter than solid bone would be. If your bones were as solid as they look on a skeleton, you'd hardly be able to walk. Gerard Tortora and Nicholas Anagnostakos, *Principles of Anatomy and Physiology* (Canfield Press, 1978).

WHAT PART OF THE BODY IS AFFECTED BY TUBERCULOSIS?

In the nineteenth century the fashionable sickness among the European literati was consumption, that wasting disease which was popularly known as the White Death. Among the notables who suffered from tubercular ravages were John Keats, Friedrich Schiller, Frederic Chopin, the Brontë sisters, and Robert Louis Stevenson. Thousands of other, lesser-known folk also succumbed to it, in a most unfashionable manner. Before 1882, when Robert Koch isolated the responsible microorganism, *Mycobacterium tuberculosis*, about four people in every thousand died from the disease. The figure is now one-tenth of that.

Anyone who has ever had a chest X ray realizes that tuberculosis attacks the lungs. But lung, or pulmonary, tuberculosis is only the most common variety of the disease. TB often moves rapidly and insidiously throughout the entire body. It most commonly affects the lungs first, but, as Brunner and Suddarth point out, "Tubercle bacilli can establish themselves in almost every type of human tissue. . . . There is no organ system that they cannot colonize." Next to the lungs, the most common infection sites are the kidneys, genitourinary tract, joints, and bones. In all of these areas the disease causes infection and progressive debilitation, and although medications have drastically cut the death rate even for the most lethal forms (such as meningeal, or spinal column, TB), the disease remains the primary killer among infectious diseases in the United States. Lillian Brunner, R.N., and Doris Suddarth, R.N., *Textbook of Medical-Surgical Nursing* (Lippincott, 1980); Harvey Shields Collins, M.D., "Tuberculosis," in *Encyclopedia Americana* (1976).

WHAT'S THE BEST HOME REMEDY FOR A BURN?

Remember when you touched the hot stove and your mother went to the refrigerator for the butter? Remember how it made the burn feel even hotter, and how you blew on the stinging finger, glad at least that your mother knew what to do in an emergency?

Well, it turns out that motherwit in this instance is off base. In spite of the fact that many families still consider butter an appropriate treatment for minor burns, there's no medical evidence this is so. Perhaps butter is popular because it looks or feels like ointment, but that's only because it's greasy; ointments have antibacterial properties, which is not true of butter. All you accomplish with butter (or margarine, for that matter) is to coat the burn with a debris-collecting goo which must later be scraped off if it interferes with healing. In addition you add fat (usually salted fat) to the fire: It's like searing your finger first, then deciding you should fry it as well.

What *is* the best home remedy? Plain, old cold tap water. By putting your finger immediately in a bowl of cold (not iced) water, you'll not only ease the pain, but prevent scarring and further damage. To ensure that, you should keep the burnt area submerged for several minutes; half an hour of such cooling is not excessive. For serious burns, of course, you should seek medical attention.   Benjamin Miller, M.D. and Claire Kean, R.N., *Encyclopedia and Dictionary of Medicine, Nursing, and Allied Health* (W.B. Saunders, 1978).

YOU SHOULD NOT RUB SNOW ON FROSTBITTEN AREAS.

Rubbing snow on a frostbitten toe sounds like a good idea, possibly because it's so quirky that those of us who have never been frostbitten imagine "those woodsmen must know," and isn't folk wisdom charming? Actually, it's an awful idea. First, rubbing a frostbitten area is likely to cause further damage to already brittle cells. Second (as any city slicker can tell you), snow is *cold;* the last thing you should do to an area suffering from cold is to make it colder still. What you want to do is to warm it up, gently and gradually, and the best way to do this is to immerse it in warm (not hot) water. The trick is to bring the area slowly back to normal body temperature, while avoiding scalding or rough treatment. It may not be folk wisdom, but it does make common sense.   Barry Behrstock, M.D., with Richard Trubo, *The Parent's*

When-Not-to-Worry Book (Harper & Row, 1981); Carol Ann Rinzler, *The Dictionary of Medical Folklore* (Crowell, 1979).

"FEED A COLD AND STARVE A FEVER." YES OR NO?

Since no one understands the common cold, this piece of folk wisdom may be as appropriate as any other medical advice in dealing with its symptoms. Traditional medical opinion, however, says that when you have either a cold or a fever—in fact, when you have any infection—your body burns up energy faster than normal, and you should therefore increase your intake of food.

The problem with this is that neither fevers nor colds are conducive to hearty appetites, and so doing the "right" thing is seldom a welcome task. The common medical compromise is to eat lightly but increase fluid intake: "Drinking plenty of liquids" is a way of keeping up your strength without forcing yourself to eat. Certain liquids, like the time-honored chicken soup, have the additional advantage of being salty enough to break through what Carol Rinzler calls the "tasteless, smell-less barrier" of the infection.

Sometimes the folk maxim is reversed to read "Starve a cold and feed a fever." As Rinzler wryly points out, this advice is "still at least half wrong."   Carol Ann Rinzler, *The Dictionary of Medical Folklore* (Crowell, 1979).

WHERE IS OUR FOOD DIGESTED?

Only a very minute part of the digestive process takes place in the human stomach. By far the greatest amount happens further down the gastrointestinal tract, in that twenty-foot-long coil supreme of guts, the small intestine. What the stomach really does is to store ingested food and soften it up by bathing it in hydrochloric acid, pepsin, and other enzymes. The real business of food breakdown is done by the bile, pancreatic and intestinal juices in the small intestine, where the bulk of absorption into the cell walls also takes place. The stomach, therefore, is a kind of preprocessing plant, creating a pulpy mass, called chyme, which the intestines analyze, process, and absorb. Harold Wellington

Jones, M.D., "Stomach," and Jeffrey Wenig, "Intestine," in *Encyclopedia Americana* (1976).

HOW MANY "SQUARE MEALS" A DAY SHOULD YOU EAT?

It's a persistent article of folk wisdom that nibbling between meals is bad for you; three well-balanced meals a day (starting, of course, with a "hearty breakfast") is supposed to be the ideal eating regimen. Recent studies suggest, however, that this dietary maxim may be bunk. It's now thought that four, five, or even six meals a day may be better for you than those time-honored three squares—no matter how well balanced they are.

Eating frequent small meals helps keep the body's metabolic activity fairly constant, and this is thought to be preferable to the "on again, off again" spurts of energy which the body must generate to effectively handle three heavy intakes a day. The only real difficulty with the spaced, lower-intake method is that it's potentially hazardous to your teeth, unless you're willing to brush five times a day as well. And, of course, eating five meals a day is not going to do you any good if each of those meals is full size. The ideal is to consume the same amount of food each day, but to do it at more frequent intervals.   Ashley Montagu and Edward Darling, *The Prevalence of Nonsense* (Harper & Row, 1967).

GROUND GLASS IS HARMLESS WHEN EATEN.

As numerous mystery writers have noted, ground glass seems the ideal murder weapon: quiet, untraceable, effective. The only trouble with it, though, is that it is *not* effective. As long ago as the seventeenth century, the British scientist Sir Thomas Browne demonstrated, on a dog, that ground glass could be ingested without any ill effects whatever. When you stop to consider that the basic component of glass, silica, is the same as that of sand, its innocuousness becomes less surprising: Think of all the infants who have gobbled down handfuls of sand with more glee than they have their carrots; none of them keel over from the "poison." As long as the substance itself is not toxic, almost anything taken in powdered form is harmless.

Ingesting glass can be fatal, of course, if you don't bother to grind it down first. A splinter or small chunk of glass can shred your innards up pretty well, and for this reason you would be wise to take Sir Thomas's word for it, and not experiment on yourself. Unless you're a whiz with a mortar and pestle, you could end up with small splinters in your powder, and even silica in that form can be deadly.   A. S. E. Ackerman, *Popular Fallacies* (1950, repr. Gale Research, 1970).

WHICH OF THE FOLLOWING LEAD TO COLDS? A) WET FEET, B) CHILLS, OR C) COLD WEATHER.

The connection between the common cold and "coldness" is so enshrined in the given wisdom that many of us think it is "obvious" that all three of the above lead to colds. As several studies have demonstrated, though, the correct answer is "none of the above."

Grandma's warnings aside, neither wet feet nor chilling seems to enhance the cold virus's activity. In experiments at England's Common Cold Research Center, subjects wearing wet socks and wet swimsuits stood in drafty, unheated areas for half an hour at a time; although this led to much shivering and chattering of teeth, none of the subjects developed a cold. The conclusion, which was confirmed by similar studies at Baylor and the University of Illinois, was that coldness does not lead to colds. The commonly observed "link" between chills and colds is often an early symptom of the infection, not its cause.

It's true that the "cold season" generally comes in the colder months of the year, but that does not mean necessarily that cold weather leads to colds. Some scientists explain the seasonal rise as a result of the fact that cold weather forces people indoors, where closer contact spreads the virus. Others speculate that cold weather may increase the virus's survival rate. The best way of avoiding a winter cold, then, might be to spend a lot of time in the snow. By yourself, of course.   Barry Behrstock, M.D., with Richard Trubo, *The Parent's When-Not-to-Worry Book* (Harper & Row, 1981).

COLDS ARE NOT SPREAD BY SNEEZING.

"Cover your mouth when you sneeze" may be good advice from the point of view of manners, but medically it can be just the opposite. Few colds seem to be transmitted through the air; the vast majority are carried and spread by hand. The common cold virus apparently occurs in such low concentrations in saliva that a sneeze or a cough, which contains particles mostly from the mouth, is very ineffective in transmitting the ailment. University of Virginia doctors had great difficulty in even finding the cold virus in sneezed material, and a University of Wisconsin team estimated that even if you are directly sneezed on, your chances of thus "catching" a cold are only about one in ten.

The hands are a different matter. The Virginia physicians found the cold virus on the hands of 65 percent of cold sufferers, and after comparing manual with airborne transmission, they concluded that hands were over 70 percent effective in doing the job—as opposed to less than 10 percent success rate with sneezing. One doctor found that when a cold virus was placed on subjects' hands, 40 percent of them developed a cold simply by touching their eyes or noses (the sites where mucous membranes pick up the virus).

It's possible, therefore, that the "hypochondriacs" who fear human contact have been right all along. Refusing to shake hands with a cold sufferer may not be very polite, but it does make medical sense, while sneezing into your hand (the polite thing to do) turns out to be asking for trouble. Unless, of course, you use a tissue—and discard it immediately afterward.   Barry Behrstock, M.D., with Richard Trubo, *The Parent's When-Not-to-Worry Book* (Harper & Row, 1981).

HEMOPHILIACS DO NOT "BLEED TO DEATH FROM A SCRATCH."

Hemophilia is an inherited genetic defect characterized by the lack of clotting factors in the blood. Because of this deficiency, a person with the disease is susceptible to a much higher risk than most people from minor scrapes and cuts: An injury that would close rapidly in a normal person might take hours or days to stop bleeding in a hemophiliac.

This is known to most people, and it has led some to exaggerate the dangers of the condition beyond what they really are. Some hemophiliacs, it is true, do die from minor scrapes, and tooth extractions can be fatal, but in most cases the bleeding of pinpricks and the like can be stopped by direct pressure, while more serious injuries can be managed by the infusion of frozen plasma and, more recently, the clotting factors themselves. The real danger in the disease is not external but internal: Internal bleeding can lead to subcutaneous swelling, and can even invade muscles and joints. Blood-swollen joints are the hemophiliac's biggest problem: Recurrent joint hemorrhage can cause chronic pain, ankylosis (stiffening) of the joint, and even crippling. Lillian Brunner, R.N., and Doris Suddarth, R.N., *Textbook of Medical-Surgical Nursing* (Lippincott, 1980). Carol Ann Rinzler, *The Dictionary of Medical Folklore* (Crowell, 1979).

WILL STEPPING ON A RUSTY NAIL GIVE YOU TETANUS?

Only if the nail is not only rusty, but covered with horse or cow dung as well. Tetanus, or "lockjaw," is caused not by rust or dirt or even puncture wounds per se, but by the bacterium *Clostridium tetani,* which attacks the central nervous system, causing muscular stiffness and spasms. The bacterium's preferred environment is the feces of farm animals, which is why the old folk treatment of rubbing a newborn's naval with pasture droppings led to lockjaw in countless infants. The disease has nothing to do with rust.

When I was a child, those of us who were immunized against it used to think of "lockjaw" as a pretty funny disease; the most callous of us would respond to the slightest pinprick by adopting the *risus sardonicus,* or sardonic smile, characteristic of tetanus victims. We know now, of course, that tetanus is no laughing matter; even with expert treatment, approximately a quarter of those who contract it die. This means that you should take very seriously *any* cut or puncture wound that could introduce *C. tetani* into the body—including, but not limited to, rusty nails. You could get cut by a glisteningly clean nail, but if it had come into contact with the bacterium before it contacted you, you might be smiling right into the grave.

Tetanus immunization is now considered effective for about seven to ten years. William A. R. Thomson, M.D., *Black's Medical Dictionary* (Harper & Row, 1979).

READING IN POOR LIGHT WILL NOT DAMAGE YOUR EYES.

It was a shock for me to discover this. As a child I logged numerous hours under the covers with a flashlight, reading while I was supposed to be asleep, and up until recently I blamed my imperfect vision on that transgression. I now find out it ain't so. Reading in a bad light may cause muscular tension, eye fatigue, and headaches, but it cannot damage your vision any more than reading in good light, or "resting" your eyes periodically, can improve it. Because poor vision is the result generally of a structural defect, lighting has no effect on it. According to Dr. Edward S. Gifford, the same can be said about "excessive reading, small print, fine work at close range, poor illumination, fluorescent lighting, lack of glasses, incorrect glasses, glasses in need of adjustment, cheap sunglasses, or devotion to television." Edward S. Gifford, Jr., *The Evil Eye* (Macmillan, 1958), quoted in Ashley Montagu and Edward Darling, *The Prevalence of Nonsense* (Harper & Row, 1967).

WHAT'S THE MOST COMMONLY ABUSED OVER-THE-COUNTER DRUG?

There is no doubt that acetylsalicylic acid, commonly known as aspirin, is an effective analgesic (painkiller) for a great deal of low-level pain: Throughout this century it has been used to give symptomatic relief for everything from headaches to menstrual cramps, from the discomfort of flu to rheumatism. That it is widely abused, however, seems obvious when you consider how frequently it is recommended for quite minor aches and pains, and when you recall that the U.S. sales of this popular "wonder drug" are in the neighborhood of three-quarters of a billion dollars a year. Popping two aspirin every four hours may seem harmless enough, but not all health professionals agree.

Aspirin is abused in two ways. First, it is ingested unthinkingly by many people who are ignorant of its possible dangers. The most notorious of these is its irritative effect on the stomach lining, which can lead to iron-deficiency anemia. Aspirin also retards blood clotting and, if used to excess, can cause a ringing in the ears. This is not to mention the fact that, because of its ubiquity in American medicine chests, the drug is responsible for hundreds of accidental children's deaths a year.

Second, aspirin is abused by the companies who manufacture it. Over-the-counter drugs are such big business today that the makers of Anacin, Bayer, Bufferin and their competitors allot huge advertising budgets to convince you that their brands are superior to Brand X. In many cases, according to a 1973 Federal Trade Commission investigation, their efforts are misleading or deceptive. The brouhaha about which brand is best, the FTC says, is largely a commercial smoke screen designed to disguise the fact that taken in equivalent doses, one firm's aspirin is indistinguishable from another's.

Consumers Union, investigating the analgesic mongers' claims, found the same thing. Anacin, for example, contains 6.17 grains of aspirin (as opposed to Bayer's 5 grains) and a dollop of caffeine. It costs four times as much as generic aspirin. CU concluded that "this is a high premium to pay for an additional 1.17 grains of aspirin plus the amount of caffeine in a quarter cup of coffee." If you must buy aspirin, they said, there is absolutely "no reason to buy anything but the least expensive brand." The Editors of *Consumer Reports, The Medicine Show* (Consumers Union, 1976).

DO PLACEBOS HAVE ANY PHYSICAL EFFECT ON THE BODY?

My *Webster's* gives the first definition of placebo as "a medication prescribed more for the mental relief of the patient than for its actual effect on his disorder." That's a clear-cut, conventional view, mirroring the traditional Western belief that the distinction between mind and matter, "mental" and "actual," is absolute. To most people, a placebo is something that cures a "nonexistent" problem by convincing the sufferer that it's an actual medicine: Hypochondriacs are thus seen as the most appropriate candidates for its use.

Modern health professionals take a more holistic view, one that realizes that the mind-body distinction is fuzzy, and sees psychosomatic illness as a real illness for which a specific organic origin cannot be found—which does not mean it is "imaginary." Placebos today are used to bridge that tenuous, often shifting gap between mental and physical ailments by enlisting the body's own defenses to combat "imagined" ills, and actual organic problems as well.

The principal mechanisms activated by a placebo are the nervous and limbic systems, which together both register pain and apparently can also overcome it. Recent research has led health professionals to believe that the suggestion of health afforded by the placebo may be assimilated in the temporal lobe, then transmitted to the adjacent limbic system, which in turn activates the hypothalamus. This part of the brain in turn affects the pituitary gland, which releases pain-killing hormones called endorphins. With the release of the very real endorphins, the "imaginary" pain subsides. So, in many cases, does "real" pain.

The range of physical responses effected by placebos is extraordinarily wide. Placebos, according to two Cornell Medical Center researchers, can "constrict the pupils, alter blood pressure, change heart and respiratory rate, influence gastrointestinal secretions and peristalsis, cause a change in body temperature," and bring about various changes in the immune response. They have also proved effective in treating such conditions as "rheumatoid arthritis, GI disorders, angina, hypertension, rashes, sinusitis, bronchitis and allergic reactions." Pretty good work for a sugar pill.   Samuel W. Perry and George Heidrich, "Placebo Response: Myth and Matter," in *American Journal of Nursing* (April 1981).

WHAT IS SCHIZOPHRENIA?

So common is the impression that "schizophrenia" means "split personality" that even in casual parlance we speak of a divided attitude toward something as being a "schizoid" approach. Because of the similarity in derivation to the word "schism," schizophrenia is commonly assumed to be the clinical description of a person who displays radically "divided" behavior, suggesting the presence in his or her psychological makeup of two or more distinct "personalities." The Sybil character played so ably by Sally Field a few years ago or the Eve character played by Joanne Woodward are seen as typical schizophrenic types.

This is a mischaracterization of the ailment. When health professionals speak of schizophrenia, they mean a psychotic disorder characterized by acute melancholy, delusions, catatonia, hallucinations, delirium, paranoia, and a range of other symptoms which, taken together, effectively prohibit the schizophrenic from participating in "normal" society. Clinicians call this condition schizophrenic (meaning "split mind") because it used to be thought that it was the result of a "splitting off of portions of the psyche, which portions may then dominate the psychic life of the subject for a time and lead an independent existence even though these may be contrary and contradictory to the personality as a whole."

This is not the same thing as a "split personality." The Jekyll-Hyde kind of disorder is diagnosed not as schizophrenia but as a "dissociation" or "dissociative reaction," a somewhat less serious condition in which "the same individual at different times appears to be in possession of entirely different mental content, disposition and character, and [in which] one of the different phases shows complete ignorance of the other, an ignorance which may be reciprocal." Multiple personality is usually described as a neurosis, schizophrenia as a psychosis.

Of course, you can classify an aberrant behavior in any way you choose, and doctors, who invented the above categories, are not generally much sharper than the rest of us when it comes to making fine distinctions; as a result, the lines between psychosis and neurosis are fuzzy, and one diagnostician's dissociative reaction may be another's schizoid fit.   Leland Hinsie, M.D., and Robert Campbell, M.D., *Psychiatric Dictionary* (Oxford, 1976).

IN HUMAN REPRODUCTION, HOW MANY SPERM DOES IT TAKE TO FERTILIZE AN EGG?

As anyone who has ever taken a high-school health education course can tell you, a single sperm is all that is needed for the fertilization of the ovum. Once fertilization takes place, the egg blocks further entry and proceeds to the business of gestation. This is taken as one of the chief wonders of biology: all those millions of sperm clamoring for the honor of paternity, and only one getting the nod. Conception comes out looking like a prize given to the swiftest swimmer: The first one to reach the ovum, it's generally assumed, is the one who gets the gold.

As congenial as this notion is to those of us who feel evolution has everything to do with fitness and nothing to do with luck, it's not entirely accurate. It is not the first (or the strongest) sperm which fertilizes the egg, but the first to pop into the ovum after its external membrane has been broken down by the combined action of *all* the finishers in the "race." (Many sperm, of course, do not finish.)

Every unfertilized egg is surrounded by a protective membrane and that membrane can be broken down only by an enzyme called hyaluronidase. This is secreted, conveniently enough, by sperm. But—and here's the rub—such enormous quantities of hyaluronidase are needed to dissolve the protective shell that even if the swiftest swimming sperm set a world record getting to the egg, it would do him absolutely no good until his slower buddies arrived. The protective shell will not dissolve until hundreds of millions of sperm have secreted the needed enzyme. That's why men with low "sperm counts" (less than about eighty million sperm per milliliter of seminal fluid) are considered infertile.

So while it is true that only one sperm is permitted to fertilize the egg, it could never have reached the goal if it had not been carried along on millions of its comrades' "shoulders." Gerard Tortora and Nicholas Anagnostakos, *Principles of Anatomy and Physiology* (Canfield Press, 1978).

CASTRATED MEN ARE NOT IMPOTENT.

We are speaking, of course, of men who have had not their entire genitals, but only their testicles, removed. In ancient Rome such men were called *spadones,* and there is ample evidence that they were, in the coy phrasing of A. S. E. Ackermann, as "apt for coitus" as their noncastrated fellows. Indeed, according to Saint Jerome, such men were often much sought after by some Roman ladies, *ad securas libidinationes,* that is because intercourse with them ran no risk of pregnancy. This is because testicular castration removes the site of sperm production (the testicles) while leaving intact the bodily mechanisms which provide for semen production, erection, and even ejaculation.

Castrated men were often employed as harem guards in ancient Eastern countries, and, in fact, the word "eunuch," signifying such supposed unfortunates, comes from the Greek word *eunouchos,* meaning one who guards a couch. It is a joke on the eunuch's employers—all those cocksure sultans—that their presumed impotence was a myth: Ackermann suggests the popularity of eunuchs with their charges may have stemmed not only from the impunity of intercourse but also "the longer duration of erection in the castrated." All you macho dudes, take note. A. S. E. Ackermann, *Popular Fallacies* (1950; repr. Gale Research, 1970).

LIVER SPOTS HAVE NOTHING TO DO WITH THE LIVER.

Explanations of liver spots—those brownish discolorations that appear generally on the torso and arms of people in late middle age—vary depending on whom you ask. In Britain the term generally is used to refer to the condition pityriasis versicolor, in which the microorganism *Malassezia furfur* causes irregular blotches of darkened skin. In America it is the popular term for one of two types of melanotic hyperpigmentation: lentigo sinilis and chloasma. The former is characterized by what Sutton calls "benign, discrete, pigmentary macules developing on senile, keratotic, xerotic or xerodermatous subjects." The latter is a similar condition sometimes associated with "pregnancy, chronic illness, malnutrition, hypoproteinemia, avitaminosis and hypothyroidism." Let your dermatologist explain the mumbo-jumbo to you; I only know that nobody mentions the liver. Arthur Rook, M.D., et al., *Textbook of Dermatology* (Blackwell Scientific Publications, 1968); Richard L. Sutton, M.D., *Diseases of the Skin* (C. V. Mosby, 1956).

WHAT IS A BLACKHEAD?

Teen-agers are often counseled to wash their faces frequently because if they don't they will develop pimples and blackheads:

The latter, it's often thought, are actually pockets of dirt which collect on the surface of unclean skin.

The advice is good, but it's given for the wrong reason. It's true that washed skin is less likely to develop these irregularities than unwashed skin, but this is not because your soap is removing the "dirt." Blackheads are not composed of dirt, but of oil that has turned black because it oxidized on contact with the air. Whiteheads (those little devils that youngsters call "zits") are composed of nonoxidized oil. Pimples are infected pores, where bacteria grow in the skin's own natural oils.

All these skin problems are the result of the accumulation of oil on the surface of the skin. Normally, the sebaceous (oil-producing) glands, just under the surface, pass their oil, or sebum, out through the pores, keeping the skin soft and preventing excessive evaporation of moisture. If the pores are blocked—by dirt, for example—the oil may back up and create trouble. Washing will open the pores, and thus reduce the chances of your getting those black marks. Reduce but not eliminate: Because of the vagaries of sebum emission, even clean skin can develop blackheads.   Gerard Tortora and Nicholas Anagnostakos, *Principles of Anatomy and Physiology* (Canfield Press, 1978).

WHAT ORGAN IS MOST AFFECTED BY ALCOHOL?

Although there is some debate about whether alcoholism is a predisposing, causative, or merely aggravating factor in cirrhosis of the liver, there is no doubt that alcohol abuse adversely affects that organ. "Only" about half of tested alcoholics develop cirrhosis after about fifteen years of drinking, but even the unaffected ones generally suffer from either alcoholic fatty liver or alcoholic hepatitis, or both; both of these conditions, moreover, are often precursors to the more serious disease of cirrhosis.

But as devastating as alcohol is to the liver, it is even more rapidly destructive of another organ, the brain. In a 1978 study conducted by five Danish scientists, thirty-seven young male alcoholics were tested for both liver damage and "intellectual impairment." Only 19 percent of the subjects had developed cirrhosis, but a whopping 59 percent were found to be intellectually impaired. This was a young sample (the subjects' average age was thirty), and cirrhosis takes a long time to develop, so it is

possible that many of the men with sound livers will ruin them
later in life; what is shocking is that after an average of only ten
years of drinking, they had already damaged their brains.

Intellectual impairment, the authors of the study conclude,
may be "the earliest complication of chronic alcoholism"; they
even offer it as a principal unrecognized cause of presenile de-
mentia. So if you think you can keep at the heavy tippling for
twenty or thirty years before you do yourself in, think again:
Even if your liver is all right, you may be too far gone to notice.
And if you think organ damage happens only to winos or guzz-
lers of booze, you should know that the preferred drink among
the Danish subjects was beer.   Kirsten Lee, et al., "Alcohol-In-
duced Brain Damage and Liver Damage in Young Males," in
The Lancet (October 13, 1979); Charles Lieber, "Ethanol and the
Liver," in *Alcoholism: Progress in Research and Treatment*, Peter
Bourne, M.D., and Ruth Fox, M.D., eds. (Academic Press, 1973).

ALCOHOL DOES NOT HELP YOU SLEEP.

Many of us have been known to take a nip now and then to
"help us sleep," and there are, sadly, even some individuals who
use alcohol's supposed sleep-inducing property as an excuse for
constant indulgence—much as others use liquor to help them
"calm down" or "perk up." It's true that if you drink enough
before going to bed, you can make yourself pass out, and end up
"sleeping it off," but that is not quite the same thing as drinking
yourself into rest.

The distinction between sleep and rest is crucial here because
while drinking can knock you out, it cannot give you a good
night's rest. This is because the ingestion of alcohol inhibits that
deep restful state known as Rapid Eye Movement, or REM,
sleep, and without enough REM sleep you are likely to wake up
the next morning just as bushed as if you hadn't slept at all.

One of the secondary problems associated with alcholism, in
fact, is the constant suppression of REM sleep. The person who
passes out regularly from booze is really getting very little solid
sleep, and this contributes to his bodily and mental debility. In
acute alcohol withdrawal, REM sleep seems to "rebound," and it
has been suggested that this return of the REM state, and its
associated dream activity, may be connected to the hallucina-

tions experienced by alcoholics going "cold turkey." Unused to dream images, they perceive them as a flood of uncontrollable nightmares. Milton M. Gross, M.D., et al., "Acute Alcohol Withdrawal Syndrome," in *The Biology of Alcoholism*, Vol. 3, Benjamin Kissin and Henri Begleiter, eds. (Plenum Press, 1974).

WHAT WILL COFFEE DO FOR A DRUNK?

You can't sober anybody up with coffee. Although countless movies have suggested otherwise, drinking strong black coffee does nothing to make a drunken person less inebriated, or to make him come around quicker. It's the level of unprocessed alcohol in the blood that creates drunkenness, and there's really nothing you can do to hasten the departure of that intoxicant from the body before it's ready to go. Drinking coffee may be a good way to while away an hour or two as your body does its work; but so is drinking water, or sleeping.

Black coffee may make your tipsy buddy look more alert, because of the caffeine, but it will do nothing for his motor reflexes or judgment. What alcohol plus coffee leads to, therefore, is simply a wide-awake drunk.

Academic opinion on this score is divided. Pharmacologically, ethanol (the active agent in alcohol) and caffeine are "antagonists," and that means you would expect coffee to offset the effects of drunkenness. But that depends on what effects you measure. In the words of Benjamin Kissin, "Where ethanol is acting as a depressant, caffeine may act as an antagonist. Where ethanol is acting as a disinhibiting agent (excitatory), caffeine may actually increase deterioration of performance." Of course, alcohol commonly acts as both a depressant and a "disinhibiting agent," so if you're trying to decide whether or not to stoke your raving buddy with java and send him out on the road, don't. The connections between ethanol and caffeine are still too poorly understood to make that anything but a gamble with disaster. Benjamin Kissin, "Interactions of Ethyl Alcohol and Other Drugs," in *The Biology of Alcoholism*, Vol. 3, Benjamin Kissin and Henri Begleiter, eds. (Plenum Press, 1974).

FOOD:

YOU ERR WHAT YOU EAT

WHAT COLOR IS A FLORIDA ORANGE?

It depends on how old it is. Oranges picked early in the season are slightly greenish, though ripe; those that are harvested in midseason tend to be the yellow of grapefruits. But since neither of these hues approximates the near reddish tone that an orange is "supposed" to have, the magi who run the United States food-processing industry have decided that in the interests of "sales appeal," they had better perform some alchemy on the poor, palefaced fruits to make them look more "natural." What this means is that much of the early crop is sprayed with a degreening (that is, chlorophyll-killing) ethylene gas, and the late crop is dipped in red dye.

Nobody seems to know what the gas and the dye do to humans, but since few Americans ingest large quantities of orange peel, the industry has not bothered much about it; presumably, the fruit itself is not harmed. For my money, such tinctorial wizardry belongs on the same shelf as manufactured vinegar-and-water douches and realistic plastic plants. I've thrown out my marmalade, too. I figure in a choice between cancer and chlorophyll, I'll take a green orange any day. *Prevention* (July 1980).

WHAT'S THE DISTINGUISHING MARK OF SWISS CHEESE?

The Swiss have been master cheesemakers for more than two thousand years—longer than any other people—and through much of their history, the manufacture and export of what André Simon calls "the adult form of milk" have been mainstays of the economy. Next to the Swiss Knights, the nation's far-ranging mercenaries, cheeses were for hundreds of years the Alpine country's principal ambassadors abroad.

The cheeses we know as "Swiss" are generally domestic copies of the most famous of the Alpine varieties, Emmenthal and Gruyère. Because these cheeses, both domestic and imported, are so popular, many shoppers have learned to identify them both, without discrimination, as typically "Swiss." The reason for this is that both varieties have the characteristic holes, or "eyes," that appear in some Swiss cheeses during the ripening process.

But these holes are not distinctively Swiss. They occur in the cheeses of many countries, and they are present in only a few of the many cheeses that Switzerland produces. Emmenthal and Gruyère have large, distinctive eyes; in Sbrinz and Appenzell cheese they are extremely small; and in the majority of Swiss cheeses—such as the nonexported Raclette, Saanen, Piora, Toggenburger, and Bellelay—they do not occur at all. The soft, triangular processed cheese that is so popular in American supermarkets is a further example of a Swiss cheese without holes.

In Switzerland, the holes are caused by expanding gases which are emitted by bacteria in the ripening cheese. In some domestic "Swiss" cheeses, they have sometimes been mechanically added (or rather subtracted) after the cheese is formed. According to Vivienne Marquis and Patricia Haskell, holeless, or "blind," cheeses used to be gouged with a utensil like a melon baller and then packaged as genuine Swiss. This type of chicanery is, of course, frowned upon by serious cheese lovers, even here; even though most Swiss cheeses are naturally "blind," in America the eyes definitely have it.   Vivienne Marquis and Patricia Haskell, *The Cheese Book* (Simon & Schuster, 1965); André L. Simon, *Cheeses of the World* (Faber and Faber, 1965).

WHICH ARE MORE NUTRITIOUS, BROWN OR WHITE EGGS?

Both brown and white eggs have their champions, some claiming that any color at all in an eggshell is a sign of imperfection, others claiming with equal fervor that the darker the egg, the better it is for you. The defenders of both types are in error, for nutritionally, brown and white eggs are identical. The only peo-

ple to whom egg color should make any difference are those who
package and market the eggs: A uniform shade among the eggs
of a given dozen is thought to be aesthetically (and therefore
commercially) preferable to a hodgepodge, while certain local
markets seem to show a preference for one type of shell over
another. In England and New England, for example, tinted eggs
used to fetch a higher price than white eggs; in the New York
area, the reverse was true.

Special coloring in the eggs of wild fowl usually functions as
protective camouflage against predators, and the shades of domestic eggs are thought to be survivals of that variety in nature.
The speckled eggs of farm-bred turkeys, for example, clearly derive from the similarly patterned eggs of these birds' wild ancestors. Coloration also seems to be related to ancestral geographical
range: Chicken breeds whose ancestors were Asiatic generally lay
brown eggs, while those of Mediterranean descent lay white.
None of this is of importance in terms of food value. "The eggs of
any given breed of hens, whatever the color of the shells, are, on
an average, as nutritious as those of another breed, provided the
eggs are of the same size and freshness and the fowls are equally
well fed." C. F. Langworthy, "Eggs and Their Value as Food,"
in U.S. Department of Agriculture Bulletin 471 (January 31,
1917).

OPENED TIN CANS DON'T SPOIL FOOD.

The fear of being poisoned keeps many people from putting
half-empty cans of food back into the refrigerator. Once you
open a can, it's thought, you should empty the unused contents
into another container; if kept in the can, the metal (which is
really steel with a tin coating) will spoil the food. This injunction,
which must make the Tupperware people happy, has no basis in
fact. Food in an opened can will spoil no faster than food in any
other vessel. Provided you keep the can covered and refrigerated
(to guard against airborne bacteria), your unused beans will keep
just as well there as they would in a glass, china, or plastic container. Uncovered or left too long, they will rot just as fast in
these containers as in their original can. Acid foods sometimes
take on an unpleasant taste if kept in opened cans, but as Montagu and Darling point out, that is not the taste of poison. Ash-

ley Montagu and Edward Darling, *The Prevalence of Nonsense* (Harper & Row, 1967).

SPINACH WILL NOT MAKE YOU STRONG.

Popeye notwithstanding, spinach will not put hair on your chest, radiant health in your eye, or muscles on your scrawny frame. There is a fair amount of the vitamins A, B, and C in it, but the element for which it is famed, iron, is present in only modest amounts, and even those modest amounts cannot be fully absorbed by the body in the form they exist in the vegetable. Carol Rinzler estimates that, for you to get your daily requirement of iron from spinach alone, you would have to consume, each year, twice your body weight of the stuff. Even if you were inclined to do this, it wouldn't be such a good idea, because spinach also contains oxalic acid (which gives it its bitter taste) and that much oxalic acid could easily concentrate in the urine, causing kidney stones. Besides, who ever said iron would make you strong? You're a human being, not a skyscraper. A lack of iron in your diet can give you iron deficiency anemia, true, but merely ingesting iron will no more make you another Popeye than eating feathers will make you a bird. Carol Ann Rinzler, *The Dictionary of Medical Folklore* (Crowell, 1979).

EATING CARROTS WILL NOT IMPROVE YOUR EYESIGHT.

It is often said that eating carrots is a good way of ensuring better eyesight; in World War II, American pilots were fed mounds of the vegetable to improve their vision, and next to the notion that "Spinach makes you strong," the idea that carrot eating and 20-20 vision are related is probably the nation's most cherished dinner-table observation.

But it is only partly true. Carrots (which belong to the parsley family) are a good source of vitamin A, and a vitamin A deficiency can damage the epithelial tissues throughout the body and inhibit the manufacture of the retinal pigment rhodopsin. In both human and nonhuman animals, this can lead to a decreased ability to see in dim light—the "night blindness" against which the

World War II aces were being guarded. But the body can use only a limited amount of vitamin A, so that gorging yourself on carrots (or fish liver oil and egg yolks, also good sources of the vitamin) will do nothing for your eyesight: The excess vitamins cannot be used by the body.

Moreover, overindulging in carrots can actually have a detrimental effect on your health because in addition to vitamin A. they contain a yellowish pigment known as carotene. If you eat enough carotene, you'll end up *looking* like a carrot: Your skin will take on an orange tinge, and will keep it until you cut back your consumption. Carotenization is not terribly dangerous, but unless you're in a punk-rock band, do you really want orange skin? Barry Behrstock, M.D., with Richard Trubo, *The Parent's When-Not-to-Worry Book* (Harper & Row, 1981); Louise J. Daniel, "Vitamin," in *Encyclopedia Americana* (1976).

IN WHAT MONTHS IS IT UNSAFE TO EAT OYSTERS?

Years ago, when refrigerators were still unknown and the iceman cameth every day to keep your icebox filled, you had to be pretty particular about what you put in your mouth, especially in the summer months, when food spoilage was a common occurrence. In those days lovers of shellfish developed a fairly reliable rule of thumb to remind themselves when to be wary. You could eat oysters and other shellfish in any month with an "r" in it; months without an "r" (that is, the summer months, May through August) were taboo. This was a pretty good rule then, at least in the northern hemisphere, but it became obsolete with the advent of modern refrigeration. No oyster now travels cross-country in anything but an air-conditioned car, and as a result, you can enjoy them just as safely in June as in March. Ashley Montagu and Edward Darling, *The Prevalence of Nonsense* (Harper & Row, 1967).

WHAT'S IN AN EGG CREAM?

Unless you're from the New York metropolitan area, you may never have had the good fortune to have tasted an egg cream. Born and bred in Brooklyn, the drink is still made to perfection in that borough's many delis and luncheonette hangouts, although you can get an acceptable version as far north as Connecticut and as far west as New Jersey. A light and refreshing concoction, the egg cream is, to my mind, the ideal summer drink: as bracing as a beer or a soft drink, but without the former's bloating action or the latter's cloying sweetness. The name, however, is a misnomer. As my Brooklyn informant Mitch Sudolsky points out, the drink contains neither egg nor cream. It's made with a squirt of either vanilla or chocolate syrup, a generous splash of milk, and seltzer. Not the mineralized, artificially carbonated stuff you get in the supermarket, but honest-to-goodness, two-cents-plain soda fountain seltzer. The combination can't be beat.

FOR WHOM WAS THE BABY RUTH CANDY BAR NAMED?

This very popular confection got its start in the early 1920s, when George Herman "Babe" Ruth was the pride of the New York Yankees. It's commonly thought that the candy bar was named after him, but this is not so. The National Confectioners Association says it was named for President Grover Cleveland's daughter, Ruth; according to Tom Burnam, this is not so either. He notes that "Baby Ruth" Cleveland, who died of diphtheria in 1904, had already been gone for over fifteen years by the time the bar was invented—making the connection with the child even less likely than the one with the Yankee slugger.

A more likely candidate, he says, is the granddaughter of Mr. and Mrs. George Williamson. Citing the columnist L. M. Boyd, who had the story from a Williamson family friend, he says that the Williamsons developed the bar in honor of their own favorite baby, then marketed it through the Williamson Candy Company, of which Grandpa George was president. Tom Burnam, *More Misinformation* (Lippincott & Crowell, 1980).

CHOCOLATE DOES NOT CAUSE ACNE.

All those television doctors who told you to lay off chocolate because it would make you break out were wrong. There is no evidence to connect the eating of chocolate with either the beginning or the worsening of acne. It can make you break out if you're allergic to it, sure; but acne is not an allergy.

A 1969 dermatological study found that there was no significant difference in skin change between subjects who had eaten real chocolate bars for a month and those who had eaten similar-tasting "control" bars without chocolate. A 1978 article in the *Journal of the American Medical Association* agreed. "Even large amounts of chocolate," it concluded, "have not clinically exacerbated acne."   Barry Behrstock, M.D., with Richard Trubo, *The Parent's When-Not-to-Worry Book* (Harper & Row, 1981); Carol Ann Rinzler, *The Dictionary of Medical Folklore* (Crowell, 1979).

BEER MAKES YOU URINATE?

Beer drinkers are supposed to be notorious for running to the bathroom. You sit in a beer joint for three hours, consume three times your body weight in Budweiser, and leave most of it in the john because, as every beer drinker knows, the stuff "just goes right through you." What very few beer drinkers know is that the reason it goes right through you has little to do with its liquid volume: It's a function of something called vasopressin or, as it's more commonly known, antidiuretic hormone, or ADH. ADH, which is produced in your hypothalamus, regulates urine production and indirecty affects the amount of water in your bloodstream. When you're dehydrated, the hormone signals the kidneys to stop producing urine, so more water can be retained by the blood and you aren't done in by a concentration of salt in your plasma. Thus ADH helps you to maintain a healthy balance between internal water and salt; without it you'd be in serious trouble.

Certain substances, though, inhibit the secretion of ADH, and when that happens the kidneys don't know they are supposed to stop producing urine. They keep drawing water out of the body as if nothing were amiss, filling the bladder, sending you to the john, and further dehydrating your body. You guessed it: One of the substances that inhibits ADH is alcohol. When you drink a lot of beer, therefore, you make it impossible for the kidneys to work efficiently. Without the signals from ADH, they work overtime, so that your bladder seems always full. Exactly the same thing would happen, though, if you spent those three hours in a bar guzzling whiskey sours—or if you spent them at a truck stop sipping coffee. Caffeine, like alcohol, is an ADH inhibitor, and if you drink enough of it, it will foul up your kidneys just as well. It's not the beer, but the alcohol, which increases your urine supply.

It should be evident from this explanation that one of the major elements in drunkenness is dehydration. Thirst, in fact, is a common symptom of a hangover: Your body is letting you know you drained it too dry the night before. That's why one way of diminishing the effect of a hangover is to gulp down a quart or two of water after you come back from the bar. It may not be exactly the bedtime snack you have in mind, but it will replace some of the water you've lost, and you'll feel less run over in the morning.   Gerard Tortora and Nicholas Anagnostakos, *Principles of Anatomy and Physiology* (Canfield Press, 1978).

THERE'S NO SUCH DISH AS "WELSH RAREBIT."

"Rabbit" sounds pedestrian and quaint, "rarebit" refined and delicious. Maybe that's why that Welsh version of a grilled cheese sandwich, the poor man's delicacy Welsh rabbit, has so often been dignified by the quite erroneous name "rarebit." You see "rarebit" on elegant menus every so often, and are expected to smile indulgently when someone with more hunger than breeding asks how Welsh "rabbit" is prepared. The term is a shibboleth for snobs.

But the joke is on those in the know. "Rarebit" is a highbrow distortion; the original and accepted term is "rabbit." It arose as a putdown of the Welsh, who in the eighteenth century were already passionately devoted to cheese, and who (so said their critics) had gone so far as to substitute it for good British game. Calling melted cheese on toast "Welsh rabbit" was thus an ethnic barb, like referring to codfish as "Cape Cod turkey," to the Indian *bummalo* fish as "Bombay duck," or to scrambled eggs with anchovies as "Scotch woodcock." "Rarebit" dates from 1785, when Francis Grose inserted it in his *Classical Dictionary of the Vulgar Tongue*. His mistake persists today, having replaced the original quip as a way of separating the ravenous from the refined.   *Oxford English Dictionary* (Oxford, 1961); Ashley

Montagu and Edward Darling, *The Prevalence of Nonsense* (Harper & Row, 1967); Eric Partridge, *A Dictionary of Slang and Unconventional English* (Macmillan, 1956).

WHERE DO THE FOLLOWING FOODS COME FROM?

a) *croissants*

b) *Jordan almonds*

c) *pineapples*

d) *Jerusalem artichokes*

e) *French fries*

f) *chop suey*

g) *corned beef and cabbage*

a) *Croissants.* The ultimate French breakfast roll is not French but Austrian. It was devised by Viennese bakers sometime in 1683, just before or just after (accounts vary) the Turks who had been besieging the city were routed by a Polish army under John Sobieski. Some say the bakers devised the crescent in obsequious imitation of the Turkish crescent moon symbol, so that when the city fell, their bread, at least, would be buttered. Others say the roll appeared after the siege was lifted, as a memento of the deliverance. In either case, the *croissant* was Viennese for a century before it was brought to Paris by a young Austrian princess who was to become the French queen Marie Antoinette.

b) *Jordan almonds.* They come from Malaga, in Spain. "Jordan" is a corruption, as Tom Burnam points out, of the Middle English *jardyne almaunde,* meaning "garden almond"—although the delicious Jordans we know today are anything but garden variety. They were prized by European chefs as far back as the Renaissance, and used to be eaten in the nineteenth century in a fruit and nut mix with raisins.

c) *Pineapple.* Although most of the world's crop is now produced in Hawaii, pineapples did not reach the Islands until 1790, and were not cultivated there until a century later. Their first home was the tropical regions of the Americas, and it was from there that Columbus secured the first samples seen by Europeans; the Guarani Indian name was *nana,* meaning "excellent fruit"; Columbus renamed it *piña* because of its resemblance to a pine cone. So it remains in Spanish, although it is *ananas* in French. An interesting sidelight to this "excellent fruit" is that the European vogue for pineapple-shaped finials and escutcheons is an indirect imitation of the West Indian custom of placing the fruits over doorways as a sign of welcome.

d) *Jerusalem artichokes.* They are not artichokes, and if any of them has ever been to Jerusalem, it's because it was smuggled in by a tourist. The plant is actually a sunflower native to the Americas, and it was recognized as such by the Spaniards, who called it *girasol,* the Spanish word for sunflower, from the mistaken belief that they turn *(gira-)* toward the sun *(sol)* all day long. It's easy to see, says James Trager, "how *girasol* came to be tortured into 'Jerusalem,' but how the root came to be called an artichoke is anybody's guess." Somewhat of a specialty item today, the plant was widely cultivated by both the Indians and the early colonists, who called it (with as much justification as "artichoke") a "Canadian potato."

e) *French fries.* Tom Burnam rightly points out that French fries, sometimes thought to be an American invention, originated neither in America nor in France, but in Belgium, where since the nineteenth century they have been made and served on the street—traditionally in waxed paper "cones" which are the precursor of the less sanitary but just as traditional British newspaper cones. Popular in France and soon afterward in England, they have recently been brought to a high degree of uniform perfection by, of all places, McDonald's. The English still call them by their original import name, "chips." (True potato chips they call "crisps.")

f) *Chop suey.* Mathews's *Dictionary of Americanisms* gives chop suey as a derivation of *tsa-sui,* which is supposed to be Chinese for "odds and ends." Theories vary as to the dish's place of origin, but nobody claims it was China. In a 1928 description of New York City gangs, one authority says that the tongs—those Chinese vigilante street gangs—are "as American as chop suey": He gives the Western gold fields as the origin of the former and a San Francisco restaurant as the birthplace of the latter. The journal *Democrat* in 1947 suggested New York and an unknown American chef; according to this interpretation, the term is Chinese for "hash." You can take your pick (one from column A *or* one from column B). At least it's clear that the mainland Chinese had nothing to do with the dish.

g) *Corned beef and cabbage.* Although it's standard fare for Saint Patrick's Day dinner throughout America, this dish is not

Irish in origin; nor has it ever been frequently eaten in Ireland. Around the turn of the century, when corned beef was considerably cheaper than it is today, impoverished Irish immigrants in the great American cities did enjoy the dish regularly, but they did not bring the recipe from Ireland; it was an Irish-American innovation. Tom Burnam, *The Dictionary of Misinformation* (Crowell, 1975); Mitford Mathews, ed., *A Dictionary of Americanisms on Historical Principles* (University of Chicago Press, 1951); *Oxford English Dictionary* (Oxford, 1961); James Trager, *The Foodbook* (Grossman, 1970); *Ireland* (Life World Library), cited in Robert Jones, *Can Elephants Swim? Unlikely Answers to Improbable Questions* (Time-Life, 1969).

ANIMALS:

THROWING THE BULL

WHAT COLOR MAKES A BULL SEE RED?

I was chased by a bull when I was five. This was on a visit to a local farm with my grandmother, and I had just begun to scale a pasture fence when the bull, taking umbrage at the intrusion, waddled toward me shaking his head. I scuttled off the fence, grabbed my grandmother's hand, and for the next three years got the maximum distance from the episode in every "What I Did Last Summer" essay I turned in.

As it happened I was wearing a red shirt that day, so I was easily roped in by the notion that a bull will go crazy over red. This is a given of folk wisdom, so much so that even the Spanish, who ought to know better, generally make their *muletas* (the matador's "capes") in red so the beast will be properly infuriated before he is killed. But the whole idea is a sham. Bulls, as Philip Ward and Bergen Evans agree, are completely color-blind: What they react to is motion. The matador could shake a purple or white or aquamarine *muleta* in a bull's face and get him just as riled as he does with the traditional red.

This is really only common sense. If you were a bull, standing in a dusty, noisy, hot arena with thousands of people screaming for your death, a dozen darts sticking out of your back, and a guy with a pink suit and a sword taunting you to charge, would you really need to see red to see red?   Bergen Evans, *The Natural History of Nonsense* (Knopf, 1946); Philip Ward, *A Dictionary of Common Fallacies* (Oleander Press, 1980).

WHERE DOES THE BISON COME FROM?

The tragedy of the American buffalo, and its subsequent impact on the population of the Plains Indian tribes, has led many of us to think of the buffalo, more properly known as the bison, as a distinctly American beast. Actually the genus name *Bison* applies to two different species: the *Bison bison* of North America and the *Bison bonasus,* or wisent, of Europe.

The European wisent, like its American cousin, has been largely obliterated from the scene by the efforts of *Homo* so-called *sapiens.* In Eastern Europe and in the United States today selected preserves contain the last remnants of a breed that once covered the forests and plains of two continents. In America, too, the bison lived in woodlands as well as on the plains with which we normally associate them. Before hunting altered their ancestral patterns, they thundered from sea nearly to sea. (Imagine buffalo in Manhattan, before the Manhattan Indians came.) What the Indians began the Europeans accelerated with a vengeance. Within a single day William F. Cody, the celebrated huntsman and guide of royalty, is said to have killed sixty-nine buffalos singlehandedly, to settle a bet with a friend. This at a time when the beasts were so numerous that picking them off from a slow-moving train was a popular tourist sport.

The decimation of a species, of course, is not a matter of grave concern to "civilized" peoples. To the aboriginal nomads whom the railroad and the army and the farmer were displacing, the passing of the buffalo meant the end. The tribes and the buffalo were one: two halves of a symbiotic system in which the beasts provided everything the humans needed, and the humans in turn kept their numbers down. When white hunters destroyed that balance, the demise of Indian culture was inevitable. Phil Sheridan, the Civil War general who later managed many Indian campaigns, once observed that buffalo hunters had done more to "settle the Indian question" than the army had done in thirty years. John Burke, *Buffalo Bill: The Noblest Whiteskin* (Putnam's, 1973).

WHAT MAKES A BUCKING BRONCO BUCK?

Folks unfamiliar with rodeos generally believe that bucking broncos and bulls just naturally like to rip-snort around: It's their natural assertiveness, their love of independence, that makes them want to hurl riders off their backs. This is partly true, but in fact, their natural instincts are seldom enough for the rodeo circuit. To enhance their desire to buck, a strap called a flank girth is tied tightly around their sensitive flanks while they are still in the chute; it's the resulting discomfort that makes these "natural" buckers go wild. Douglas Kent Hall, *Let 'Er Buck!* (Saturday Review Press/Dutton, 1973); Giles Tipette, *The Brave Men* (Macmillan, 1972).

WHAT ANIMAL GIVES US CATGUT?

Etymologically, the word "catgut" obviously refers to the guts, or intestines, of the cat, and since catgut has been used for centuries for stringing musical instruments, it has been suggested that the name arose because of the screeching, "caterwauling" sound emitted by these instruments in the hands of a poor player. It is not known whether or not cats' intestines were ever used for this purpose, though; virtually all catgut strings are made of *sheep's* intestines, with a few exceptions in the past having been of horse or ass guts. *Oxford English Dictionary* (Oxford, 1961).

WHY DO BIRDS FLY SOUTH FOR THE WINTER?

Any child can tell you that birds go south for the winter for the same reason that college students go to Fort Lauderdale: It's just too cold in the north. But this explanation, obvious as it seems, does not really account for the complexities of bird migration; specifically, it does not explain why some birds take flight for "warmer" climates long before cold weather sets in—in other words, long before the reduction of available food becomes so severe that they must either take off or starve.

Theories of bird migration used to revolve around the notion that it was an ancestral habit picked up no later than Pleistocene times: Modern birds migrate, it was suggested, in response to ancient ice shifts, or in search of an ancestral winter home, destroyed when the continents divided. Contemporary ornithologists put less weight on these speculative scenarios and seek to explain the birds' behavior in terms of complex physiological and environmental factors. Chief among these are 1) the influence of changing photoperiods, which affect the birds' hormonal systems, fat deposition, and consequent readiness for flight, and 2) the influence of changing weather, which seems to act as a catalyst in their ultimate decision to leave.

Fat deposition seems crucial to this curious annual phenomenon. Because it takes so much energy to migrate, birds must store enormous quantities of fat before they are ready to fly: A skinny bird could not make the journey, since fat is the airborne "fuel." The accumulation of this fuel, it has been shown, is influenced by the birds' pituitary glands, and these in turn are influenced by varying day length and sunshine. All of this takes place long before temperature change sets in. So while it is true that autumn chills kick off the journey, the birds have been packing for that journey in the warmest months of the year. They may not "know" the snows are coming, but their pituitary glands certainly do. "Animal Migration" in *Encyclopaedia Britannica* (1976); Josselyn Van Tyne and Andrew Berger, *Fundamentals of Ornithology* (Wiley, 1976).

OSTRICHES DO NOT HIDE THEIR HEADS IN THE SAND.

Ostriches may not be the whiz kids of the bird world, but they are certainly not so stupid as to suppose that sticking their heads in sand can save them from a hungry predator or the vanity of milliners' clients. The "head in the sand" story is a myth that began among the ancient Arabs and was passed on by credulous writers from Roman naturalists on. It may have been inspired by the fact that ostriches occasionally sleep with their necks extended along the ground, or the fact that, when running away from danger, they sometimes adopt the same posture momentarily, either to listen at the ground or, thinking they have already escaped, to rest. Bernhard Grzimek notes that young ostriches are particularly fond of such impromptu siestas.

The great flightless birds, which are related to the rheas, moas, cassowaries, kiwis, and emus, would have no need of such a foolish stratagem, anyway—even if it worked. Their hearing and eyesight are so good that they generally are the first on a plain to spot danger; as a result they frequently act as "unintentional but reliable sentinels" for duller-sighted antelopes and gazelles. They are phenomenal runners, leaping ten or twelve feet high in full stride, and reaching speeds of over thirty-five miles an hour. Even when they are cornered, they are not totally at a loss, since they are powerful kickers as well: In the Hanover Zoo a while back, an ostrich bent a quarter-inch-thick iron bar into a right angle with a single blow of its leg.

This means nothing against a gun, of course, and in the last century, when ostrich feathers became fashionable, the birds were almost wiped out by hunters supplying miladies in Mayfair. Oddly enough, it was the opening of ostrich farms that saved their necks. Bred for market, they soon became less rare; consequently, the demand for their feathers went down, and like the chinchilla and the sable, they were saved from extinction. This is known as the domestication of folly.   *Grzimek's Animal Life Encyclopedia* (Van Nostrand Reinhold, 1975).

WHAT IS THE LARGEST MEMBER OF THE CAT FAMILY?

Although the lion is commonly called "the king of beasts," it is not the largest of the great cats, or felids, as the scientists call them. That honor belongs to its lesser-sung but much more powerful cousin, the tiger. Male lions *(Leo leo)* are generally six to eight feet long (excluding the tail), about three feet high at the shoulder, and four to five hundred pounds in weight. The tiger *(Panthera tigris)* can exceed that by a foot in length, several inches in height, and a hundred pounds in weight. The massive Siberian tiger, which like most tigers is an endangered species, is really the king of the felids.   Everett Sentman, "Lion" and "Tiger," in *Academic American Encyclopedia* (1980).

NOT ALL MAMMALS BEAR LIVE YOUNG.

In high-school biology you learn that one of the distinguishing characteristics of the mammals is that they bear their young live; indeed, live birth is often thought of as the magical border separating us "higher" animals from our inferior, egg-laying cousins. The exceptions that disprove this rule are to be found in the order Monotremata, containing five species of spiny anteaters and the bizarre, single-species duck-billed platypus. All six of these animals are found in Australia, and all of them are oviparous, which is to say, they lay eggs.

These egg-laying mammals were discovered only toward the end of the last century, and the initial reaction in Europe was pretty skeptical. The platypus in particular, with its broad flat bill and its webbed *and* clawed feet, was thought to be not a real animal at all but a hoax, like the stuffed "mermaids" of the time, which turned out to be monkey's heads sewn onto fish tails. Only after zoologists found and killed pregnant monotremes in the wild were their colleagues convinced. W. H. Caldwell, for example, dissected a just-killed platypus in 1884 and discovered in the oviduct a large-yolked egg, of the type scientists called "meroblastic." He sent an immediate telegram to Montreal, where the British Zoological Society was convening, to register his discovery with remarkably economic zeal: It read simply, "Monotremes oviparous, ovum meroblastic." *Grzimek's Animal Life Encyclopedia* (Van Nostrand Reinhold, 1975).

PORCUPINES DO NOT THROW THEIR QUILLS.

Since antiquity people have believed that in order to protect themselves, porcupines hurl their quills at aggressors. Aristotle said that the animals employ them like darts to repulse hunters and dogs. Isidore of Seville, several centuries later, spoke of the humming of these darts as they flew through the air, and William Shakespeare, in *Hamlet,* referred to "the terrible porcupine." These authorities have plenty of company in the general population: Even today, city folks on a weekend camping trip are cautioned to watch for skunks who throw their scent and porcupines who throw their quills.

The latter is an unnecessary worry. The porcupine's quills are indeed a defensive adaptation, but there is no real evidence that their use of them involves throwing. Usually, when they are threatened, they turn their backs to the antagonist, extend their quills so they bristle, and sometimes shake their bodies, so that they resemble dancing pincushions. In the course of this defensive maneuvering, loose quills occasionally are dislodged, and a quill shaken loose, it is true, can become embedded in the attacking animal. But that is accidental, not planned. If porcupines could effectively use their quills as darts, no dog would dare threaten them, and experienced hunting dogs frequently overpower the animals.

This does not mean that you should approach a frightened

porcupine lightly. Their quills can do you damage, if you are careless enough to get stuck. They can grow well over a foot long, and the tips of some of them are equipped with bristles and hooks that can cause a painful injury. African hunters, in fact, used to use the quills as dart and arrow points. The traditional view is hyperbole, but the reality can be unpleasant enough. *Grzimek's Animal Life Encyclopedia* (Van Nostrand Reinhold, 1975).

WHERE ARE THE FOLLOWING DOGS FROM?

a) Afghan hound,
b) Brittany spaniel, and
c) Great Dane.

a) *Afghan hound.* The elegant, long-haired Afghan, now so prized as a show dog, was originally, like its cousin the greyhound, used for hunting gazelles, foxes, and other game. Europeans first encountered the breed toward the end of the nineteenth century, when Victorian England and czarist Russia both had their eyes on unhospitable, but strategically important, Afghanistan. The first Afghan to reach the British Isles arrived in 1894. Afghanistan, though, was not the dogs' first home. An Egyptian papyrus from the third millennium B.C. refers to "a baboon- or monkey-faced hound," and illustrations on contemporary tombs suggest that this hound was, in fact, the Afghan. Three millennia before that, the ancient inhabitants of Greece depicted such a dog in fabric, and a legend persists in the Middle East that the dogs saved from the flood by Noah were these same wiry, aristocratic hounds. How they traveled from the Eastern Mediterranean to Afghanistan is not known.

b) *Brittany spaniel.* The world's only pointing spaniel, the Brittany spaniel, like its working relations the setters and pointers, is principally a sporting dog, used by bird hunters to locate fowl. In spite of the designation "Brittany," it is more likely that the dog originated in Spain than in France. "Spaniel," it is believed, is a corruption of "Español," so that this entire group of bird dogs may have gotten its start south of the Pyrennees. The breed was widely used in Brittany, expecially by British fowlers who found the area a congenial hunting spot, and the Brittany branch of the spaniels, it is likely, was inbred with English setters centuries ago. This gives them an Anglo-Iberian descent.

c) *Great Dane.* These stately, gentle dogs were bred originally to attack and destroy wild boar: hence, their massive size and the custom, still widely observed, of cropping their ears lest they be torn in battle. Similar dogs were known as far back as the Fourth Dynasty of Egypt, but it was in Germany that the breed reached perfection. They were considered indispensable there as guard dogs for palaces and castles, and the nation's Iron Chancellor, Bismarck, kept them as personal bodyguards. "Great Dane" is a translation of the old French term *grand Danois,* which was (and is) a misnomer, since the breed has no connection with Denmark. An alternate French term *dogue Allemand,* which may be translated "German mastiff," has been lost but is far more accurate. Stanley Dangerfield and Elsworth Howell, eds., *The International Encyclopedia of Dogs* (McGraw-Hill, 1971).

WHAT SMALL ANIMALS ARE ELEPHANTS AFRAID OF?

The notion that the world's largest land animal can be sent into a tizzy by one of the smallest animals appeals to our sense of paradox and also alleviates any doubts we may entertain about which species is lord of the earth. Since elephants are huge, immensely strong, intelligent, unaggressive, and kindly, they must be given an Achilles' heel in compensation, lest they seem nobler than ourselves. Let it be timidity; let us say that a pachyderm will run from a mouse.

By some such process of self-elevation, perhaps, was hatched the belief that elephants are afraid of mice. Bernhard Grzimek has demonstrated that it is quite fallacious. Testing several elephants' timidity against a number of small animals, he found that among those that made the beasts really nervous were rabbits and, of all things, dachshunds. Perhaps the elephants were unsettled by the skitteriness of these creatures; when they were placed nearby, the elephants "moved back in fear and threw sand and rocks . . . by stamping their feet against the ground." When the same experiment was tried with mice, no such nervousness was displayed. The elephants merely inspected the rodents with their trunks, and then stomped them underfoot.

It used to be thought, by folks who never tried this experiment, that the reason elephants were afraid of mice was that mice could scurry up their trunks, and thus interfere with their breathing. Nobody likes a mouse up the nose, but this explanation is still hooey: Even if a mouse did happen to make its way up an elephant's trunk (an extremely unlikely prospect), the beast could easily dislodge it merely by blowing outward. Any animal that can shoot a bucketful of water into its mouth with its trunk (they drink through their mouths, not their trunks) would surely have no trouble with a mouse. *Grzimek's Animal Life Encyclopedia* (Van Nostrand Reinhold, 1975).

SNAKE CHARMERS DO NOT HYPNOTIZE THEIR REPTILIAN FRIENDS WITH FLUTES.

Since the legendary days of ancient Greece, humans have wanted to believe that they have not quite lost the art of communicating with animals. In one of the oldest of Hellenic folktales, Orpheus is accorded the privilege of soothing beasts by his transcendent touch on the lyre. The Pied Piper legend continues the myth with more modern, sadistic overtones.

Music may or may not have charms to soothe the savage beast, but one beast it will never soothe is the snake. In spite of the popular notion that snakes are hypnotized by the music of rustic flutes, it is not the music, but the swaying of the flutes, the rhythmic undulation of those tweeting magic wands, that apparently makes them docile. Experimenters have tried to show that snakes can be made to respond to certain electrical vibrations, but the biological consensus remains that snakes do not hear as we do, and certainly not well enough to respond to music. They are virtually earless as well as hairless. The music, in a snake charmer's act, therefore, is strictly for the humans in the audience. Herndon Dowling, "Snake," *in Encyclopedia Americana* (1979).

WHAT IS THE MONGOOSE'S FAVORITE PREY?

Thanks to Rudyard Kipling's classic story "Rikki-Tikki-Tavi," many of us have grown up thinking that the mongoose and the cobra are sworn-for-life enemies, and that it is the chief delight of

Rikki's relatives to hunt down, confront, and dispatch snakes of any description at all. This is a distortion of the facts. There are several species of mongoose inhabiting areas of south Asia, Africa, the East Indies, and Spain, and although many of them will kill and eat venomous snakes, the reptiles do not by any means comprise the major portion of their diet—or of their entertainment. Mongooses are omniverous carnivores, and will eat pretty much anything in their path, including small rodents, birds, eggs, shellfish, fruit, and a wide variety of insects. Most mongooses exist largely on insects and spiders, while certain species have very specialized diets: One African species favors crocodile eggs, and an Indian variety subsists almost entirely on crab.

Rikki's antagonism toward snakes, therefore, was a bit idiosyncratic. Mongooses can and do kill cobras, the cobra being a relatively slow striker and thus farily easy to dispatch. But against other snakes the mongoose does not always fare so well. Fights staged in the West Indies between the Indian mongoose and pit vipers gave most of the victories to the latter, and many observers have reported that when confronted by snakes, mongooses prefer to keep their distance than to fight.

Even in India, where Rikki's exploits took place, cobras and mongooses in the wild tend to ignore each other. Mongooses are not immune to snakebite, although they are very resistant, and there is much evidence that in the long-running snake-mongoose feud, the snake is a little ahead. In Trinidad, where boa constrictors eat mongooses, snakes are an insignificant portion of the mongoose diet, and almost all of those killed are nonpoisonous. The Caribbean mongooses must know something that Kipling and his hero did not.   H. E. Hinton and A. M. S. Dunn, *Mongooses: Their Natural History and Behavior* (University of California Press, 1967).

WHAT'S THE MOST POISONOUS SPIDER?

The spiders of the genus *Latrodectus* are the most notorious of all arachnids. With their glistening black bodies, their bright red or white markings, and the female's reputation for devouring her mate, the "widow" spiders seem to have earned their name; if you're bitten by a black widow, popular wisdom says, you may as well start making out your will.

This bad reputation is not really deserved. The black widow (the common name for three species of *Latrodectus*) can inflict a painful bite, and it's true that some of those bitten die within a day or so of asphyxiation: The venom, which is neurotoxic, stiffens the internal muscles, causing convulsions and ultimately strangulation. But most of those bitten survive, and, in addition, it has been shown that the widows, like most spiders, are timid and show no special inclination to bite humans. Even when disturbed in their webs, they prefer to run than fight.

Tarantulas, too, have gotten a worse press than they deserve. These large hairy beasts look so fierce that they have been unjustly labeled as dangerous. Some South American species are deadly, but most tarantulas are pretty tame, their bites being no worse than a bee sting. Some folks even keep them as pets.

The spider you really *should* fear is the *Loxosceles reclusa,* the "brown recluse" of the central and southwestern states. This is a yellowish brown spider less than a half inch in length, with long legs and a violin-shaped dark spot on its carapace. This spot gives it its other common name, violin spider, and also makes it easy to identify. Which is a good thing, considering that the recluse likes to sleep under piles of dirty clothes, in dark closets, and behind furniture.

The toxin of these spiders, which is much more virulent than that of black widows, causes fever, nausea, skin loss, ulceration, and damage to the liver and kidneys. There are medications that are effective against the toxin (corticosteroids are commonly used), but getting bitten is still no fun. The last person I knew who had been kissed by one of these little devils was on his back in the hospital for a week.   B. J. Kaston, *How to Know the Spiders* (Wm. C. Brown Co., 1978).

WHY DO BIRDS SING?

Contrary to the wishful thinking of songwriters, birdsong has little to do with contentment, love, or good spirits. Birds do not sing because they are happy, or to welcome the sunrise, or to croon each other lullabies. The great majority of bird sounds serve a far more serious function, or rather set of functions, since it is now clear to ornithologists that avian song can be broken down into a small number of distinct categories.

The major categories are three. Birds sing firstly to announce their presence within a given territory, secondly to coordinate some activity with a mate, and only thirdly as an aesthetic or purely "emotional" exercise. These three types of song—advertising song, signal song, and emotional song—are varieties of *primary song;* ornithologists also recognize varieties of soft, nonterritorial *secondary song,* such as the "whisper song" by which the bird repeats "under its breath" the notes of the primary song, and the trial attempts by young birds that are called "rehearsal songs." In addition, birds emit *call notes,* which are shorter, less melodious utterances designed to register alarm and coordinate defensive activities.

Birdsong varies considerably from species to species, and is also affected by the time of day and season of the year. Songs are more frequent during the nesting season, while daily variations may have something to do with light intensity: At least this seems to be the case among birds who sing at dawn. A few species, moreover, sing continuously from sunup to sundown, with some warblers producing over a thousand songs in a day. The record songster, though, was a red-eyed vireo observed by a birdwatcher in the 1950s: In a single day, it gave out 22,197 songs. It sounds like a joyous feat, but it was probably borne of worry. The most likely explanation of the bird's virtuosity is that it feared invasion of its turf. Josselyn Van Tyne and Andrew Berger, *Fundamentals of Ornithology* (Wiley, 1976).

LEMMINGS DO NOT MARCH TO THE SEA AND DROWN.

That plucky, prolific little rodent, the Scandinavian lemming, has had a bad reputation for centuries. In the 1500s it was believed that lemmings were generated spontaneously in clouds, fell to the earth in massive swarms, and devoured everything in their way, like a misplaced Egyptian "plague." More recently, they have been characterized as stupid rather than vicious. In the popular view, once a year they leave the safety of their tundra homes to hurl themselves foolishly into the sea: People who have never seen a lemming, speak confidently of the animals' "suicidal urge," and think of "lemminglike" behavior as the blind following of a leader to destruction.

This is unfair to the species. Lemmings do undertake hazardous mass migrations, but these are neither annual occurrences nor as mindlessly "suicidal" as the popular picture suggests. The animals are incredibly prolific, with one lemming mother sometimes bearing over twenty young in a year; as a result, overpopulation is a constant problem, and it is this problem that the migrations seem designed to alleviate. When the food supply in a given region is nearly depleted, the animals pick up and take off, seeking greener pastures and elbow room. They may wander for weeks at a time, losing numbers along the way, until they are suitably reduced to enable them to utilize the vegetation properly, and it is because of this attrition that they may seem bent on "killing themselves." Actually, the destructive journeys serve as a population check, which ensures the species' survival.

As for the "march to the sea," that is pure hyperbole. Migrating lemmings do cross wide bodies of water, and many drown in the process, but they are fair swimmers, and the best evidence suggests that when they plunge into a lake or stream, they have every intention of getting to the other side, and drown only when they misgauge the distance. No doubt lemmings have been swallowed up by the ocean, but not as a regular pattern: If suicide in the surf were a pattern, the breed would have died out long ago.

Walter Marsden suggests that the belief about mass suicide may be "an awesome parable of original sin" or "an unconscious transfer of human guilt and expiation feelings" into the scurrying horde. They may serve, in folk tradition, as a kind of communal scape-beast, first visiting wrath on farmers by ravaging their crops, then expiating their sins by washing them clean in the sea. It's a provocative speculation, though a heavy burden to lay on an animal only six inches long.   Walter Marsden, *The Lemming Year* (Chatto & Windus, 1964).

RABBITS ARE NOT RODENTS.

Because of their prominent incisors, rabbits used to be classed as rodents, and among nonscientists, that classification has stuck. But it's an outmoded view. Rodents, such as squirrels, hamsters, beavers, and mice, characteristically chew their food in an up-and-down gnawing manner; the word "rodent" comes from the Latin *rodere,* to gnaw. Rabbits, along with hares and pikas, chew in a lateral fashion, and are also morphologically distinct from the rodents; taxonomists call them all *lagomorphs* (from the Greek *lagos,* for "hare").

Lagomorphs, in spite of their similarity in appearance to the rodents, are actually morphologically closer to the large, hoofed beasts, such as camels and cows. They share with these animals a kind of two-phase digestive system, but with a curious twist. In ruminants like the cows, food is chewed, swallowed, regurgitated, chewed, and swallowed again; the chewing of the partially digested cud is what makes the animal a ruminant. In the rabbits and hares, food is eaten, passed through the entire digestive system, excreted in both hard and soft pellets, and then the soft pellets are eaten again. The "cud" of these ex-rodents thus passes through the entire body twice.   *Grzimek's Animal Life Encyclopedia* (Van Nostrand Reinhold, 1975).

BEARS DO NOT SLEEP THROUGH THE WINTER.

Bears are not true hibernators. They do "den in" for the winter, but their activity in the den is distinct from what zoologists call hibernation. In hibernation, an animal's body temperature drops dramatically, breathing and heartbeat slow down, a general torpor sets in, and external bodily functions cease. Bears enter their lethargic winter state in response to the same stimuli—cold, hunger, darkness, and quiet—that impel other animals to hibernate, and they make preparations similar to those of hibernators: They acquire a layer of fat, seclude themselves, and gradually reduce their movements. But whereas in the smaller, true hibernators this leads to a very low body temperature and a lengthy period of unconsciousness, in the bear the reaction is less severe. Body temperature drops only slightly, the animals remain drowsy rather than dormant, and physiological functions—such as suckling the cubs, who are usually born in January—continue without alteration. Many male bears remain active all winter long, sleeping lightly not in dens but on the ground. Remember this the next time you come upon a "hibernating" mound of fur in the woods.   Ann Haven Morgan, *Field Book of Animals in Winter* (Putnam's, 1939).

SNAKES ARE NOT SLIMY AND COLD.

It's amazing what people will believe about snakes. Since ancient times these lithe, elegant reptiles have been both revered and abhorred, as emblems of the mysterious, the tempting, the unknown; the number of myths associated with them has been very little reduced by the rise of modern "reason." Among the snake tales that have persisted in certain areas to the present day are the following quaint phantasms:

• That a rattlesnake's age can be determined by counting the number of its rattles—and that this snake always gives a "warning" by shaking those rattles before it strikes

• That the milk snake is so named because it attacks cows at night, "milking" them with its fangs and thus depriving its calves of nourishment

• That the "hoop snake" takes its tail in its mouth and rolls after you like a frenzied hula hoop

• That snakes hypnotize their victims before striking by staring directly into their eyes

• That placing a horsehair or a cowhair rope around you on the ground will keep you safe from rattlers as you sleep, since snakes will not cross such a rope; and

• That whiskey, juniper berries, or two scoops of pistachio ice cream will save your life if you are bitten.

All these notions are nonsense, as is the far more common idea that snake's skin is clammy and cold. Snakes are cold-blooded creatures, so their skin is usually colder than ours, especially if the temperature is low. But on a warm day, after a snake's been lying around in the sun, its skin is warm and dry. The only time it gets at all moist is when it's just come out of the water. Your skin is probably far clammier than that of your neighborhood snake. Roy Pinney, *The Snake Book* (Doubleday, 1981).

SHARKS ARE NOT VORACIOUS KILLERS.

Thanks to the mechanical monster "Bruce" of Steven Spielberg's *Jaws*, sharks have now replaced snakes as the most feared animals alive—in spite of the fact that, according to veteran shark researcher Eugenie Clark, "It is far safer to swim with these animals than to drive on an average city street or highway." The popular image of the shark has been established by the scanty and sensational information we have about that most fearsome member of the breed, the great white. It's Ms. Clark's contention that this is pretty unfair; there is, she says, no such thing as *the* shark—sharks are a large and fascinating group of extremely varied animals.

Even the great white, that notorious people-eater, probably attacks only in defense of its supposed territory, and not in response to some imagined primitive "urge to kill"; the number of people who die each year because of shark attacks rarely exceeds ten or twelve, and that's all types of sharks, worldwide. The great white, moreover, is the only shark that normally feeds on "objects as large as humans." The vast majority are what zoologist William Beebe calls "chinless cowards," and three species—the mammoth whale shark, the basking shark, and the recently discovered "megamouth"—feed exclusively on plankton. The nearly three hundred and fifty species in this "killer" group of fish include such oddities as the grotesque "pig shark," which feeds on sea urchins and mollusks; the sprawling "angel shark," which looks like (and is often confused with) a ray; and the diminutive "devil shark," a deep-dwelling phosphorescent variety that is all of one foot long.

Ms. Clark, who has studied sharks for more than twenty-five years, feels that they have a lot more to fear from us than we do from them. Certain species, such as the indolent basking sharks, are being widely hunted by the Japanese, while along Australian and South African beaches, many hundreds of sharks are killed yearly in nets designed to protect bathers. Sharks present no risk to our species, she says, but unfortunately the reverse is not true. "When it comes to sharing the sea, we insist that the sharks take all the risks." Eugenie Clark, "Sharks: Magnificent and Misunderstood," in *National Geographic* (August 1981).

JACKALS ARE NOT CRAVEN SCAVENGERS.

The popular image of the jackal is that of a slinking, shifty-eyed low dog, whimpering around the heels of the real macho beasts, the leopards and lions, for a stray bone shoved their way. Jackals are dogs, all right (like the domestic dogs, they are in the *Canis* group), but the rest of the picture is bunk. As field worker

Patricia Moehlman has shown, the African jackal is a hardworking, family-conscious hunter whose occasional scavenged meals are few and far between.

Jackals mate for life, often live in extended families, and are intensely protective of younger siblings. Some of their diet, it's true, consists of leavings from larger beasts, but the bulk of it they win by their own courageousness and agility: Only in times of privation do they have to forgo their customary diet of fruit, rodents, and other small animals to horn in on the big cats' prey. And they are no more craven than they are lazy: In defense of their dens, jackals are known to have taken on cheetahs, vultures, hyenas, honey badgers, and lions. Not too bad for cowards. Patricia D. Moehlman, "Jackals of the Serengeti," in *National Geographic* (December 1980).

HOW BLIND IS A BAT?

"Blind as a bat" entered the vernacular as a metaphor for total sightlessness long before anyone had ever heard of echolocation. Now that we understand something about that mysterious sonar-like mechanism, the sightlessness of these flying mammals seems even more certain: If they can get around so well by bouncing sound waves off objects, what use would they have of eyes?

It's true that most bats do not see very well (although all have working eyes), but in the members of one suborder, Megachiroptera, eyesight has evolved quite well, and echolocation is used hardly at all. These Old World "fruit bats" have large, specially adapted eyes that enable them to see well in dim light; they navigate by means of sight, and locate the fruit and flowers on which they feed by smell. Of the fruit bats, only the members of the genus *Rousettus*, which live in caves, have the ability to navigate by sound. Lacking this ability, the others must rely on sight: They are the eagles of a half-blind world. Clive Roots, *Animals of the Dark* (Praeger, 1974).

WHAT BIRD SEES IN THE DARK?

Owls are such effective nocturnal hunters that it's often supposed they can see in total darkness. Poetic license, and the legends of many lands, have given them almost supernatural powers of seeing. "With Wisdom's eyes," poet Joel Peters once observed, "Athena's bird turns darkness into light." This must be taken as metaphor, not fact. Owls do have exceptionally sharp eyes, but, as naturalists John Sparks and Tony Soper note, all eyes are *light receptors;* "the generously proportioned ones of owls are no exception." An owl in total darkness, therefore, would be as blind as you or I. Fortunately for them, "total darkness" exists in nature only in subterranean caves, where the birds do none of their hunting.

As for that "Wisdom's eyes," the wiseness of owls is legendary, but only that. Athena, Greek goddess of wisdom, took the bird as her personal symbol, but there is no evidence that she was much of a naturalist. The great raptors of the night were first associated with wisdom, no doubt, because of their immobility and silence. If still waters really do run deep, then the owl might easily be taken for a Buddha. In the anonymous traditional poem we read:

A wise old owl sat in an oak;
The more he saw the less he spoke;
The less he spoke the more he heard;
Why can't we all be like that wise old bird?

Good advice, though we might be wary of concluding that *all* silence is a mask for wisdom. There are as many quiet dullards as Buddhas. Maybe the owl is silent because it can't think of anything to say.   John Sparks and Tony Soper, *Owls: Their Natural and Unnatural History* (David & Charles, 1970).

WHAT FARM ANIMAL IS FILTHY AND STUPID?

Pity the poor pig. For ages it's been assumed that the entire porcine population loves nothing better than to muck about in the muck, while its genius colleagues the horses and the cows do second-degree equations in their heads. Think of the names we give the poor critters. Swine. Hogs. Sow. Every one of them an insult to us nonfilthy, nonstupid humans. To all of us raised on the conventional image of the farm, the pig is dirty and dumb.

Farmers, however, do not agree with us. At least not all of them do. Roger North, a British keeper of pigs, claimed that "contrary to popular belief, the pig is extremely clean if allowed to live in a clean condition." Pigs are dirty, he says, because their owners don't have the decency to clean their sties regularly, but prefer to let the muck pile up in the mistaken belief that on the outlook for a good place to wallow in the heat, swine will choose swill every time. Actually, they will choose whatever they have at hand; there is no evidence (since nobody has ever tested for it) that pigs prefer mud to clean pens.

As for brains, it's hard to understand how the notion got started that swine are fat between the ears. Numerous farmers have pointed out that pigs have been known, regularly, to open complicated bolts on gates, to seek greener pastures or the call of swinish amour. North says, "If that is not intelligence in an animal, I don't know what is."   A. S. E. Ackermann, *Popular Fallacies* (1950; repr. Gale Research, 1970).

HOW MANY EYES DOES A FOUR-EYED FISH HAVE?

Anableps anableps, a curious toothed carp of Central and South American rivers, is called the four-eyed fish because its eyes are adapted to enable it to see above and below the water surface simultaneously. Each eye is divided by a slender band of skin. Above the band, the eye focuses on flying insects; below it, on underwater prey. Lying on the surface, the fish may thus appear to have four distinct eyes, but, in fact, each of its two divided eyes has but a single lens.

In the past icthyologists have occasionally referred to members of the *Chaetodon* family as four-eyed fish as well. There is no morphological justification for this. These gaily colored "butterfly fish" (relatives of the angelfish) sport prominent dark spots near their tails, which whimsical taxonomists used to identify as extra "eyes." Their actual eyes are conventional and undivided.   John Oliver La Gorce, ed., *The Book of Fishes* (National Geographic Society, 1939); *Grzimek's Animal Life Encyclopedia* (Van Nostrand Reinhold, 1975).

WHAT KIND OF BIRD IS A PUFFINUS PUFFINUS?

The Procellariidae family of birds includes fifty-three species of shearwaters, so named because, in their search for fish and squid, they characteristically sweep low and swiftly over the water. The *Puffinus* genus, which has nothing to do with puffins, includes *P. puffinus,* the Manx shearwater; *P. pacificus,* the wedge-tailed shearwater; and *P. tenuirostris,* the short-tailed shearwater. All are great flyers, and the short-tailed species is exceptional: Its migratory zone extends from Australia to the Bering Strait.

The puffins belong to an entirely different family, the Alcidae or auks, a kind of northern penguin, but related to the gulls. Like the *Puffinus* genus, puffins are colonial shorebirds, but as flyers they're strictly bush league. The now extinct Great Auk, in fact, couldn't fly at all, and most of its surviving relations are better at diving for food (like ducks) than at "shearing" the waves. These richly colored, exotic birds are rapidly on the decline—victims of industrial spillage. Ornithologist Bruce Campbell notes their only chance of avoiding extinction: "Provided we stop using the sea as a dump, and that we run out of oil within the next twenty years as predicted, it is just possible that some of these birds will survive."   Bruce Campbell, *The Dictionary of Birds in Color* (Viking, 1974); Josselyn Van Tyne and Andrew Berger, *Fundamentals of Ornithology* (Wiley, 1976).

WHAT KIND OF ANIMAL IS A KOALA?

In the stuffed-toy industry, the koala is giving old teddy a run for his money; thousands of American kids now go to sleep clutching their "koala bears," and you even find the littlest ones being referred to as "cubs." Even in Australia, where they ought to know better, a pet name for the cuddlies is "Teddy Bear."

But koalas are marsupials, not bears. Like kangaroos, bandicoots, and wombats, they carry their young in a pouch. You won't find a grizzly doing that. Or spending its whole life up a tree. Nor do koalas live entirely on eucalyptus leaves. Those leaves are their preferred diet—so much so that they commonly smell of eucalyptus—but in a pinch they will eat the leaves of the box tree, and even nibble on mistletoe.   Ernest P. Walker, *Mammals of the World* (Johns Hopkins University Press, 1975).

WHALEBONE IS NOT BONE.

For much of the nineteenth century, when the underwear industry enjoyed its finest hour, the retaining ribs, or "stays," of corsets were made of a substance called whalebone. Firm yet flexible, it remained a valued raw material for corset makers until steel and synthetic materials edged it out of the market. In the early part of the century a ton of whalebone might be worth well over two thousand British pounds, and since a single bowhead whale might yield a ton and a half of the stuff, one of these giants dead might be worth seven or eight thousand dollars, for the whalebone alone.

"Whalebone," however, is a misnomer. The whales which yield whalebone are in the *Mystacoceti* group, and are called "baleen" whales because of a peculiar feeding apparatus that they carry in their mouths. This apparatus, called baleen, is the whale "bone" of popular usage. It consists of "winglike horn plates hanging from the palate, one behind the other, which are equipped with fembriae (fringes) on the inner border." Baleen whales eat plankton, small fish, and crustaceans, and the apparatus that gives them their name is actually a mammoth straining system that enables them to squeeze their food out of vast quantities of ingested water.

The baleen of the bowhead whale was particularly prized for corsets, not only because it was more suitable for stays than the baleen of other species but also because the whale itself was relatively easy to capture. Other baleen species are the right whales, the humpback whales, and the earth's largest-ever living creature, the blue whale. All of these are threatened with extinction, and the bowhead whale remains the rarest of all whale species. A heavy price to pay for the luxury of an eighteen-inch waist. *Grzimek's Animal Life Encyclopedia* (Van Nostrand Reinhold, 1975).

PLANTS:

WHAT COLOR IS GRASS?

Most of us see grass as a uniformly green substance whose function is to serve as lawn. Yet the grass that covers America from patio to fairway represents only a fraction of the planet's various grasses. Grasses cover a third of the earth's land, and even if they are less decorative than a suburban lawn, they are economically of infinitely greater value.

To botanists, a grass is "a plant in the Grass family," that huge collection of flowing grains classified officially as Gramineae. They have narrow leaves with parallel veins and small inconspicuous flowers (yes, flowers), and they come in a variety of shades. Timothy grass and wheat can run from various shades of green to tan; purple love grass, barnyard grass, and northern dropseed come in differing shades of purple, from straight purple with the first to black with the last; prairies three-awn is a lovely shade of white; and tall oats grass ranges from green to purple to silver.

In spite of the garden industry's success in convincing most of us that lawnliness is next to godliness, a neatly mowed lawn is, in terms of economic efficiency, a pretty bad business. It takes a lot of energy to keep a lawn from doing what it wants to do naturally—which is to revert to forest or weed—and after spending that energy, you cannot even eat it. Not so with the world's other grasses. For most of the people of the world, grass is a staple of life: Entire cultures subsist on rice or corn, while even as profligate a civilization as ours would find it difficult to do without oats, barley, wheat, or rye.   Lauren Brown, *Grasses: An Identification Guide* (Houghton Mifflin, 1979).

WHAT KIND OF TREE IS POISON OAK?

The members of the Rhus family are trouble. Imbued with a resinous irritant called urushiol, they are responsible for the majority of cases of skin poisoning by plants in the United States. The most populous (not to say popular) species of this group is the trifoliate imp *Rhus toxicodendron,* which, although it is known as both poison oak and poison ivy, is neither an oak nor an ivy. Nor is its cousin *Rhus vernix,* commonly known as poison sumac, very similar, at least in behavior, to the majority of sumacs. Poison sumac is also known in Latin as *Toxicodendron vernix* and, in English, as poison dogwood, poison elder, and poison ash, which will give you some idea of the confusion involved with these plants. Among the few things about them that are not confusing are the fact that they make everybody who touches them (even those who claim to be "immune") itch like the devil and the fact that according to the taxonomists, they belong to the family Anacardiaceae, which makes them, in a word, cashews.   Walter Conrad Muenscher, *Poisonous Plants of the United States* (Macmillan, 1961).

WHAT'S THE DIFFERENCE BETWEEN A MUSHROOM AND A TOADSTOOL?

In his charming treatise on the edible fungi, mycologist W. Hamilton Gibson describes an interview between himself and a "rustic mushroom oracle" that, he says, illustrates the ease with which people can be scared away from "toadstools" by self-appointed sages. Gibson has just picked a basketful of wild mushrooms when the "authority" crosses his path.

" 'Ye ain't a-goin to eat *them,* air ye?' he asks, anxiously, by way of introduction.

" 'I am, most certainly,' I respond.

" 'Waal, then, I'll say good-bye to ye,' he responds with emphasis. 'Why, don't ye know them's tudstools, 'n' they'll kill ye *sartin* as *pizen?* I wonder they ain't fetched ye afore this. . . . Come into my garden yender 'n' I'll show ye how to tell the *reel mushroom.* ' "

The "real" mushroom, it turns out, is the variety called *Agaricus campestris;* all others, the "oracle" insists, will put you in your grave, because they are not mushrooms but toadstools. Shaking his head in dismay, Gibson leaves the man to his wisdom and goes home to cook up a batch of the delicious, despised "toadstools." They are, as he knows, quite harmless.

It's an extreme example, but illustrative of the nervousness that the ignorant have always brought to the subject of wild fungi. Because a few varieties are deadly, conservative gatherers steer clear of all but the safest, blandest types, while their more daring fellows, equipped with surefire "tests" for telling mushrooms from toadstools, frequently put themselves in the hospital. For the simple fact is that the rustic tests aside, the only way of determining whether or not a fungus is edible is to have an expert identify it. Mushroom is merely the popular term for "edible mushroom," and toadstool the popular term for its poisonous cousins. To a mycologist the terms are interchangeable.

The poisonous (and unidentifiable) mushrooms apparently began to be called toadstools in the late fourteenth century, when it was thought that "venomous" toads sat on and infected them. This was utter nonsense. *Amanita phalloides* needs no toad to make it deadly, and *Agaricus campestris* would remain harmless if sat on by an army of toads. The noisomeness of the inedible varieties comes from toxins that attack, generally, the human nervous and gastrointestinal systems. You may call the toxic mushrooms "toadstools" if you like, but from the scientist's point of view, the designation is meaningless.   W. Hamilton Gibson, *Our Edible Toadstools and Mushrooms and How to Distinguish Them* (Harper, 1899); R. T. and F. W. Rolfe, *The Romance of the Fungus World* (1925; repr. Johnson Reprint Corp., 1966).

WHAT COLOR GRAPES GIVE WHITE WINE?

Grapes come in a huge range of colors, but the ones that are used in winemaking—the fifty or so varieties of the species *Vitis vinifera*—are generally classified as either "white" or "black," with white grapes ranging in color from yellow to green and black grapes from red to bluish black. While red and rosé wines are made from the black grapes, it is not true that white wines are made only from the white. The deep colors of red wine come from the fruits' fermenting skins; as long as you remove the skin, you can make a perfectly acceptable white wine from either white or black grapes. Many light Rhine wines use the red-skinned Traminer grape, while the Semillon variety, which turns a musty brown when overripe, produces the golden Sauternes.   Alec Waugh, *Wines and Spirits* (Time-Life Books, 1968).

STRAWBERRIES ARE NOT BERRIES.

The succulent, aromatic strawberry is actually the fruit of a plant that belongs to the same family as the rose. An herb of the genus *Fragaria,* which is within the Rosaceae family, it has been cultivated in Europe since the fourteenth century and is now a popular cash crop throughout the temperate regions of the world. The part of the plant we eat is not a true berry, but a fleshy fruit receptacle, or *torus,* housing on its surface the plant's numerous single-seeded fruits; the presence of this torus makes the strawberry, like the blackberry and the raspberry, an "aggregate fruit." True berries, which have no such structure, are pulpy, pitless fruits in which the pericarp, or ovary wall, is mostly fleshy and soft. Examples include the blueberry, the grape—and the tomato. Richard S. Cowan, "Fruit," in *Encyclopedia Americana* (1976).

BAMBOO IS NOT A TREE.

Bamboo is a hardy, prolific, and extremely versatile plant whose usefulness in tropical climates is difficult to exaggerate. In many Asian countries, both the grain and the shoots are eaten; silica taken from the joints is used as a folk medicine; pipes and receptacles are made from the stems; split and flattened, these stems also provide material for weaving, planking, wickerwork, and thatching; the unsplit stem of the larger species is a strong and flexible timber. Without bamboo, Oriental material culture would have evolved in a dramatically different direction.

The plant is not a tree, in spite of its appearance, but a grass, belonging to the group Bambuseae, within the large Gramineae family. Of the more than two hundred species in this group, many are as tall as trees, though they reach their impressive height much faster than their woody lookalikes. Charles Snow reported that one Philippine specimen was measured at eighteen inches one day, and three days later had grown an additional two feet. Florida varieties, he said, were known to have reached heights of over seventy feet in one season. This gives the bamboo—which with the cane is the only grass that provides structural material—an advantage over the tree. Its stems are just as strong as wood, but far more easily replenished. "Bamboo" in

Encyclopedia Americana (1976); Charles Henry Snow, *The Principal Species of Wood: Their Characteristic Properties* (Wiley, 1908).

THE DOUGLAS FIR IS NOT A FIR.

Nor is the Douglas spruce a spruce, or the Oregon pine a true pine. All three names are among the many common misnomers applied to the stately lumber tree *Pseudotsuga manziesii,* which forests hundreds of thousands of acres in the American and Canadian West. Second only to the sequoias in height, these trees are reported to have grown three hundred and fifty feet and ten or twelve feet in girth: two-hundred-foot specimens are common.

One of the most important timber trees, the Douglas fir provides a hard, strong wood used in posts, poles, railway ties, flooring, and many varieties of lumber. The trees give West Coast lumberjacks their principal work, danger, and excitement. They were originally classified as *Pinus taxifolia* or *Abies taxifolia,* and although they are still grouped with the pines, they are neither true pines nor true firs. The current name, *Pseudotsuga,* comes from *pseudo* for "false" and *tsuga* for "hemlock." Taxonomist Charles Snow called the tree "a sort of bastard hemlock." Charles Henry Snow, *The Principal Species of Wood: Their Characteristic Properties* (Wiley, 1908).

NOT ALL "GIRDLED" TREES ARE DOOMED.

"Girdling," or stripping off a layer of bark in a complete circuit around a tree trunk, is usually thought to be equivalent to a death sentence for the tree. Since water and nutrients travel from the roots to the leaves through the inner bark, circumferential stripping interferes with the flow of these necessities and thus, it is thought, dooms the tree. By and large this is true, but it is interesting to note that for many tropical trees, the death sentence is subject to reprieve.

Any girdled tree will generate new bark cells if given time; the reason that many victims of girdling die is that they cannot regenerate fast enough. Jungle species are an exception. Tropical growth is so rapid, for trees as well as other plants, that girdling almost never kills a tropical tree unless the cut is also bathed in poison: Sodium arsenate is sometimes used to ensure the death of an unwanted tropical tree after it has been girdled. The tapping of rubber trees and the frequent girdling by forest dwellers of trees whose bark is used for clothing and baskets are only two examples of jungle trees being stripped all around and surviving. As botanist E. J. H. Corner admits, "Such trees reveal the vivacity of trunks as well as our imperfect understanding of their organization." E. J. H. Corner, *The Life of Plants* (World Publishing, 1964).

WHERE DOES BRAZILWOOD COME FROM?

In spite of its name, brazilwood was not originally found in Brazil; nor was it named after the country. In fact, just the reverse is true. In the Middle Ages *brasil* was a reddish dye much desired by European clothiers. Marco Polo had come upon it in the East, and up until the sixteenth century it was imported in large quantities from the East Indies, where the *Caesalpinia sappan* tree, from which it was obtained, grew in profusion. Then during the Renaissance voyages of discovery Portuguese mariners found a new source of the dye: the *Caesalpinia echinata* tree, which grew in the South American jungles. So widespread was this *brasil*-bearing tree in the tropical New World that seamen began referring to its habitat as *terra de brasil,* or "the land of *brasil";* later they shortened this simply to "Brasil." Thus, the country was named for the dye, not vice versa. Ackermann points out that the Portuguese named the island of Madeira in the same way, from the thick stands of timber (*madeira*) they discovered growing there. A. S. E. Ackermann, *Popular Fallacies* (1950; repr. Gale Research, 1970); E. S. Harrar, "Brazilwood," in *Encyclopedia Americana* (1979).

WHAT TREE GIVES US MAHOGANY WOOD?

Because of its rich reddish color, the beauty of its grain, and the ease with which it takes a finish, mahogany is highly prized as a decorative wood and veneer. But most of the world's "mahogany" is not true mahogany at all. Originally, the term applied to the wood of a single species, the *Swietania mahogani* found in Central America. When seventeenth- and eighteenth-century woodworkers spoke of mahogany, it was the wood of this tree they meant. Imprecision soon set in, and by the nineteenth century "mahogany" was being used to describe the wood of the so-called African mahogany and the Indian mahogany tree too. Neither of these is even in the same genus as *Swietania*.

Today's "mahogany" comes from an even wider assortment of trees. As early as 1917 the term was being applied commercially to the woods of over fifty different plants, and the general watering-down of the designation has not slowed since then. If your furniture dealer tells you, therefore, that an item is "real mahogany," you should take it *cum grano Swietaniae.*   C. D. Mell, "True Mahogany," U.S. Department of Agriculture Bulletin 474 (February 9, 1917); Charles Henry Snow, *The Principal Species of Wood: Their Characteristic Properties* (Wiley, 1908).

HOW OFTEN DOES THE CENTURY PLANT BLOOM?

The striking *Agave americana* plant is both a favorite ornamental throughout the Southwest and, in much of Mexico, a valued "beverage crop." With its tall, straight flowering stalks, or panicles, it suggests an exotic, miniaturized fir tree; from its flower rosettes the Mexicans extract a sap which, when fermented, yields the drink *pulque,* a fetid, milky intoxicant which, in much of rural Mexico, performs the same social service that muscatel does on the Bowery; a related species yields *mescal,* a more fiery form of the drink.

In Mexico the agave is known as the maguey plant. In English-speaking countries it is called the century plant, from the traditional but erroneous belief that it blooms only once every one hundred years. The plant is a slow starter, but not that slow. Most "century plants" bloom, and then die, after about eight to ten years; the flowering process may take as long as fifty years, but never as long as a century. Perhaps it should be renamed the "half century plant."   H. C. D. deWit, *Plants of the World* (Dutton, 1967).

WHERE DO TULIPS COME FROM?

Today tulips are a staple of the Dutch economy, with countless bulbs being exported each year to garden shops abroad. But this colorful symbol of the Netherlands has been known in Europe only for a little over four hundred years; before that, the flowers were confined to their native soils in Asia and Northern Africa. Wild tulip varieties had been known in the Eastern Mediterranean for many centuries; and it was there that the first cultivated varieties made their appearance. Turkey was a popular growing spot, and it was from a Turkish garden that, around 1554, an Austrian diplomat named O. G. de Busbec took bulbs to bring back to Europe.

These first imports altered European history, for by the 1630s tulips had become extremely hot items in the north of the continent. In Germany and Holland, during the "tulipomania" of 1634–1636, customers paid insanely extravagant sums for bulbs, and speculated wildly in tulip "futures." One Amsterdam dealer is reported to have sold a single bulb for a new carriage, two horses, and the equivalent of about twelve hundred dollars. When the bubble burst in 1636, the Dutch who had not been ruined by the crash settled down to less bullish labor, and soon made tulip growing one of the country's most stable and lucrative enterprises. T. Berger, "Tulipomania Was No Dutch Treat to Gambling Burghers," in *Smithsonian* (April 1977); Robert S. Lemmon and Charles L. Sherman, *Flowers of the World* (Hanover House, 1958).

WHAT IS PETRIFIED WOOD?

Both the name and the appearance of petrified wood suggest that it is simply wood that has turned to stone. This is not the case. Petrified wood is wood that has been fossilized by a process known as petrifaction or permineralization. In this process wood that has been buried in sediment is invaded by mineral-rich groundwater, which then deposits its minerals—usually silica, calcite, and iron compounds—in the pores and other open spaces of the wood. This makes it extremely heavy and far more resistant to weathering than living wood could ever be.

"Petrifaction" is somewhat of a misnomer, since the wood does not really "turn to stone." Instead mineral matter replaces the cellulose in the wood by dissolving it and taking its shape. This process, which can happen to animal as well as plant remains, effectively preserves minute details so that a permineralized stump or branch or insect appears exact in every particular, except for its "stoned" condition. In fossilized insect and spider remains found in a California lake deposit, the replacement process was so exact that the muscles, heart, and other internal organs of the creatures are perfectly "preserved." Cornelius S. Hurlbut, Jr., ed., *The Planet We Live on: Illustrated History of the Earth Sciences* (Abrams, 1976).

EARTH:

BOTCHING THE COMPASS

WHAT DIRECTION DOES A COMPASS NEEDLE POINT?

The earth is often described as a massive magnet, with its lines of magnetic force emanating from, and returning to, the North and South poles. This is a useful description, but it's wrong in several particulars. First of all, the lines of force you generally see drawn as regular, closed loops are in fact far more irregular than that, because forces in the planet's crust and interior create what are called "magnetic anomalies" in the field.

Secondly, when we refer to the North Pole, we generally mean the *geographical* pole, or the northern tip of the axis of rotation; to say that a compass points "north" to this pole is inaccurate. What it actually points to is the *magnetic* north pole, which is about eleven degrees away from geographical or "true" north. If you were to use a compass to reach true north, therefore, you would never get there. Where you would end up is at seventy-eight and a half north latitude by sixty-nine degrees west longitude—miles away from your destination.

Thirdly, and most surprisingly, scientists are now convinced that the magnetic poles are not stable, fixed points, but are wandering in space over time. "Polar wandering" has taken place constantly through geologic time, and in addition the magnetic integrity of the two poles has also been inconstant: Geologists say the planet's magnetic field in the past flowed often in the reverse of its present direction, indicating that the poles have changed position not once but many times. If you could be transported back a few million years with your compass, then, you might find that it pointed south. Not "true" south, of course, but geomagnetic south. Cornelius S. Hurlbut, Jr., ed., *The Planet We Live on: The Illustrated Encyclopedia of the Earth Sciences* (Abrams, 1976).

IN WHAT SEASON IS THE EARTH CLOSEST TO THE SUN?

Since the earth is heated by the sun, and since it is heated more in summer than in winter, it seems reasonable to suppose that the planet is closer to the star in the summer than in the winter. This is not true; if it were, we would have a great deal of trouble explaining why when it is summer in the northern hemisphere it is winter south of the equator.

The seasons are caused not by the planet's distance from the sun, but by the varying amounts of direct sunlight that each hemisphere receives as the planet revolves around the heat source. The earth, you will recall, is tilted on its axis with respect to its orbit around the sun; because of the tilt, or inclination, the northern hemisphere receives more direct rays from about March through September, and the southern hemisphere receives more in the other half of the year. That's why it's hot here when it's cold there, and vice versa.

The distance between the earth and the sun changes constantly as the planet goes through its elliptical orbit, but that distance has nothing to do with the seasons. We are actually closest to the sun around January 1, in the middle of the northern winter, and farthest away in July; but the difference in the two distances is a mere 3 million miles—not enough to make an appreciable difference in heat, when compared to the average distance of 92.9 million miles. "For this reason," says Robert E. Boyer, "directness of the sun's rays and total daylight time, rather than distance, control our seasons."   Robert E. Boyer, "Earth's Planetary Motions," in Cornelius S. Hurlbut, Jr., ed., *The Planet We Live on: The Illustrated Encyclopedia of the Earth Sciences* (Abrams, 1976).

IT'S NOT HOTTEST AT THE EQUATOR AND COLDEST AT THE POLES.

"Hottest at the equator, coldest at the poles" is not a bad basic rule of thumb for determining surface temperatures around the globe, but it comes to grief rapidly because of the variety of land masses, convection currents, and bodies of water of which the earth is composed. If the planet were a uniform, undifferentiated sphere, the rule would work pretty well; as it is, climate is affected, as Montagu and Darling wrote, not only by absolute distance from the poles, but by such variables as topography, prevailing winds, ocean currents, and a host of other factors. Thus Seattle, partly because of the proximity of a warming ocean current, is significantly warmer than East Coast cities on a similar latitude. Mount Kenya, in equatorial Africa, is capped with a permanent glacier. And there are palm trees in Cornwall. "It would be convenient," they lament, if our world were simple and followed certain basic, understandable rules . . . like the rule that it shall cool off in direct proportion to one's distance from the equator." Alas, it is not so. If only our world were not so *messy!* Ashley Montagu and Edward Darling, *The Prevalence of Nonsense* (Harper & Row, 1967).

NOT COUNTING ALASKA, WHAT IS THE NORTHERNMOST STATE?

A quick glance at the map suggests that Maine, its great snowy forests thrusting toward Greenland, is the closest of the "lower forty-eight" to the Pole. As the most northeastern part of the Northeast, this moose-laden, bone-chilling region seems like New England's own Yukon. The impression you get from the map is that from Washington into the Great Lakes, the forty-ninth parallel is the boundary, and that Maine juts slightly above it.

A closer investigation of latitudes, though, puts Maine below, not above, the line. The only state, in fact, whose borders extend north of the forty-ninth is the Great Lakes dairy giant, Minnesota. The state's so-called Northwest Angle, ceded to the United States by an 1818 agreement with Great Britain, is an approximate rectangle of flatland separated from the rest of the state (and the nation at large) by an arm of the Lake of the Woods. Sparsely populated and bitterly cold, it was the site of the French Fort St. Charles, built in 1732. Its northernmost point, near the town of Angle Inlet, is about 130 miles north of Maine's northernmost point, Escourt Station. Theodore Blegen, *Minnesota: A History of the State* (University of Minnesota Press, 1963).

HOW MANY OF THE UNITED STATES HAVE
TERRITORY NORTH OF CANADA?

Maine is obvious, and Alaska. If you glance at a map, so are Vermont, New Hampshire, New York, Michigan, and Wisconsin. You might miss Washington, Oregon, Minnesota, North and South Dakota, Montana, and Idaho. Canada's southernmost point is tiny Middle Island, which lies west of Toledo in Lake Erie, just south of the larger Pelee Island. If you run a latitude line east to west through Middle Island, the states you'll intersect are Massachusetts, Rhode Island, Connecticut, New York, Pennsylvania, Ohio, Indiana, Illinois, Iowa, Nebraska, Wyoming, Utah, Nevada, and California. All in all, twenty-seven of our states lie to some degree north of our northern neighbor. *The National Atlas of the United States of America* (U.S. Department of the Interior, 1970).

WHICH EXTENDS FARTHER WEST:
VIRGINIA OR WEST VIRGINIA?

The designation "West" might lead one to suppose that the creation of West Virginia was an aspect of that early stage of colonial expansion when the seaboard population was gradually pushing toward the sun: One imagines Appalachian mountaineers and Ethan Allen's Green Mountain Boys as contemporaries.

But West Virginia was not created until almost a century after Allen. It came about as a result of the animosities between slaveholders and abolitionists just before the Civil War: With Virginia split between the two, the best solution seemed to be to acknowledge the division on the map. In 1861, when Virginia seceded from the Union, residents of the more mountainous regions refused to go along and proclaimed themselves loyal to the Union. That is how West Virginia was born, two years later, as the thirty-fifth state.

It's northwest rather than west from Virginia, and although a lot of it is west of a lot of Virginia, the Old Dominion has the edge on the upstart for looking farthest west. The westernmost point of West Virginia is a loop of the Big Sandy River a little bit north of Louisa. Virginia extends over fifty miles farther west, to Cumberland Gap National Park. Charles H. Ambler and Festus P. Summers, "West Virginia," in *Encyclopedia Americana* (1980).

WHAT IS THE DEEPEST CANYON IN THE UNITED STATES?

Arizona's spectacular Grand Canyon, that phantasmagoric monument to the patience of running water, is the deepest of the many canyons that have been carved by the Colorado River. It ranges from four to eighteen miles in width, and at its deepest drops about fifty-seven hundred feet from the canyon rim to the water. This is a mighty fair plunge, but nothing like that of a canyon several hundred miles to the north. Part of the "Grand Canyon of the Snake," it is Idaho's noted Hell's Canyon. Cut by the winding Snake River, it extends for about a hundred miles from Brownlee Dam on the Idaho-Oregon border north to just above Lewiston, Idaho, where the river runs west to join the Columbia. It's not particularly wide, but it is deep: From the Seven Devils Mountains to the east, the valley floor drops seventy-nine hundred feet—twenty-two hundred feet deeper than the deepest part of Arizona's marvel.

The Snake River was in the news back in 1974, when motorcycle daredevil Evel Knievel attempted unsuccessfully to rocket across it in engineer Robert Truax's Sky Cycle X-2. Even Kneivel was not loony enough to try this at Hell's Canyon; he took off upriver, at Twin Falls.   Ronald L. Ives, "Grand Canyon," and Clifford I. Dobler, "Hell's Canyon," in *Encyclopedia Americana* (1980).

IN WHAT COUNTRY IS MISSISSIPPI BAY?

Below the delta of the "Mighty Mississip," there is a stretch of the Gulf of Mexico that is named after the river; this stretch, however, is Mississippi Sound, not Bay. To find Mississippi Bay, you would have to travel halfway around the world to the unlikely location of Japan. There, in Tokyo Bay, just off Yokohama, you would find an inlet called Mississippi Bay, another called Susquehanna Bay, and a third called American Anchorage. The names were bestowed in July 1853, while Commodore Matthew

C. Perry, squadron commander of the American naval expedition
that opened up trade with Japan, was waiting in Tokyo Bay (then
called Yedo Bay) to learn whether President Millard Fillmore's
overtures to the emperor were going to be accepted or rebuffed.

The origin of American Anchorage is obvious: It was a harbor
for the Commodore's fleet. The *Mississippi* and the *Susquehanna*
were two of his flotilla's warships, and he was so fond of their
names that he also gave them to a couple of small islands in the
bay. His other ships, the *Saratoga* and the *Plymouth,* also got
islands named after them, as did Perry himself. I am indebted to
Leo Rosten for leading me to this interesting tidbit, although I
must respectfully point out that it was the Americans, and not the
Japanese, as he says, who distributed the names. Whether or not
they are still used I do not know; they do appear on Perry's own
charts. Francis L. Hawks, *Narrative of the Expedition of an
American Squadron to the China Seas and Japan* (Appleton and
Company, 1856); Leo Rosten, *The Power of Positive Nonsense*
(McGraw-Hill, 1977).

WHEN DID THE MASON AND DIXON LINE ORIGINATE?

The Mason and Dixon Line is still considered the unofficial
dividing line between the North and the South, and because of
this it's often supposed that the line was laid out sometime in the
early nineteenth century to divide the free states of the North
from the slave states of the South. This is not so. It was laid out
between 1763 and 1767 by the English surveyors Charles Mason
and Jeremiah Dixon, to settle a boundary dispute between the
Calvert family, proprietors of Maryland, and the Penn family,
proprietors of Pennsylvania. For nearly a hundred years the two
families had battled over who should collect taxes in the disputed
area; Mason and Dixon were called in to settle the legal feud.

In 1820, when the Missouri Compromise divided western lands
into slave and free, the term "Mason and Dixon Line" came to
refer not only to the Pennsylvania-Maryland border but also to
the rest of the slave-free latitudinal divisions: the Ohio River
to the Mississippi, and the 36′30″ parallel which the Compromise
itself had established for states west of the Mississippi. The extended meaning soon became commonly accepted, although it
was quite inaccurate. Mason and Dixon would certainly have
been surprised to learn that a half century after their task was

completed, they were being credited with having surveyed the Midwest. "Mason and Dixon Line" in *Encyclopedia Americana* (1980).

THE OZARK MOUNTAINS ARE PART OF WHAT MOUNTAIN RANGE?

The Ozarks, those rugged highlands that have contributed so much to American folklore, certainly look like they belong to the Appalachian range. Their soft contours and rolling, forested slopes evoke images of buckskin and log cabins far more eloquently than do the craggy, ice-capped peaks of the Rockies.

But they're really distinct from both the Appalachian and the Rocky chains. Geologically speaking, they are no more closely related to, say, the Blue Ridge Mountains of Virginia than they are to the Bighorn or Bitterroot ranges of the West. The Ozarks were formed over 600 million years ago, during that vast, ill-defined period of geological history known as the Precambrian era. They are thus among the oldest mountains on the continent. By comparison the Appalachians are youngsters. Most of their rocks are Paleozoic, which means less than 600 million years old, and there are sections of the chain in West Virginia and Pennsylvania that are no more than 275 million years old.

The Rockies are, of course, even younger than that. The infants of American mountains, they were formed largely during the great Laramide disturbance, around 65 million years ago—just about the time that the dinosaurs were becoming extinct. When the Ozarks were being formed, the vertebrates had yet to emerge. "Ozark Mountains" and Albert V. Carozzi, "Geology: The Earth's History," in *Encyclopedia Americana* (1980).

WHAT COUNTRY HAS THE WORLD'S HIGHEST STANDARD OF LIVING?

It depends on how you measure it, of course. Americans are accustomed to thinking of the United States as "the greatest country on earth," and what they mean by that, usually, is that this nation has both a high degree of personal freedom and a wide range of economic opportunities. To the more cynical chauvinists, it simply means that we're the richest nation on earth. The

Nepalese may be quite happy in their medieval squalor, and blissfully unaware that a color TV is a necessity of the Good Life, but no American will claim that because they are happy with little they have achieved a higher "standard of living" than our own. In measuring this elusive quality, the yardstick is almost always material.

Even by the material standard, though, the United States is not at the top of the heap. Measured in terms of Gross National Product (the amount of generated wealth per capita), the United States is topped by at least three other nations. In 1976 the World Bank estimated our GNP at $7890; Sweden's was $8670, Switzerland's was $8800, and oil-rich Kuwait's was a staggering $15,480. The poorest countries, measured in GNP, were in Asia, with India weighing in at an annual $140 per person.

But that's only money talking. To get a slightly more reliable outlook on "standard of living," you really should measure something more than the weight of a nation's purse. That's what the Overseas Development Council did in compiling its recent Physical Quality of Life Index. The PQLI is a composite of life expectancy, infant mortality, and literacy figures, rated on an index from one to one hundred. The top runners here were all in the industrialized West, which was no surprise. What was surprising was that there was little correlation between PQLI and GNP. Wealthy Switzerland had a PQLI of 95, but so did relatively poorer Canada. Ireland, with a GNP of only $2560, and Austria, with $5330, both had a PQLI of 93. The United States and poorer Great Britain both measured in at an average 94.

On both scales, the industrial trailers were the Soviet Union and Spain—although Norway, with a quite respectable GNP of $7420, had like them a PQLI of 91. Third-world countries fared much worse. India's PQLI was 41, Gabon's only 21. Kuwait's enormous wealth must still be very badly managed, for its PQLI was only 74—eight points behind dirt-poor Sri Lanka. What is it that money can't buy? *The Book of Numbers* (Heron House Publishing, 1978).

OUTER SPACE IS NOT "SPACE."

That is to say, it is not empty. Considering the enormous distances between the stellar and galactic bodies, it is common for us here on earth to consider "space" a vast, empty medium in which the planets, asteroids, and stars float around like motes in a primordial ether. Actually, what lies between the stars is not the great *nada* of popular conception, but a stew (admittedly a very thin stew) of gases, cosmic rays, and dust. There is approximately one dust grain for every 100,000 cubic meters of space. That may not sound like much, but it's enough to render many distant stars almost invisible. Simon Mitton, ed., *The Cambridge Encyclopaedia of Astronomy* (Crown, 1977).

WHAT COUNTRY GIVES AWAY THE LARGEST PERCENTAGE OF ITS GROSS NATIONAL PRODUCT AS FOREIGN AID?

Americans like to think of themselves as a generous people, and if you measure our international aid in flat, whole-figure terms, the notion is justified: We do give less advantaged countries more total aid than any of the other industrialized nations. In 1976 that total was $4.3 billion, a figure which dwarfs the $2.1 billion of our nearest competitor, France.

But if we measure the aid given as a percentage of GNP, we come out smelling less rosy. The United States, remember, is among the most affluent nations in the West, and that $4.3 billion, when compared to 1976's mammoth GNP, comes out to only 0.25 percent. Canada, which gave away only $886 million, sacrificed 0.46 percent of its GNP, and France, with half our total contribution, weighed in at 0.62 percent.

The biggest givers, though, were Sweden and the tiny Netherlands, who gave respectively $608 and $720 million. In their smaller economies those figures represented 0.82 percent of Gross National Product. To equal their largess, we would have to have contributed over three times as much as we did. *The Book of Numbers* (Heron House Publishing, 1978).

IN WHAT STATE IS THE STATUE OF LIBERTY?

The preeminent symbol of American opportunity has so long been associated with the image of immigrants reaching New York City that it is seldom realized that the statue actually stands in New Jersey. Bedloe's Island (renamed Liberty Island only in 1956), on which Frederic Bartholdi and Gustave Eiffel erected their colossus in the 1880s, sits in New York Harbor but is within Jersey City's waters. It is only because of an 1834 compact that New York has any control over the island at all: Sales taxes from the statue's concessions go to Albany, not to Trenton, as do non-federal income taxes paid by the few families who live there. The statue is a beacon, however, only because of New Jersey, since the island's power comes from a Jersey City utility. (Ultimate jurisdiction is, of course, federal, since the island has been a national monument since 1924, and is maintained by the National Park Service.)

The statue's name, incidentally, was originally "Liberty Enlightening the World," referring to French republican hopes that it would serve as a galvanizing symbol for the spread of democracy throughout the globe. In the century since its erection American pride of ownership has tended to dim the builders' evangelical intention, and the colossus has become not so much an enlightening model as a simple image of welcome. Thanks in part to Emma Lazarus's famous poem, "Miss Liberty" now symbolizes an open, "golden" door, not an attitude of militant republicanism; even more at variance with her makers' intentions, she is seen not as a "universal icon," but as a national one. She has been "not only neutralized, but naturalized as well." Marvin Trachtenberg, *The Statue of Liberty* (Allen Lane, 1976).

WHAT HARBOR DID THE COLOSSUS OF RHODES STRADDLE?

The Colossus of Rhodes, designed by the sculptor Chares in the third century B.C., was a huge bronze likeness of the sun god Helios, which was considered one of the seven wonders of the ancient world. The work was supposed to have taken twelve years, and when the statue was complete, it stood over one hundred feet high. It stood by the harbor at Rhodes for not quite sixty years, and was destroyed by an earthquake in 224 B.C. The shattered pieces, which lay on the ground for centuries, were finally plundered by Saracens, who sold them to Jewish merchants in A.D. 653.

Some time in the late Middle Ages the colorful idea got started that in its prime the Colossus had actually straddled the harbor, and that ships approaching the Greek city had to sail through its legs to reach port. This belief was widespread in Europe by the sixteenth century, but there is no contemporary evidence to support it. The statue probably stood "near" the harbor rather than "over" it, for when the earthquake struck, the pieces fell on the land. "The precise spot of the colossus remains a mystery, for it was never described by reliable eyewitnesses." Brian Dicks, *Rhodes* (Stackpole Books, 1974).

FRANCE'S BASTILLE WAS NOT BUILT AS A PRISON.

The most notorious prison in eighteenth-century Europe, the Bastille was originally erected in the fourteenth century as a citadel to protect the royal residence during the so-called Hundred Years' War. Until the early seventeenth century, it was used exclusively as a fortress; it only became a state prison under the ministry of Cardinal Richelieu in the 1620s, and although the mob which destroyed it in 1789 had reason to resent it as a symbol of royal tyranny, in fact it was never as monstrous a "dungeon" as Alexandre Dumas led many to suppose. The French government considered demolishing it in 1784, and five years later, when it fell to the revolutionaries, only seven prisoners were found inside. "Bastille" in *Encyclopedia Americana* (1980).

WHAT IS LONDON'S "BIG BEN"?

Big Ben is as much a symbol of the British capital as the Eiffel Tower is of Paris or the Statue of Liberty is of New York. It's generally supposed, though, that Big Ben is the great tower clock that sits above the Houses of Parliament, but this is not the case. Big Ben is actually the clock's largest bell, a thirteen-ton behemoth that began striking the hours in 1859, and that was named after Sir Benjamin Hall, commissioner of works at the time of its installation. The term began to be applied to the famous clock only later, and is today used indiscriminately for the clock and the tower. Every London guidebook has a picture of the noted clock; few show you the real Big Ben. "Big Ben" in *Encyclopaedia Britannica* (1978).

WHERE IS THE LARGEST PYRAMID IN THE WORLD?

Ask any random ten people this question and nine will immediately answer "Egypt." Actually, although most of the planet's large pyramids do grace the Nile delta, the largest one of all broods half a world away, in Cholula de Rivadabia, Mexico. Built between the second and the sixth centuries A.D., it was dedicated to the Aztec god Quetzalcoatl, the "feathered serpent" of many legends. At 177 feet tall and an estimated 4.3 million cubic yards in volume, it covers an area of nearly forty-five acres, making it not only the largest pyramid, but the largest monument of any kind ever constructed. By comparison the more famous Great Pyramid of Cheops, west of Cairo, covers a paltry thirteen acres. Its volume is about 3.4 million cubic yards, its height a mere 130 feet. It was built, of course, in the third millennium B.C. —when people were a good deal shorter. *Guinness Book of World Records* (1980); Peter Tomkins, *Secrets of the Great Pyramid* (Harper & Row, 1978).

AFTER WHAT ANIMALS WERE THE CANARY ISLANDS NAMED?

The Canary Islands are rich volcanic islands that lie in an archipelago just off the northwestern coast of Africa. Now owned by Spain, they have been known to sailors since antiquity. The Phoenicians, Greeks, Carthaginians, Arabs, and Romans all set in there during their explorations of the African coast. An ancient tradition associates them with the Fortunate Isles, or Isles of the Blessed, because of their agreeable climate. They were also thought to be remnants of lost Atlantis.

Canaries abound on the islands, but the birds did not give them their name. The Romans called them *insulae canariae,* which means "islands of the dogs," or "doggy isles," because wild dogs *(canes)* were even more populous there than canaries. From *canariae* came the English name Canary, and from that in turn came the common term "canary" for the birds. These small finches still grow wild on the islands, although you might have trouble recognizing them as canaries: The domesticated canary is usually yellow; the wild ones, while they have some yellow markings, are mostly gray, gray-brown, or olive green.   M. M. Lasley,

"Canary Islands," and Carl Welty, "Canary," in *Encyclopedia Americana* (1980)

WHAT MODERN COUNTRY CORRESPONDS TO ANCIENT GAUL?

By "Gaul" we moderns mean France, but as Philip Ward points out, in Julius Caesar's day Gaul extended over far more of Europe than its supposed contemporary counterpart. The eastern border was the Rhine, the northern and western borders the sea, the southern one the Pyrennees chain. This meant that Gaul covered not only most of what is now France but also the Low Countries (where the Belgae, or Belgians, lived); Switzerland (home of the Helvetii, or Helvetians); and even a thin strip of Spain.

And that's only Transalpine Gaul, or Gaul "beyond the Alps." The region called Cisalpine Gaul (Gaul "this side of the Alps") extended into Italy itself. Before their subjugation by the Romans beginning in the second century B.C., the Gauls had advanced as far as the Tiber. Modern France got that far only in the dreams of Charles de Gaulle.   Philip Ward, *A Dictionary of Common Fallacies* (Oleander Press, 1980).

HOW DO YOU GET AROUND VENICE?

"By gondola, of course" would be the prospective tourist's answer, and for many in Venice the gondola is indeed a principal means of transport. But it is not the only one. The romance of the canals has led many to suppose that they are the only thoroughfares in the city, and this is simply not so. Venice, the jewel of the Mediterranean, is built around its canals, and it is on the canals— by gondola and by other forms of water taxi—that visitors generally travel. But there are plenty of footpaths as well, and it is therefore a mistake to suppose that if you want to get anywhere in Venice, you must pay to be poled around.

Much of the freight and other business traffic in Venice is conducted by water, and private vehicular traffic is restricted. The walker, however, can see the whole city by land. The elaborate canal system is crisscrossed by an equally elaborate bridge system (there are over four hundred bridges in the city), and even the

Grand Canal is spanned by three bridges, including the famous
Ponte di Rialto. E. V. Lucas devoted four chapters of his *A Wanderer in Venice* to the delights of Venetian strolling. So it is entirely possible to get around the fabled city without ever getting
into a boat.   E. V. Lucas, *A Wanderer in Venice* (Macmillan,
1914).

WHAT DIRECTION IS IT FROM THE ATLANTIC TO THE PACIFIC SIDE OF THE PANAMA CANAL?

When the United States opened the Panama Canal in August
1914, it was fulfilling a dream that had spanned four centuries.
Ever since Balboa reported that the Atlantic and Pacific oceans
were, at the isthmus of Panama, only about fifty miles apart,
European surveyors had been weighing the feasibility of digging
a canal. Down the years such luminaries as Ben Franklin, Simón
Bolívar, and Goethe had advocated the project, and in 1881 Ferdinand de Lesseps, architect of the Suez Canal, actually set out to
begin it. Finding the rocks of the Continental Divide less tracta-
ble than the Egyptian sand dunes he was used to, he abandoned
the effort eight years later, leaving thousands of investors irate. In
spite of his failure, though, he had laid out a reasonable route,
and it was basically this route that American engineers followed a
generation later.

It wasn't an east-west route. Because the Atlantic is east of the
Pacific, many Pacific-bound travelers assume that when they pass
through the Canal, they will be sailing west. The isthmus curves
in such a way, though, that the direction is really southeast. From
Colon on the Atlantic to Gatun Lake ten miles away, ships sail
approximately to the south. Once in the lake, however, they veer
sharply to the left, and for the rest of the fifty-mile journey they
move southeast. The geographical oddity of the isthmus means
that the Atlantic's Caribbean Sea is at this point *west* of the Pacific's Gulf of Panama.   Lawrence O. Ealy, "Panama Canal," in
Encyclopedia Americana (1979).

WHERE IS MONT BLANC LOCATED?

With the possible exceptions of the Matterhorn and the Jung-
frau, Mont Blanc has probably been more frequently discussed,
painted, and photographed than any other mountain in Europe.

As early as 1786, when European mountaineering was still in its infancy, a team of Swiss climbers reached its summit, and it has remained a climbers' lodestone ever since. Perhaps because the Swiss were its first conquerors, perhaps because the Swiss Alps are Europe's most celebrated range, it is often assumed that Mont Blanc, the "highest peak in Europe," is the pièce de résistance of the Swiss crown jewels.

But the mountain is French, not Swiss. It stands in the department of Haute-Savoie on the border of Italy and France, a good dozen miles from Switzerland. Nor is it really the highest peak in Europe, only the highest in Western Europe. If in "Europe" you include (as geographers do) that portion of the Soviet Union that lies west of the Urals, then Mont Blanc is not even in the running, for, compared to the Russian Caucasus range, the Alpine peaks are pikers. Mont Blanc stands at 15,771 feet; Mt. Elbrus, the pride of European Russia, tops that by more than half a mile. *Academic American Encyclopedia* (1981).

WHAT CAUSES THE TIDES?

Most of us learned in school that the tides are caused by the moon. This is not inaccurate, but it is only part of the story. Actually, the gravitational fields of both the moon and the sun have an effect on the fluctuations of water level that we refer to as tides. The moon's pull is the dominant factor, because of its relative closeness, but even at 92.9 million miles away, the sun affects our planet's tidal flows, since it is so much larger than the moon. Solar tides, which occur at approximately twelve-hour intervals, are smaller than the slightly wider-spaced lunar tides, and they occur at different times. But they are not insignificant, and in some parts of the world, such as the southern coast of Australia, they are more influential than those caused by the moon.

Of course, separating lunar and solar tides is something of an exercise in futility, since the planet is a holistic system, and the ebb and flow of ocean waters should really be seen as part of a three-part configuration (the earth, the sun, and the moon) rather than two distinct, two-part arrangements. Lunar and solar gravitational forces act both in concert with and in contrast to each other, and this means that at certain times of the year tides will be enhanced by the cooperation of solar and lunar influences, while at other times those influences will balance each other out, resulting in tides of only modest variations. Typically, tides at the new and full moons, called spring tides, are exceptionally large, while tides at the first and last lunar quarters, called neap tides, are significantly smaller. This is because in spring tides the solar and lunar influences work together, and in the neap tides they are opposed.

One fascinating note should be added, and that is that both celestial bodies influence not only the liquid bodies on our planet, but the solid and gaseous ones as well. The term "tides" generally implies water, but, in fact, every particle of matter on the earth—and in the earth's atmosphere—is affected by the pull of the sun and the moon. Extraplanetary gravitation is known to have an effect on both terrestrial gravitation (as measured, for example, by a plumb line) and on the "weight" of the atmosphere. Atmospheric pressure is clearly influenced by both the sun and the moon, and although the mechanisms of the atmospheric tides are as yet imperfectly understood, it is clear that, contrary to the evidence of the oceans, in the atmosphere it is the sun, not the moon, which makes the difference.   Bernard D. Zetler, "Tide," in *Encyclopedia Americana* (1980).

THE EARTH IS NOT A SPHERE.

There is nothing as impermanent as truth. The notion for which Columbus gambled his life, his fortune, and his sacred honor turns out to have been an illusion. In spite of what the Greeks observed, in spite of the Genoan's proof, in spite of the calumny that has been heaped on defenders of the flat or hollow earth, the planet is not, finally, a sphere; it is actually an "oblate spheroid," which is a mathematician's gibberish for an object that is slightly flattened at the poles and correspondingly bulging in the middle—like the beach ball your child is sitting on. (Newton accounted for this by showing that the rotating earth's centrifugal force would naturally cause the bulge.)

In technical terms this means that the planet's equatorial radius (call it a) is longer than its polar radius (b); the degree of oblateness is defined by the formula $(a - b)/a$. Or in real planetary terms, (3,963 miles - 3,947 miles)/3,963 miles. Which equals 0.003367, or about 1/298. So the round earth is no more. Is there nothing sacred?   J. T. Wilson, "Earth," in *Encyclopedia Americana* (1980).

SOURCES

In compiling this miscellany of misapprehensions, I have used, in addition to the individual sources noted after the entries, a kind of core reference library—the combined work of several fellow researchers without whose earlier spadework my digging would have been immeasurably more difficult.

Chief among these allies in the battle against given wisdom, I must mention the editors of, and contributors to, four fine encyclopedias. In more instances than I can recall, my first research stop in this book was either the *Encyclopaedia Britannica* or the *Encyclopedia Americana.* Their usefulness to me far exceeded the evidence provided by their several citations after the entries. In addition, the excellent one-volume *Columbia Encyclopedia* and the new *Academic American Encyclopedia,* on which I had the pleasure of working, were also of constant value. So, too, was the *Oxford English Dictionary,* which almost a century after its first volumes appeared remains a lexicographer's Shangri-la.

Of the numerous "fallacy books" that have been published in the last century or so, I have found a couple of dozen to be particularly fruitful. These I have kept by me as a bedside reading shelf, and from them I have drawn not only information, but an acute sense of the resilience of human gullibility. With deep thanks to their authors, I am pleased to list them here.

Ackermann, A. S. E., *Popular Fallacies* (Gale Research Co., 1970; reprint of 1950 London edition).

Bombaugh, Charles C., *Facts and Fancies for the Curious* (Lippincott, 1934).

Burnam, Tom, *The Dictionary of Misinformation* (Crowell, 1975), and *More Misinformation* (Lippincott & Crowell, 1980).

Evans, Bergen, *The Natural History of Nonsense* (Knopf, 1946), and *The Spoor of Spooks and Other Nonsense* (Knopf, 1954).

Kane, Joseph Nathan, *Famous First Facts* (H. W. Wilson, 1964).

Louis, David, *Fascinating Facts* (Ridge Press, 1977), and *More Fascinating Facts* (Ridge Press, 1979).

Montagu, Ashley, and Edward Darling, *The Ignorance of Certainty* (Harper & Row, 1970) and *The Prevalence of Nonsense* (Harper & Row, 1967).

Phyfe, William Henry, *5000 Facts and Fancies* (Gale Research Co., 1966).

Reddall, Henry Frederic, *Fact, Fancy and Fable* (Gale Research Co., 1968).

Robertson, Patrick, *The Book of Firsts* (Clarkson Potter, 1977).

Rosten, Leo, *The Power of Positive Nonsense* (McGraw-Hill, 1977).

Stefansson, Vilhjalmur, *Adventures in Error* (Robert McBride & Co., 1936).

Stimpson, George, *A Book About a Thousand Things* (Harper, 1946), and *Information Roundup* (Harper, 1948).

Wallechinsky, David, and Irving Wallace, *The People's Almanac* (Bantam, 1975), and *The Peoples Almanac #2* (Bantam, 1978).

Ward, Philip, *A Dictionary of Common Fallacies* (Oleander Press, 1980).